Ancient Mysteries Tarot
Keys to Divination
and Initiation

By

Roger Calverley

LOTUS PRESS
Twin Lakes, WI
USA

Copyright © Roger Calverley 2004
Cover design © Mary Sullivan 2004
Text design and format: Eclectica Publications 2004

ISBN 0 940985 72 1
Library of Congress Control Number: 2004101604
1st edition
Publisher: Lotus Press,
          PO Box 325
          Twin Lakes, WI
          53181, USA
          Telephone: 262 889-8561
          Email: lotuspress@lotuspress.com
          Website: www.lotuspress.com

TABLE OF CONTENTS

FOREWORD

When I heard that love was the mother of knowledge, I was ready to become a child of stillness. If I can love, what needs to be said? If I cannot, what is worth saying? Love comes down to express itself in form; love goes up to lose itself in spirit. Love smiles to awaken slumbering hearts, and love weeps to remember itself when overcome by slumber. Love moves to share itself. Love moves not to realize itself. The mind of man and the heart of God are united by love. His love and ours are not different. They are parts of a single whole. Love makes all parts whole. Love is all.

PREFACE

Ancient Mysteries Tarot is about the primal sources of the Tarot tradition. Long before Tarot cards were used in early Renaissance Europe, the Mystery School traditions of initiation and divination were working with earth, air, fire and water, the power of numbers, and the great archetypal beings that we refer to as the Major Arcanum. To assemble symbolic expressions of these forces on cards and then make the cards widely available became possible with the advent of printing between 1400 and 1600 AD in Europe. Thus, in a popularized and somewhat debased form, with many variations, symbolic expressions of the ancient Mystery School teachings were dispersed in veiled imagery into the European mind.

The general intolerance of the Christian mindset in Europe from the Middle Ages to the end of the Enlightenment, and well beyond into our own century, made it necessary to cloak the spiritual and occult possibilities of Tarot with quasi-Christian, European symbolism. The earliest European decks also included some Hermetic and Alchemical symbols, which do come closer to the primal roots of the ancient tradition. Packaged for the European mind, the High Priest (or Hierophant) was illustrated as the Pope, and the Priestess was represented as the "Papesse" – which is just about as close to heresy as one might want to risk. The official position of the churches, both Protestant and Catholic has usually been that Tarot is the work of the devil. Yet, if we want to truly understand what Tarot is, it is necessary to know its roots, its original meaning, the nature of its symbols and the energies to which they refer, and to see how Tarot evolved as it journeyed through time.

In *Ancient Mysteries Tarot*, I envisage Tarot as a tree. Its roots reach down into the obscurity of ancient historical and even pre-historical times and its branches and fruit are above the surface to be seen and touched by the outer mind. There is no evidence that the ancient seers and sages used the same 22 archetypes as we find in the earliest decks of cards produced in Europe in the fourteenth and fifteenth centuries.

But they did have a very active interaction with the archetypes both for divination and initiation. There is no evidence that the creators of early European decks of Tarot cards had the four elements of earth, air, fire and water in mind when they developed suits in symbols of pentacles (or coins), swords, wands and cups. But occultists and diviners have seen this in the cards and used them that way for centuries. There is no question that the use of numbers on Tarot cards opened up many esoteric possibilities, with echoes of Pythagoras and the traditions of Chaldea and Egypt from which he drew. But there is no evidence either that the designers of the earliest Tarot decks were thinking of the esoteric meanings of Pythagorean numerology. We cannot say therefore that the earliest decks in existence prove a link with the ancient mystery schools. Yet when we see how the seed of the Tarot tree has risen up from its hidden roots and flowered into a variety of decks which are currently used far more for magic, meditation, healing and divination than for card games, we have to conclude that the inner life, spirit, or reality of Tarot has much more resonance than the earliest decks of European Tarot cards might suggest.

Ancient Mysteries Tarot draws its imagery from the Mystery Schools of pre-Christian Egypt, India, Greece, Mesopotamia, and Meso-America. These cultures flourished from the earliest times well into the Roman, imperial period of world history. Their art resonates with a sense of ancient, magical, primal, archetypal and mysterious realities. Between 1987 and 2003, I had the good fortune to visit places where the ancient mystery schools flourished, to meditate, photograph, sketch and paint what remains of their temples, their statues, and their art. In the Parthenon at Athens, in the ruins of Knossos on the isle of Crete, in the Valley of the Kings, the Temples of Luxor, at the Pyramids and in the museums of Alexandria, in Southern India, in the old Inca temples of Peru and in the Khmer temples of ancient Thailand, I was able to take in the energies and consciousness of the mystical past, and to document much of it in watercolour. As a historian and amateur archaeologist, I was also able to have first hand experience of North American sites where the sacred realities of the past were still strongly resonant. All of this direct experience, enriched by thirty years as a daily meditator, went into the writing of the book *The Ancient Mysteries Tarot*, and the painting of a deck of cards to accompany it.

My own spiritual journey is relevant because through it I came to an in-depth and personal experience of the Wisdom Tradition. In the course of about thirty years of spiritual seeking, I was very fortunate to discover the work of Sri Aurobindo and The Mother and to spend time living at their Ashram. Together, these two spiritual pioneers opened a new chapter of evolution on our planet by connecting the earthly consciousness to the very highest sources of spiritual reality. Sri Aurobindo called this highest plane of energy and consciousness the Supermind. From about 1920 until his death in 1950, he attempted to bring it down into the earth atmosphere. In 1956, The Mother, his spiritual collaborator, announced that a door in the inner world had finally opened, and that the golden light from above had begun to descend into the earth. From that time to this, momentous spiritual changes and shifts in consciousness have been taking place all around us, including the New Age movement, the growth in popularity of yoga and meditation, mutation of human DNA into greater degrees of complexity, and increasing experiences of mystical reality on the part of spiritual seekers in all traditions.

The Universal Truth that is being expressed in the symbols of Tarot was well articulated in ancient India, but was also widely revered in many other pre-Christian cultures. The Mystery Schools are important because they were the repositories and the universities of ancient spiritual traditions (as contrasted with official state rituals and priesthoods). The ancient wisdom was transmitted from master to disciple by direct initiation for thousands of years until eventually, by the end of the Roman Empire, the last traces of the mystery schools were obliterated. By the time that Rome was waning, Christianity was a dominant influence. From the time of late antiquity (roughly 300 to 400 AD) until the twentieth century, Christian dogmatism held sway over the European mind, as Islamic theology gripped the Middle East and large parts beyond. Yet within the last quarter century much of the ancient European and Mediterranean tradition has been re-discovered, and re-constructed. There are now many communities of practitioners who have embraced primal, archetypal forms of divination and initiation as well as the wisdom teachings that support them. These people are in the vanguard of a universalized spiritual awareness which is spreading ever wider, and the result is that Tarot books and decks have become best sellers in the mainstream market.

Still, most people who read Tarot books and use Tarot cards do not understand its ancient roots. History suggests that Tarot decks first appeared in early Renaissance or late Mediaeval Europe. But for many, its internal structure and symbology suggest that its roots reach back to the primal wellsprings of civilization itself. When we know more about the primal powers to which Tarot refers, we begin to see that Tarot is a Book of Truth, a wide and universal truth that cannot be contained within any religion, because it speaks the language of symbolism, number and archetypal form. Tarot truth appeals not to the dogmatic or theologically inclined mind, but to the love of spiritual adventure and the importance of intuitive revelation. These are the building blocks of all true spiritual expression. It is for this reason that personal meditation, and the writings of the great spiritual masters become indispensable for plumbing the depths of consciousness from which Tarot comes. Those who practice a spiritual path, and those who have progressed their consciousness in spiritual matters, are likely to be more deeply aware of the *inner* lineage of esoteric energies and symbols than academic scholars who write about the same matters. For example, the meaning of The Fool can be better understood in its deeper sense when we come to know the reality of the soul, and its representative, the 'psychic being'. In any case, Tarot is not merely an arcane mental amusement, it is a way of moving into deeper levels of engagement with Truth in all its varied forms of self-presentation. Those who, like The Fool, set forth on their own inner adventure will be best able to discover the richness with which Tarot can speak about the journey of self-discovery. Skeptics, positivist historians and debunkers will be able to split hairs and sift limited evidence for many years to come with a view to grounding Tarot in a much more mundane matrix of so-called hard facts.

In *Ancient Mysteries Tarot*, you will find that earth, air, fire and water are referred to directly, rather than mediated by symbols such as pentacles, swords, wands and cups. Stone is very important because it is the bones of the earth, the crystalline repository of earth's wisdom and power. Ancient temples, statues and sacred power spots all relied on the energetic properties of stone to hold and transmit the energies of awakening. Stones were libraries and batteries and canvasses for the sacred energies of initiation. For this reason, stone figures prominently in this deck. In fact, there is hardly a card that does not have stone on it. For the Earth-Energy cards (pentacles), stones are used; for the Water-Energy cards, you will find streams of water emerging from stones; for the Air cards, you will find windows in stone. Only among the Fire cards, sometimes, will you find less stone. But then, Fire-energy is, in the given cosmic scheme of things, furthest removed from that of stone.

Stone is a powerful medium of artistic expression. If you place your hand on certain of the statues in our modern museums, you will often be able to feel a certain kind of energy that indicates a living presence inside the stone. Many of the ancient carvings were true power objects, homes to living entities that had been invoked to take residence there. Indian temples carry on the practice to this very day.

There is a great deal of superstitious misunderstanding that has been attached to Tarot. It helps to appreciate that Tarot expresses universal spiritual wisdom, not any limited religious version of it. The Highest Truth is One. But in its expression, in this universe into which we are born, Truth is manifold, varied and complex. Consciousness is infinite, but as it manifests in this three-dimensional time-space continuum in which we live, consciousness takes on many guises. It can manifest as energy. Or it can manifest as matter. In matter, it is not fluid, but becomes fixated or crystallized into specific forms. These forms arise and appear in three dimensional space. They change and evolve in time. The ultimate Reality is beyond time and space, but its varied expressions are crystallized, fixed and delimited when they occur in this dimension. In other words, all forms must be situated in some specific relation to north, west, south and east, as well as up, down and centre. Thus, geometry and number become means by which the expression of truth can be accomplished in a multi-faceted way. Colour and sound are also means by which the unity of truth can be given varied expression. Tarot is about the expression of Truth in form.

Either we take the position that all expression of the Divine Reality is idolatrous, or we admit that all expression involves some distortion, yet it is worth the effort. Tarot takes the latter position. Whereas in the Bible God is a Father figure, in Tarot, Divine Authority can be expressed in both genders, and it is understood to be beyond gender. The Emperor is not "better than" or "superior to" the Empress. They have different but complimentary roles, just as males and females do. The patriarchal position has for much of recorded history been that female energy is inferior. Thus, in the New Testament we find St. Paul advising women to take a subservient position to men, and we find also in Islam and Judaism that women have traditionally been kept to the background. However, Tarot gives a place to the feminine aspect of the Divine, and considers it indispensable to our human wholeness.

Initiation and divination are about the search for wholeness. Tarot, which I sometimes refer to as The Book of Truth, ranges freely through the many forms of expression in which Infinity has clothed itself and by means of which higher consciousness has been revealed to humans in quest of greater wisdom. Both the dark and the light are necessary for the full revelation of Truth on earth. Therefore, in Tarot we find images of Death, The Devil, The Tower and The Hanged Man (The Prisoner), as well as many aspects of challenge and negativity in the numbered cards, particularly swords.

It came as a complete surprise to me to experience that I was being guided by The Muse to start writing about Tarot. But a series of revelations took place, often in my morning meditations, that showed me, chapter by chapter how to proceed. I learned to follow the thread of what was being shown and unfolded and to keep at it daily as long as the inspiration lasted. I supplemented my writing by doing as much reading as I could. However, I have to say that what is original in this work comes from what I was shown inwardly in meditation day by day as the book wrote itself. This is what makes me feel and believe that deep spiritual connections are important to truly understand Tarot; the content of the book came to me largely as a revelation from these sources, supplemented of course by extensive research.

It was immediately after a trip to Peru, where I had spent weeks among the ancient ruins of the Incas and Pre-Incas, that I received the inspiration to paint a Tarot Deck. Since beginning to write *Ancient Mysteries Tarot*, I had been collecting Tarot decks which I felt to be in harmony with the earliest traditions of divination and initiation. I vividly recall one lazy afternoon in mid July 2003, when I was alone at my country retreat relaxing on the couch and drifting off to sleep. Suddenly, with a sense of urgency, I awoke and knew that I had to return home at once, that same hour, and begin putting together the art for a new Tarot Deck, which would embody a different vision of its roots. This, like the urge to begin writing, came as a bolt from the blue. I had no desire to undertake a new project as demanding as painting 78 images, right after completing a 250 page manuscript and hard on the heels of three weeks of adventure in the mountains of Peru. But the inner directive to begin painting came as clearly, imperatively and surprisingly as had the directive to begin writing. It simply could not be denied.

As a matter of fact, many pieces of art which I had completed during my years in Asia between 1989 and 1995 were ideal for certain cards within a proposed Ancient Mysteries Tarot deck. Others had to be worked up from my understanding of ancient tradition, drawing on a collection of pictures and photographs that I had assembled during my years of travel to ancient sacred sites around the world. Important decisions and choices had to be made in creating an Ancient Mysteries Tarot Deck. To illustrate the Minor Arcana or not – this was one important question. My choice and direction in this matter can best be understood by looking at other Tarot decks from the past.

The modern Tarot traditions which we find in the Tarot of Marseilles, the Etteilla Tarot, and most of all the Rider-Waite Deck, with paintings by Pamela Colman Smith, have shaped our understanding of Tarot in modern times. The Waite deck in particular accomplished a popularization of Tarot, but at a great cost. The nature of what was lost can best be explained if we understand the importance of numerology in Tarot.

Numerology is a very profound field of study going back thousands of years and known in all parts of the globe. Each of the numbers from one to ten has a set of meanings, perhaps on average five or more highly significant meanings, as well as a number of subsidiary ones. Arthur Edward Waite decided to illustrate the Minor Arcana, (which was something new) and to do this he commissioned Pamela Smith to paint a picture that would express for each card one of the numerological meanings. Let us take one example. The number five carries an energy of movement, change, progress, freedom, a need to explore, to experience new adventures, to communicate and to gather fresh experience. Along with change and movement five carries a vibration of adaptability, and an element of uncertainty and instability. It can, on occasion bring shifting fortune, and in the extreme, may precipitate strife, difficulty, adversity or conflict. In the Waite deck, the artwork for the Five of Swords emphasizes the challenging and crisis-like character of the number. It is one of the most unpleasant of the tarot cards, with overtones of humiliation, meanness, defeat, betrayal and violence. It suggests failure and misfortune. Obviously this is not the complete picture of the five vibration. It is a substantial reduction and even a distortion of its total meaning.

This narrowing of meaning is the price Waite paid for his decision to illustrate the Minor Arcana. Previously, the illustrators would have placed a single sword on the card for the ace of swords, then two, three, four, five and so on for the remainder of the cards up to ten. A person reading the cards would bring to bear his or her knowledge of the symbol to which swords refer, which is air, and the full range of meanings of the number, and put this together in the overall context of the reading to come up with an interpretation. Waite simplified Tarot, popularized it, and at the same time greatly reduced (and to that extent diminished) the meanings of many Minor Arcanum cards by his decision to illustrate one of many possible meanings for each number. The average, relatively untrained Tarot reader would find it quite easy to remember a given card's meaning by simply looking at the illustration and picking up its visual clues. The Ten of Swords, for example, shows complete destruction, whereas the meaning of ten and of air are in no way negative. It was Waite's destiny to create a form of Tarot which would appeal to the masses and bring about a world in which Tarot was more widely used. What Waite did made perfect sense to him, from his perspective. The pictures were more interesting than endless illustrations of swords, wands, discs and cups, and the visual clues of Waite's new, illustrated Minor Arcanum greatly simplified the problem of interpretation. Tarot has never been the same since.

Ancient Mysteries Tarot, on the other hand, has returned to the older, more demanding way of reading the Minor Arcanum. This requires a user to combine his or her knowledge of the meaning of the four elements, whether earth, air, fire or water, with the full range of significance of the ten numbers, and thereby take into account all possible meanings that any card may have. This is a richer, deeper, and more flexible way to read the Minor Arcanum than simply to settle on one meaning, often a lesser one, but the one the artist has chosen to illustrate over and above all the others. It is the ancient way, the way of those who, in the past made a lifetime study of divination. It is perhaps more demanding, but it is true to the tradition. In this, *Ancient Mysteries Tarot* parts company with the Rider-Waite deck and others of its ilk which have illustrated the Minor Arcanum with pictures, thereby forcing the numerological significance of any given card into the procrustean bed of one exclusive meaning – or at best a much reduced range of meanings related to the illustration.

I have also chosen to return to the primal elements as opposed to their cultural symbols. Thus water, not a cup, is used to designate that element, and stone, not a 'pentacle' is used to designate earth. Fire is fire, and a window framed with stone is used to designate air. This pulls Tarot back into its primal and ancient ambience, making for possibilities of richer and more complex interpretation, but also demanding a deeper study of the timeless, universal meaning of numbers and the four elements.

As to the question of whether the negative or the positive energies of any given card predominate, it is often a function of the degree of ego that is present in the person for whom the reading is being made. Mind is the most direct outflow of ego, so swords (or air) is the suite where the smallness and negativity of egocentric people is most apt to be exposed. A spiritually developed, or a very pure individual might find very positive indications in a card such as the five or the ten of swords (air) which would for a selfish and mean-spirited person, dominated by ego, spell suffering. My own practice is not to use reversed cards. But the obverse side of the cards is designed so that reverse cards can be used by those who prefer to do readings that way. The obverse side of each card has an illustration which echoes the mystery school tradition.

This book may be adding something new and valuable to our understanding of Tarot in several ways. Firstly, it recognizes the role of the Divine Mother in the processes of initiation and divination which are central to Tarot. For it is the Goddess aspect of Infinite Consciousness which imparts to humanity its capacities for intuition, creative expression, nurturing and healing.

Secondly, the hidden roots of Tarot reach back, as I have mentioned, into the ancient traditions of the Mystery Schools. If one has had past lives in this tradition, and if one examines these past lives, or if one examines the history of the Mystery Schools or of ancient religion, or if one studies the modern material which has been channeled on these subjects, it becomes very evident that this is so.

Thirdly: Each soul is evolving toward a higher level of awareness, and in that journey, we will all become more and more open to spiritual presences and energies which we call the archetypes. This is not the highest realm of spiritual experience, it is an intermediate realm, but the pilgrim soul must pass through it on the journey home to the ultimate Source. We have important things to learn in the archetypal realms. The Major Arcanum of Tarot uses imagery of the great archetypal beings to open doorways in human consciousness. In this sense it expedites our initiation. Tarot is not only a tool of divination, but also of divinisation. We will each be required to develop and unfold from within ourselves the consciousness of the Magician, the Hermit, the Empress, and the others. Many or most books on Tarot stress how the images can be used in fortune telling, but the Mystery School tradition from which Tarot places equal or greater importance on the process of initiation.

The real validation of how helpful Tarot is in the spiritual journey comes from the personal experience of its users. For me personally, the act of writing the book and painting the deck came as an inspiration from the beyond. The Muse revealed something, and I recorded what I was shown. I hope that I have set down clearly and beautifully what was given. My wish is that it will bring you, the student of Tarot and of life, an opening to a wonderful new adventure of self-discovery.

PART ONE : THE ANCIENT TRADITION

What Is Tarot?

This book grew out of an inner revelation that came to me in the form of several dreamlike experiences in meditation, both when I was sitting for formal daily practice, and at other times in a state resembling sleep. This seed of inner experience developed further by my reflections about it and later on by extensive research. Let me tell you about the initial experience, which led to all the rest.

Many of my most important dreams come in the early morning, just before I wake up. In the one I am about to describe, I was aware of being "asleep, but not asleep". Spiritual masters write about this as a kind of intermediate state between full waking and deep sleep. When I enter this realm, it feels like being in the full waking consciousness, not like dreaming. Sometimes in that state I think I am lying in bed awake. But I am not fully awake, as in meditation. The experience I am going to share was so real and convincing that I could not but believe I had lived through it. I was lying in bed early in the morning before getting up. I returned to normal waking awareness with the memory still fresh and quickly tried to set it down in words. Join me now as I try to share and relive what happened…

I am in bed with my eyes closed, but I am not aware of this. I am having an inner experience. In this experience, I am walking in the woods, a kind of woodland very like my own country retreat. It is rocky terrain, and the trees are a mixture of mature hemlock and pine, with some cedar and oak interspersed here and there. I can also see the occasional white bark of birch trees. I come to a place deep in the woods where everything is very still. It is a clearing among the trees. Directly ahead of me I see a rocky granite hill, and in its side an opening or grotto. Sitting in front of this dark opening is a strange lady.

She is wearing grey robes, and across her face is a veil. She is quite still, and there is a mood of solemnity about her. With some hesitancy, I begin to draw closer to her. I sense that she is aware of my approach while at the same time being absorbed in her own interior reverie. Her features are dimly visible behind the veil, but I cannot say that I would be able to recognize her on the street, or that I could pick her out again from a photo.

Crossing the opening in the forest, I stand before her in silence. I had the feeling of her gaze resting on me. There is utter stillness all about. Then, I hear a voice within my mind, a female voice. Softly, the words are pronounced: Sybilla sum.

I know what these words mean. I do not have to make any mental effort at remembering my high school Latin, because the understanding comes automatically. "I am the Sybil", she says. Then, she speaks again: Intro ibo ad altari Dei.

"I go in to the altar of God." Her voice inside my mind is soft and solemn, its cadences soothing and kind. These words I know and remember from my childhood as an altar boy. I have the feeling of being in a sacred place, and the smell of pine is intense, like incense.

At this point, her mind guides mine to look behind her physical form into the dark mouth of the grotto. I become aware of steps that lead downward into its dark interior. She turns away from me and slowly begins to walk down those steps. I follow her. I have no hesitation to do so.

Slowly we descend into the darkness. It is cool, with dank, sweet smells of earth, and a feeling of moisture in the air. We come to a level stone floor, a small circular alcove, dimly lit, and then we begin to ascend. I count fifteen steps, stone steps, as we come up again. To my right and to my left it is all granite and only a faint light from ahead makes anything visible at all. The Sibyl's grey robes rustle on the stone steps as she ascends, and I follow behind her into a growing light.

When we reach the top, we are standing in a chamber entirely cut from living stone. A circular skylight allows a gentle beam of radiance to shine down into the centre of the room. It falls upon a crystal orb, which sits on a square stone altar. On four sides of this altar are stone pillars. The crystal orb glows with the light, and there is enough radiance to see that the room is circular, and that the stone walls have pictures hanging on them. But my gaze returns to the crystal ball, because its light is drawing my attention into itself.

"This is the world," says the voice within my mind. "This is the Mother."

We stand together, the veiled lady and I, gazing into the crystal ball. "Behold the Mother's Light," the voice whispers.

The silence deepens, and my gaze is drawn inside the ball. I realize that the crystal ball and the room are lit by moonlight, not sunlight. There is a sense of energy cool and pure, refreshing and peaceful. I am in a place of wholeness and peace. I want to rest there, to float in that atmosphere of silent bliss. I want to seek deeper and deeper into this wonderful feeling of lightness.

How long this experience of being in the light lasts, I cannot tell. For at this point, I wake up. I feel deeply at ease, as if emerging from a wonderful meditation, or from a profound state of contemplation.

This is what happened to me in my first experience. This was the start of my journey of discovery in Tarot. Before sitting down to write about this experience in my dream diary, I went across the hall from my bedroom to the library and opened the box where my Tarot cards were kept. There, I found the card of the High Priestess. She had the same look and feel as the Sybil of my dream. I found The Hermit. It was the same face (The deck I was using was the Spiral Deck). It took a few moments of recollection to try and understand what this experience had meant.

As I reflected, I realized that I had made an inner contact with the High Priestess, and that she had acted as my guide. She had taken me into a temple of some sort. Its key feature was a crystal sphere, which she referred to as "The World". Its light was the moon-energy, and in this light I had experienced the depths of contemplation. I had not taken in the pictures on the walls, but I had the feeling that they held Tarot associations. The Mother-power was the prime mover at work in this temple. It was a Goddess temple of some kind, but a place where I felt very much at home.

I knew from my Tarot studies that the High Priestess is the guide in matters intuitive. Her message is one of reliance on inner sensing, a knowing that comes from the heart and not from the busy intellect. And indeed the feeling I had from the figure in the dream and from this temple was one of stillness, power, and a mood of numinous moonlight bathing everything in peace and purity. The steps at first led downward into the bowels of the earth, but then they ascended into a chamber lit by a single source, a single beam of moonlight.

I knew that "The World" was also one of the 22 cards of the Major Arcana, but I was used to seeing it pictured as a human female form, not as a crystal sphere. It was the culminating card of the Major cards in the Tarot deck, and represented the primal matrix, the original time-space continuum of creation, the world-soul and the wholeness of things. But in my dream experience, the world, the crystal sphere, was lit up by moonlight. And I had experienced an entry into this silver light. And it had not been an intellectual experience. I was not making any interior dialogue or verbal commentary while all this happened, indeed my mind had been quite still. That stillness and that sense of depth endured as I wrote the experience down, and it continued to be with me through the remainder of the day.

This experience came at the start of a period of reflection and research on Tarot which resulted in the book *Ancient Mysteries Tarot*. When I began to write, I was most familiar with the artwork of the Rider-Waite Tarot deck, especially the images of the Major Arcanum. Following the above experience I had a series of meditations, in which I received inner guidance about the writing of the book. In my subsequent reflection and research, these seeds grew into a volume that suggested that there was a connection between Tarot and the ancient Mystery School Tradition. A month or so after the book was written, I was inspired to create the artwork for a new Tarot deck which would express what I had been writing about.

In *Ancient Mysteries Tarot*, I use the word "Tarot" to refer to three things. I use it firstly to mean Waite's Tarot, and other decks like it. This was my starting point, but I became familiar with many other decks, some that preceded it and many more that followed. These had been created roughly between the years 1400 and 2,000 AD. This is Tarot pretty much "as we know it".

Secondly, I use the term Tarot to refer to elements that were part of ancient divination and initiation in the Mystery Schools of Greece, Mesopotamia, Egypt and India from about the time of Christ's birth, going back four to six thousand years. I call this the Roots of the Tarot Tree. I understand that many students of Tarot may feel that this 'stretches' the meaning of the word Tarot unduly, but the book *Ancient Mystery Tarot* explains how and why I came to this understanding. Other points of view on this matter may be quite valid from their own perspective.

Thirdly, I use the word Tarot to refer to the material that I developed in *Ancient Mysteries Tarot* and the new deck of cards (*Ancient Mysteries*

Tarot Deck) which I created to formulate my ideas about Tarot's relation to ancient traditions. In my writing, I refer to certain ancient and primal realities of the inner world as "archetypes". Examples of this term include the "wise old man", the "divine king", the "earth goddess", and the "wheel of fate". These and other archetypes are pictured in the Major Arcana of most Tarot decks. In my understanding of Tarot, archetypes, the four sacred elements (conventionally symbolized by swords, wands, cups and coins) and the Pythagorean numbers, are the essence of whole system. I know very well that Tarot may have been nothing more than a game of cards for most people who used it during the several earliest centuries we can trace historically. And I understand that people who lived BC probably did not have Tarot Cards in the form of decks as we do. But they did have, in their traditions of divination and initiation, the basic elements later assembled symbolically into the form of Tarot Cards. The first makers of Tarot cards, consciously or unconsciously were creating a remarkable tool for opening consciousness to many levels of reality, including its most ancient roots.

What, then, is Tarot? For me, Tarot is a compendium of the possible meanings a human life can have. The meaning is not in the cards, but in their user. A deck of Tarot cards is an instrument, which can be used skillfully or otherwise, not unlike a violin or a piano. Each of the 78 images in a deck of Tarot cards pictures a possibility that we can experience. The meaning of a card depends on the question that is asked, the skill of the reader, the other cards in the spread, and the possible refinements of further questions that may be asked, using further cards, to elaborate the initial clue. In particular, the 22 images of the Major Arcanum express archetypal attainments, experiences, insights or capacities that we can grow into and realize. On this basis Tarot has been called a Book of Wisdom. It can be used to see into the potential of a human life and understand it better (divination), or it can be used to study, comprehend and attain deeper or higher levels of consciousness (initiation). These two uses are not mutually exclusive. Divination means seeing further and deeper, ultimately seeing the Divine, and initiation means growing into, realizing, and becoming all that we can be. Tarot offers pictures of many of the combinations and permutations of experience which a human life can encompass as it unfolds from lesser to greater dimensions of wholeness.

Tarot could not exist without symbolism. We humans have used symbols from the most ancient times right up to the present day both to express ideas, and to activate states of heightened awareness. A true symbol comes from a plane of existence beyond the three-dimensional time-space continuum, which is the normal waking world, in which we move and live. Symbols carry the energy and information of their own planes of reality. If we are intuitively alert and attuned, a symbol can convey deep meaning. As subjects for meditation, symbols can precipitate significant experiences of expanded knowledge. When our human mind contemplates spiritual symbols, it takes on their form and assimilates their resonance. Gateways of deep understanding can thereby be opened.

In history, many cultures have evolved into greatness and then declined, but they have all used symbolism to express and to empower their purposes. Tarot puts on the cultural trappings of symbolism and imagery in order to speak to us about a realm of reality that endures even as cultures rise and pass away. The archetypal structure of Tarot is its inner essence, the core foundation of its meaning. A modern Tarot deck has 22 cards designated as the Major Arcana and a further 56 cards designated as the Minor Arcana. These latter are divided into four suits known conventionally as swords, cups, wands and pentacles. The core of meanings that Tarot can express inheres in the various artistic expressions of visual content that Tarot decks take (with greater or lesser degrees of distortion) whether ancient or modern. The inner reality to which Tarot refers can be glimpsed only when we learn to read the cards, and this is a special skill. We must know something about the symbolism of the cards, and we must be able to awaken our intuitive side, which demands that we align our consciousness in the right way.

When Tarot decks first began to show up as illustrated playing cards at the beginnings of the Renaissance in Europe, the keys to understanding the esoteric teachings of the Mystery Schools had been misplaced. The Hermetic scholars and the alchemists of that period had fragments of understanding, but not the complete picture. There are intriguing hints that the earliest decks may have been expressing the arcane lore of the Renaissance magi, but this has not been conclusively proved. We do know that Italy and France were astir with renewed interest in the wisdom of the ancients, fuelled by texts from Constantinople, which fell to the Turks in 1453. Some of these texts had references to the Mystery Schools that were already old when Rome was founded.

In ancient times, from generation to generation, the Mystery Schools had preserved, deepened, and transmitted the wisdom which occultists from the Renaissance onward saw encapsulated in the symbols of Tarot. But the Roman Empire and the Christian Religion and the barbarian invasions shook that ancient world and its primal spiritual traditions to the core. In Christian Europe, right up until relatively modern times, any deviation from official dogma was treated as heresy, and heretics were hunted down and silenced. The history of the Albigensians, the Cathars, the Gnostics and other sects shows how brutal the suppression could be. In this milieu, Tarot could exist as a card game, but not as a teaching of deep truth. To use it for divination or for initiation meant risking life and limb. The dogmatic absolutism of the Roman Church would countenance nothing that could open the European mind to spiritual realities beyond its own official teaching. Even today, Ouija boards and seances are condemned as sinful.

By the time of the Enlightenment, the advent of the Freemasons and Rosicrucians and the re-discovery of the languages and writings of the Ancient Near East, the European mind was ready to begin the process of re-discovering the Mystery School tradition which lay behind much of the symbolism of Tarot. In the early 1900's, the Rider-Waite Tarot deck captured popular interest and set the direction that mainstream Tarot would go in terms of art, symbolism, and interpretation for virtually the next century. Now, with the New Age movement well in progress, we have reached a turning point. The universal, Gnostic and divinatory aspects of Tarot can more and more be seen as an expression of timeless, universal wisdom-teaching. We know more about the initiation-rites and the divination methods of the ancient Mystery School tradition. Type the words "Mystery School" into any Internet search engine and you will find references to the Greek mysteries of Orpheus and Eleusis, the mysteries of ancient Egypt, and other references to the Babylonians, Chaldeans and Celtic Druids. The particular stamp which Waite placed on our understanding of Tarot, while useful in its day, has branched off in many directions since his time. *Ancient Mysteries Tarot* is a book that begins by reviewing some of the evidence for a connection between modern Tarot and ancient traditions, and then goes on to tell the story of The Fool's journey of experience through the archetypes.

Since I had no interest in Tarot at all prior to my dream-experience described above, and the later meditations which unfolded its meaning, it was necessary to reflect, research, practice and teach the subject to make sure that I was on firm ground. I am grateful to Mary Greer and others whose advice has been invaluable in this process. Tarot history in particular is a contentious area of debate and the modern mind demands solid evidence for any claims one makes in this field. My previous 30 years of daily meditation and spiritual study have provided me with a personal perspective that might make possible a new and useful contribution. Other perspectives, from their own vantage points, may also be very valuable. Many kinds of analysis and consideration and comment on Tarot prove useful when we seek to understand all it can be, and use it to its full potential. That has been my experience. I hope that what follows will be useful in this spirit.

The student of Tarot, who is really a student of life and an apprentice of its wisdom, will master the subject more quickly if his or her mind can be transformed into a temple of knowledge. The work of ordering, informing and illumining the mind (as well as the heart) creates within us a sanctuary, and the deeper, sacred insights into Tarot can come fully to life if they are provided with that atmosphere. If you can activate the archetypes to which the Major Arcanum of Tarot refers, and make them feel at home in your consciousness, they will play their role in your life, richly enhancing its scope and meaning. Tarot symbols offer us insight and awakening exactly in the measure that this inner work of self-preparation has been done. They mirror our intentionality to us. They communicate the degree of clarity, insight, spiritual depth, range and subtlety that we have established in our own consciousness. If our core intent has been purified and motivated by our spiritual aspirations, as the Mystery School traditions have always guided students to do, Tarot will reveal the fullness of its magic.

This is the spiritual approach to Tarot. It works from the top down. If, following the advice of Master Jesus, you seek first the Kingdom of Heaven, all the rest will be added to it. In my own case, I came to feel that if I could know the lost wisdom of the Mystery Schools, I would understand better the language of number and symbol and image by which Tarot expresses its meanings. I did not feel it was absolutely indispensable to go rummaging through the rags and bones of history for scraps of "proof" to figure out what Tarot might have meant to Europeans living at the end of the Middle Ages. The earliest historical decks that still remain in no way capture the full scope of Tarot's ancient meaning or its modern possibilities. There are ages of darkness and ages of light, and a human mind's capacity to know the deep meaning and power of symbols may be adversely or beneficially affected by the circumstances of birth. History can try to document how people thought and understood at a point of European history where Tarot was being re-discovered by the western mind after a long sleep of spiritual forgetfulness and religious suppression. My interest, as I felt guided in my meditation, reflection and research, was not to sort out the history of Tarot's re-emergence so much as to grasp the fullness of its primal meaning. I wanted to have some sense of the archetypal understandings of ancient adepts who were masters in both initiation and divination. Using the power of number, the four sacred elements and the archetypes, they had scaled the heights. I was interested in Tarot as an extension or expression of the Mystery School tradition, and all that this signifies for us today when we have decks of cards to use as symbols and tools. I had the sense that initiates in the temples of ancient Egypt or Greece or Chaldea might have used clay discs with numbers or paintings, or table-tops with designs or other tools which allowed them to do the same thing as modern users of Tarot do with their printed decks.

My study was useful, and the books I read were helpful links in a long journey of discovery, but my inner guidance was the decisive factor in what I gave importance to. Tarot is a tool for putting you in touch with your own intuition and with the inner guides that teach you through the intuitive faculty. Traditional teachers in ancient times taught that only those who have studied the Universal Truth for several lifetimes, likely from a variety of traditions and perspectives, will have developed the capacities of the higher, intuitive mind necessary for the mastery of arcane wisdom. I had the immediate sense that Tarot can be used as a tool for the development of the more subtle mental faculties, and once these faculties have unfolded, it can be a book which reveals the secret teaching in ever greater depth. One lifetime is only a link, or a step, in a great journey of self-discovery. But it can become rich with meaning when we learn to read the original books of divine wisdom, and especially when we develop the necessary skills to access the deepest teachings, which invariably use symbolic language. Tarot is one such language.

Knowing what Tarot refers to, and *how* it refers, is what counts most in its use. For example, in your own spiritual development, when you discover the psychic being (which I sometimes experience as the child in the heart, the soul-child) you know more about The Fool. When you have learned the uses and abuses of power, you know much about the Emperor. When you have lived as a monk, you know something about The Hermit. A lifetime is not too much to learn the meaning of one card from the Major Arcana. In learning Tarot, you become conscious of the wisdom of many lifetimes. Tarot affords you a language of summation, a means to encapsulate the wisdom of your soul's journey of evolution.

Initiation and divination will be encountered by every soul which awakens to the spiritual adventure of life, and when we come to share the journey with others, Tarot is one of our best links to the essentials of the ancient wisdom tradition. Any teacher or author's own personal journey is intimately related to the story he can tell you about Tarot. One really only knows the terrain he has walked. Only of this does one truly have the right to speak. Thus, my own focus is defined, limited, imperfect, incomplete, but at the same time blessed by the perspective that opened to me. I tried to be a good scribe for the insights that came through, and to ground them in as firm an understanding of divination and Tarot as study would permit. The initiations and deepenings of consciousness which I have experienced in this life and others of which I have become aware determine my perspective.

In my later reflections about my dream experience, it seemed that the Sybil was one form of the Divine Mother, who is my spiritual guide and one form of the Infinite Consciousness. In the temple we've visited, the moon channels the sun's light, and in fact the Divine Sun in all its glorious fullness *needs* to be scaled down into something we can assimilate, something with transduced energies that can unfold and evolve in time and space, elements of a story that we can live and discuss.

Of all the Tarot cards, my closest sense of affinity has for some time been with The Fool. And I think I know why this is so. I feel that I know The Fool from the inside. Much of what he is, I am. So it is as The Fool that I tell my story of a journey through the archetypes in *Ancient Mystery Tarot*, a story that is a metaphor of what I have personally lived and experienced and known. My sense of The Fool is that he only appears to be a fool if you look at him from the outside, through the eyes of accumulated social conditioning, or from the perspective of the mental ego. But if you can experience who he is from the inside, he is by no means foolish. The words "fool" and "foolish" only arise when The Fool bumps up against social convention. In his own space, he is true to himself, and has much inner freedom; he is internally consistent within himself, and he only encounters dilemma or misunderstanding when he pursues his adventures in the outer world and faces the conundrums of humanity. It is his fate to be misunderstood by those who see him from the outside.

I feel that knowing The Fool is intimately related to knowing the soul. Each of us is, in essence, that divinity, but in order to manifest our divinity in material form, we must incarnate. When a human being is born, the soul enters into the three dimensional time-space continuum, taking on a mind, an astral (emotional) body, and a physical body, as well as a set of karmic limitations or challenges which are necessary for growth and expression of potential. When the Divine Self has projected a part of its timeless reality into manifest form, that portion of divinity is called the soul. The soul experiences evolution as a human being, it unfolds its capacities from life to life, but it cannot be compromised by its earthly experiences, (fire cannot burn it, water cannot drown it, etc. as the Bhagavad Gita says) it can only learn and evolve. As the soul absorbs life's lessons and assimilates its experiences, the physic being manifests more of the soul's wisdom and capacity.

The Fool, who in spiritual vocabulary can be called the "psychic being" (from the Greek word psyche, or soul) is the inner reality of our unlimited potential. He is not in any way conditioned by human history, social habits, family karma, the ego, or by the mind and its social programming. He works through all of this in an innately innocent, intuitive sense of inner purpose, to achieve an inner growth of consciousness in the adventure of life. Living through various kinds of experience is how he learns his lessons. This is how he develops the ability to express his potential in creation, and to cope with its darkness. He is forever renewing the adventure of his human incarnations for the purpose of progressing in self-mastery, but none of his experiences bind or limit him. He is naturally innocent, clear, a free spirit. By the end of his journey, The Fool has acquired all the gifts of The Magician, and all the qualities or lessons of the other 20 figures in the Major Arcana, but he always remains who he is, free from all kinds of ego-limitation. His only limitation, and it may be a form of wisdom, is that he is not shaped by social convention.

There is a certain kind of meditation you can do wherein you become the psychic being. Or, the experience of being in your soul may just happen to you outside the context of formal contemplative practice.

One of the first signs that you are having this experience is that you become childlike. You become heart-centred. The complexity of your mind, while you are in that flow, simply melts away. There is a quality of sweetness and freshness that comes forward in your inmost feelings. You walk more lightly. You feel more deeply and clearly the poignancy of life. You have a sense of inner freedom from all that is around you, and in fact the world such as it is may seem, when you look at it through the eyes of the inner child, rather stale and drab. You have the sense of how everything is inwardly, in its true essence, before it is interpreted and manipulated and tainted by the human mind, and you find it all intrinsically beautiful. This includes your experience of other people, but you see the difference between who they are in essence, and the personality-scripts they are living. You observe this from a space within yourself where you feel it is wiser not to interfere. You have the good sense to keep quiet in order to be true to the spirit of your inner vision. You find that you are naturally kind-hearted and caring in your disposition towards all life, but you may not be motivated to do anything other than to smile upon the world lovingly.

There is a quiet sense of having come home. You know what it means to be truly yourself, but you feel like a babe in the woods relative to the sophisticated and complicated world around you. You may not feel that you are able to relate to it on its own terms. Hence, the need to gather experience and to acquire an education, and hence the journey and the quest into which the Fool is always entering. The child in the heart is forever exploring, playing with experience, setting out on new avenues of discovery. His disposition is playful, and he learns by play, because his heart is light. He is never pulled away from this inner lightness of being, because he can only be true to himself. He has the "innocence of a dove" as an innate gift. He sets out on his life-adventure to acquire the wisdom of the serpent. This is The Fool I know from the inside, The Fool who experiences the adventures of the Tarot which unfold later in this tale. These are some things I can say about the Fool from my own personal experience of the psychic being. This may sound poetic or metaphorical, but I suspect that there are very few of us who can claim to be completely unacquainted with the child in the heart. Anyone who is would find the above comments meaningless.

II Priestess

III Empress

IV

Emperor

V

High Priest

VI

Lovers

VII

Chariot

VIII

Strength

IX

Hermit

X **Wheel**

XI **Justice**

XII **Prisoner**

XIII **Death**

XIV

Temperance

XV

Devil

XVI

Tower

XVII

Star

XVIII

Moon

XIX

Sun

XX

Prophecy

XXI

World

The Tarot Card illustration called "The Fool" is looking at the psychic being from the outside, and trying to illustrate his appearance by means of visual symbols which are overlays of cultural association. The earliest cards show The Fool as a beggar being attacked by a dog. Waite has him wearing a mantle decorated with spoked wheels, which express the whirling movement of the universe. In the Waite deck, seven green leaves surround each wheel-mandala, corresponding to the seven chakras, and under this mantle the Fool wears a white shirt, signifying purity of spirit. He carries a pole with a bundle, signifying his personal identity and psychological potential. The light of the sun shines on him from a yellow sky of divine intelligence. All of this, of course, reflects the perspective of the Golden Dawn magical group of which Waite was a member and sometime leader.

For me, the white dog beside the Fool represents "Sarama", or intuition. In the Vedas and the Upanishads, India's oldest scriptures, Sarama was experienced in the occult visions of the Rishis, and they symbolically referred to its action by using the symbol of a hound, or dog, who ran ahead sniffing out and discovering things unknown to the owner. The Fool is ready to step forward into the unknown, represented by a precipice. He does not have to know what lies ahead, because he is not moving forward from a place of fear or from a need to control (insecurity). He is open, unbounded, unencumbered, and he travels light. Intuition runs before him and sniffs out the truth of what lies ahead, beyond the superficial appearances. The Fool, in turn, responds to what his intuition reveals, not to the ploys of social convention. This is how he remains true to his own nature, and this is how he confronts and sometimes offends society.

It became clear to me, as I matched my inner awareness of my own psychic being with the Tarot image of The Fool that it would be very important for me to be able to enter into the consciousness of The Fool if I wanted to progress in Tarot. In other words, if I wanted to learn from the High Priestess, I would do best to approach Her from within the consciousness of my own soul-child, with openness, purity of heart, and intuitive spontaneity. In that consciousness, I become the child of

33

every mother, and link heart-to-heart with everyone and everything I encounter. She would feel this, and her guidance would be all the more assured from the intuited inner rapport. By becoming my own heart-child (who is by no means a fool), I would be transparent to the moonlit teaching beamed down into the crystal sphere at the heart of the temple. I would see the world as a repository of lessons which would be conveyed to me in symbolic visions, in magical time-space, in archetypal territory of the inner terrain. Only my own intuitive way of knowing could adequately receive and process what she had to convey, because I knew that the High Priestess would not cater to the presumptions of my mind. She came to me to liberate me from the limitations of my mental notions, not to lend them support, and it is for this reason that she spoke to me in the oracular vein, with the language of universal symbols, rather than in conversational banter.

Yes, I would have to develop greater facility at merging into my own psychic centre of being if I wanted to become her student, and move through the kingdom of archetypal lessons in the inner temple to which she had taken me.

Something else came to mind as I reflect upon the Fool, who is the protagonist of the tale to come, and his relation to the High Priestess, and it can only be explained by digressing into a few further details from my meditation. I am accustomed in my morning meditation to holding a crystal ball on my lap, cradled in my two hands. I meditate with a small group of seekers every morning at 7 am, and once or twice a week with a somewhat larger group of spiritual friends who follow the same heart-path as I do. One or two of these people had remarked that they could see gold light in the crystal ball when they looked my way during meditation. And I myself once glimpsed this light at the end of a session of meditation, when I was setting the ball aside in order to do a reading from a spiritual book, which is the normal way our group sittings are concluded. The presence of light within a crystal ball had been part of what the Sybil (High Priestess) had shown me in my dream-experience. It was the silver light of The Moon preparing the way for the descent of the Supramental Sun. It was a centrally important symbol of the spiritual work I was engaged in. It was something I needed to understand.

In three previous books that I authored about crystals, I had become aware that a fine quartz crystal is physical matter structured into an extraordinary degree of balance and harmony. All the molecules in a piece of quartz crystal (especially a clear one, without clouds) are lined up in perfectly symmetrical order. One can experience one's energy and consciousness being greatly amplified when they interact with such a piece. This was the kind of crystal ball I was holding in meditation. It was a unique piece both for size and clarity, and for some time now, various people in my group had been feeling its presence. One or two people in particular would make appointments to come and sit in the same room as the crystal ball and tune in to it for personal healing. Thus the image of the crystal orb in the temple had a real-life precedent. The image of a crystal sphere, representing "The World", resting on a square altar (spirit perfectly expressed in matter), illumined by light from above, seems clearly, as I reflect on it, to be an image of the marriage of heaven and earth. But in this case, in my dream with the Sibyl, it was moonlight which flooded down through the aperture in the ceiling of the inner temple, not the direct solar outpouring. This had its own symbolic meaning which, as I pondered it, seemed to be: the moonlight would teach me a number of lessons concerning the evolutionary unfolding that was my soul-journey on earth. The teaching would not be a silent white screen of the Supreme Self, rather it would be a tapestry of experience peopled by the archetypes of universal symbolism, and presided over by the High Priestess of perfected intuition. The crystal ball of the inner temple, like the ball I hold in meditation, would be a catalyst for initiation into a more conscious journeying of the spiritual path. Inside the grotto, in the inner temple of wisdom, which seemed to be the Sibyl's true home, the descent of celestial light into earthly matter seemed to be the central event. No doubt the pictures on the walls had their own importance for the future teaching, and I felt I would come to understand more of this if I were able to visit the place again, whether in dreams or in meditation.

As I began to write the early chapters of *Ancient Mysteries Tarot*, I knew that the cards of the Major Arcanum were 22 in number. I knew that the Fool was myself, my deeper self. I knew that "The World" was embodied in the crystal sphere at the centre of the inner temple. And I knew that the High Priestess, who called herself the Sibyl, had emerged from her own sacred space to be my guide. My inner feeling was that my sincerity in meditation and my fidelity to myself in my personal living would be all important for keeping open the channel by which I could progress further, and take in all she had to show me. This I was resolved to do.

A Crystal World

If The Fool is the protagonist and usually the first card of the Major Arcanum, The World is the final card, and the completion of The Fool's journey. When The Fool has encountered twenty different archetypal situations and their representative beings, and learned the lessons associated with each and acquired mastery of the relevant situations, he comes in the end to the experience of The World. What is this experience? Why is there a crystal sphere symbolic of the world at the centre of this temple in my dream vision?

My first intuitive answer is the evocation of another memory. It is a photograph of planet earth taken from outer space. The earth is green and blue, misted over in places by clouds, floating in the midst of the darkness of space, radiantly beautiful, and ONE. When we earthlings were first able to behold the earth from outside, and see that it was one and whole, something changed in our collective consciousness. We could see that we were sharing a single planet together, and that when we looked down from a great enough height, the earth was ONE. The Fool has always understood the underlying oneness behind the apparent diversity, but at the end of his journey he has mastered the challenges of life and he can live his knowledge of oneness in harmony with those whose attitude and actions violate the sense of inner oneness. When he began his journey as an innocent soul, he had not learned how to be *in* the world while not *of* it, but by the end of his journey, the world is truly his because he has mastered its ignorance. He is at one with the world and all it holds, because he has graduated from the school of life and attained conscious mastery and expression of his full inner potential.

But why is the sphere crystal? Crystal is matter brought to its highest degree of organization. A flawless diamond begins life as a dark lump of coal. Over long periods of time, through the forces of geology, the coal is compressed into a perfect crystalline structure, and it becomes adamant, the hardest substance known to man. True, it is still only carbon, but the alignment and harmonization of every atom into a perfect order has made it a "jewel of great price". A clear quartz crystal is a similar miracle of nature, and its many remarkable properties make it a wonderful tool for healing, for intuitive work, as an object or adjunct to meditation, and for attunement. A clear quartz crystal is, for the mineral world, what a fully realized spiritual master is in the human world, a transformed, perfected being. The earth will one day become perfect. The pure crystal sphere speaks of earth's high destiny.

Of course clear quartz crystal is one of the most important substances on earth. It is at the heart of our modern revolution in communications. It powered first our crystal radios, and later our computers, and is fundamental to most of our current technology. The development of computer chips made of pure silicone dioxide crystal has enabled us to create powerful tools of communication and calculation and to generate an inner world of information called the internet, where we can go to retrieve all sorts of facts and images, if we have the right computer setup. This is all analogous to the field of meditation, where we progressively refine our inner senses so that we can travel in various fields of consciousness and attune to the wisdom of higher levels of reality which have not yet taken material form. This is what much of the inner spiritual work is about.

Within days of my dream experience with the Sibyl, I began to reflect more deeply on the meaning of the Crystal sphere which represented The World in my dream-temple. In Tarot, The World stands for wholeness, the bringing together of separate parts into a synthesis or union. It stands for the realization of goals and quests, the achievement of the heart's aspirations and dreams. It is healing and attainment, the richness of completion and the blessedness of homecoming. It is a very good image of the completeness of a soul who has successfully completed life's journey, or indeed who has achieved full realization after a journey of many lives.

I began to reflect back and to remember how the image of a temple and the importance of its inner structure had been something I had been pondering for quite some time. For several months prior to my dream-vision, the image or concept of a temple had been impressing itself upon my mind, and I had the sense that I should be seeing my way forward to try and actually create a physical expression of my inner vision. One day in the middle of winter, I had walked out into the back yard, which is about half an acre in size, and begun to trace a large circle in the snow. I remember seeing how a structure of such a diameter would fit in the landscape, and I re-drew the circle several times until I felt that the surface area looked right. This memory reminds me that even in mid winter the temple idea was there in my mind. The dream of the Sibyl came much later, in early April.

Gradually, some of the elements of the temple's possible design and structure became clear in my mind. It was to have a floor design based on the Mother's symbol. This was a symbol which consisted of a small circle at the centre, four clover-shaped petals surrounding this, and twelve petals in the outermost ring. The central circle represents the Infinite Consciousness, the four inner petals represent the four primal powers or aspects of the Divine Mother, and the twelve outer petals represent the twelve forms of manifestation which these four powers take in the material creation.

I knew that this motif on the floor was important to the meaning of the temple, and I knew additionally that the walls were to be in the form of a circle. I had envisaged a beam of light coming down from the ceiling and hitting a crystal ball. This I had seen in the Matrimandir in Auroville, near Pondicherry India.

I must say, in retrospect, that my conscious mind had not taken in much of the detail of the temple interior in my dream experience.

Rather it had moved firstly to the Sibyl, and secondly to the crystal orb on the altar. This orb, and the light which bathed it became the focus of my awareness in that dream. My previous meditation and studies had conveyed to me a sense of the symbolic meaning of the crystal globe, and it is this which needed to be further refined after the meaning of this dream had settled into my understanding.

The crystal sphere represents earth, and a solar ray coming down from above represents the light of higher consciousness which enters into matter to transform and perfect it. It is a vision of the uniting of heaven with the earth. The perfect order of the crystal molecules is capable of receiving the light, amplifying it, and putting it to use in organizing matter to higher degrees of purity and order. The more highly ordered and refined the instrument of reception is, the greater the power it can channel. This is true both of computer chips and human beings.

A spiritual human being is a microcosm of the entire creation, and has the potential to become a conduit for the highest levels of energy and consciousness. Indeed, an evolving human being who has become aware of the presence of the soul is in one sense the true and original temple of which all the architectural expressions on earth throughout time are secondary and derivative. The inner sanctum of any temple represents the dwelling place of the Divine. In the dream-temple which I had visited, the crystal sphere represented an earth which was being bathed in pure light from above, earth in the process of being divinised. But the light flooding down from above in my vision was moonlight, which is the light of spiritual wisdom, not the solar light which is symbolic of the highest attainment. Therefore, this light represented a guiding influence on the journey through life's stages and cycles. It does not lead our consciousness to the formless Higher Self directly, but by measured stages of unfoldment. This light guides us through the progressive experiences which educate and initiate the soul into mastery, so that the soul can incarnate the highest consciousness and live it in a transformed material creation.

Many spiritual paths of the past including Buddhism and Advaita Yoga have sought to escape re-incarnation altogether and abandon earth to its fate, as if it were forever doomed to a state of ignorance and *maya* (illusion). The modern spiritual vision is that heavenly power can be brought into the earth and can lift earth into a future state of harmonious perfection. The ancient vision of a marriage of heaven and earth, and the soul's mission in effecting this, are central to our spiritual future on earth.

In spirituality, meditation is a centrally important discipline. But the understanding of meditation develops as practice matures. In the beginning, a seeker has his or her own personal reasons for practice, but in time, especially on a path where surrender is important, this develops into an aspiration to find and follow the Divine Will. In the more mature stages of spiritual practice, we meditate not so much for the fulfillment of our own will as for the surrender of it to the Divine Guidance.

The Sibyl in my dream was an archetype of inner spiritual guidance. The light which bathed the crystal orb at the centre of the temple represented a world placed in the fullness of the action of Divine Grace and Guidance. My personal world, which means my body, mind, heart and soul could be placed in the flow of Grace just like that crystal sphere. If I chose perfect surrender, this would be possible. Then, I could become a channel of the inner guiding power. I would in effect BE the crystal sphere at the heart of the temple, just as my own soul was the living divinity at the centre of my own human temple at this time. This was the teaching symbolism of the temple dream. This was the full meaning of the crystal orb.

Light will pass through a perfectly clear crystal without any distortion. Symbols which include crystal seem especially relevant to our own modern age. Any symbol is in essence a material form wherein every part is fully aligned to the expression of a single truth. All parts of a six sided star, for example, exist in total focus upon expressing the truth of that symbol. A six sided star becomes the symbol of Sri Aurobindo when, within its centre is placed a square (symbolic of perfected material expression) and within the square is placed a lotus (representing the perfected human being, or avatar) floating on wavy lines representing the ocean of consciousness. Without this addition, it may suggest the Star of David, and a Jewish or cabalistic tradition of spirituality, or even the political ambitions of Zionism.

This complete alignment of all parts to a single expressive intent which we find in all symbols is what makes them powerful tools of teaching and learning. The unifying of all parts in a single whole whose intent is to image forth a significant message is also what we find in the imagery of Tarot. It is for this reason a very helpful tool for individuals who aspire to attune many levels of the mind, including the subconscious, to a higher degree of alignment with Truth.

Research shows that symbolism in general and Tarot symbols in particular were widely used the pre-Christian Goddess tradition and in the ancient Mystery Schools. If we think of Tarot as merely a card game developed in the late Middle Ages, and if we rely on incomplete historical records and the few remaining Tarot cards of that period to determine its origins, our horizon of understanding will be quite limited. The kind of positivist thinking which is useful in hard science, or even some branches of history and archaeology, is much less useful in spiritual, creative, or intuitive disciplines. In fact, a literal minded obsession with material facts sometimes blinds a researcher to subtle energy patterns which underlie the appearance of things and frequently create the phenomena we take in through the five senses. Spiritual study makes us aware of the states of consciousness which underlie different forms of energy, and gives us progressive control in all three fields of experience, the physical, the energetic, and the realm of pure consciousness. Tarot holds many lessons for us in all three domains.

A temple is a place of sacred attunement. The structure of a sacred building and the symbols and artwork it houses constitute a doorway into the inner worlds, and possibly even a point of connection with the Infinite Consciousness which is beyond form. I knew that the temple which had been revealed to me by the Sibyl in my dream was going to help me learn and develop a new dimension of awareness, and I hoped I would be adequately prepared to make the most of this opening and opportunity. If I could find how Tarot connected with my meditation and spiritual practice, I knew I would be motivated to make the best use of it, and to give it due importance. I also sensed that it would be a language which could make it possible to reach out and communicate with many searching souls who were aspiring to become more fully conscious.

Although the accreditation of oracles died out with classical civilizations, Tarot has been making a big comeback in recent years. Tarot books outsell most others in the New Age bookstores, because people are immensely interested in understanding their lives and the patterns by which they are weaving their probable futures. Tarot can renew a sense of life's mystery and adventure. It conveys an awareness of sacred archetypes and offers us the chance to learn from them. This is something that many seekers do not seem to find in the church pews on Sunday morning.

In sum, I knew that this line of study and experience was the work I had to do. One must honour the Muse or lose the connection. I decided to go forward and to prepare myself inwardly for a new phase of revelation. That it would come, I had no doubt, but the form it would take had many surprising turns.

The Long Journey

One day in early April, I sat down to meditate early in the morning. In my hands I held the beautiful crystal ball whose energy I find so helpful for inner attunement. At the very beginning of my meditation, I had the clue to allow my visualizing abilities full scope, and this is what took place shortly after I had seated myself and closed my eyes:

I found myself mounting the fifteen steps into the darkened stone chamber. I was wearing a thin white linen shirt, and over it a many-coloured mantle of silk with many golden wheels, each of eight spokes. At the top of the stairs, I entered a stone chamber, the same circular room of my previous dream-vision, and the first thing I noticed in the darkness was the beam of moonlight that shone down from the ceiling upon a crystal ball. This crystal ball, resting on a perfectly square stone altar, was radiant in the silvery light of the moon. I took my seat upon a tripod which was placed directly before the altar, and when I was seated, I observed that the crystal ball was just below eye level. I sat there for several minutes gazing into it, and gradually my mind emptied of all thoughts.

On my two shoulders, I felt the weight of the Sibyl's hands. Then, like a pressure on the top of my head, a force began to descend. I could feel it like a heaviness moving down into the cells of my cranium and then descending to the heart. The stillness of my mind deepened immensely, and before my mind's eye came the image of The Magician, who is considered the first of the forms among the archetypes of the Major Arcanum. Then, the Sibyl's voice began to speak, but it was not so much a voice outside myself as a voice from within the depth of my own heart. My own inner wisdom was arising from its source, my soul, in association with the Sibyl's form and presence, which I took to be an emanation of the Divine Mother.

*"**Magus**! this is the work, this is the duty before you. The **earth** of your physical and practical life, the **air** of intellect, the **water** of creative and emotional power, and the **fire** of spiritual mastery, they are there before you on the table to work with. You must make yourself their master.*

*I will be there behind you as the seeing eye of the **High Priestess**, as the power of the Divine Mother. My insight, my intuitive guidance will be with you at every step. Never hesitate to enter the temple of stillness and see through my eyes and feel with my heart of tender care. Take care that you see beneath appearances to the hidden forces that shape them. Be guided by the wisdom of your heart, your feeling of what is right.*

*You will be gifted with everything you need to do the work that is before you. The **Empress** will give you nature's abundance of riches, all the endowments of culture and civilization, art and expressive power, the gift of nurturing and the sense of caring that brings forth abundance. This is your canvas, and you are the artist of your destiny. The fullness and abundance that earth can offer are yours to work with. Use them wisely, and attain mastery.*

But understand well : with great riches, comes much responsibility and a requirement to act with power and authority. You must be the lord and master of your kingdom, and you must manage all your resources with fairness, order and discipline. You must be guided by principle, and you must be firm in your adherence to the laws of truth. **The Emperor** *has power because he has submitted himself fully to his duties. This you must also do. And if you will submit to the path of duty, you will be given something more, the fullness of sacred tradition. The* **High Priest** *guides those who have been proven in action and found dependable. Sacred learning, and the path of initiation are yours if you go forward on this journey. To your practical competence will be added spiritual attainment. You will be initiated into the mysteries and given teaching authority to serve others, to release the aspiration of souls and to inspire the opening of hearts.*

But you must also experience the fullness of love and the lessons of relationship. You must experience the polarity of sexual energies and the wholeness of complete bonding with life. When you see the **Lovers,** *you will know what is between them. Only when you have mastered right relationship and found your own wholeness therein will you be ready to take hold fully of the reins of your own self mastery. You will be able to make your heart's choice and follow the truth of your inner guidance.*

This **Charioteer** *who handles power so adeptly is a fully formed individual. His ego is well developed. He has taken charge of all aspects of his life and attained competence in many spheres of action. But if he is to go forward, he must begin an even higher path than that which he has heretofore covered. He must preside over the dissolution of his own ego.*

In this higher path, the power of love will be his greatest strength and support. He must tame and master his own impulses, and he must pass all his tests and trials. He will draw upon the **Strength** *of compassion, using the magic of his heart's oneness with all life. In doing this, he will attain to the path of complete mastery. One who has true strength of heart masters the beast, not by compulsion, but by gentle influence.*

The **Hermit** *is one who has surrendered to the Mother's guidance. His entire life is devoted to contemplative seeking. He has already experienced the* *mastery of the world, but he foregoes worldly concerns in order to focus exclusively on the quest for higher wisdom. To him, the ups and downs of fortune, symbolized by the **Wheel**, are no source of dismay. He goes forward steadily, with great detachment while the wheel moves through its cycles. Every upswing and every downturn carries its lessons home to his open heart. He follows the light as it leads him forward. He comes to know the cycles of the wheel and to make use of their alterations for his own learning.*

*He has attained that perfect balance which is sometimes called **Justice**, but which he experiences in his heart as perfect equilibrium. In his life there is no excess, no imbalance. He willingly chooses right action. He is fully aware, and sincerely committed to integrity.*

*Notwithstanding the progress he has already made, this seeker of truth will come to a point in time when he is suspended in a void of unknowing. He will find that all which he has relied on at every previous stage of the journey is of no avail. He will be a like a Hanged Man, a **Prisoner** suspended in a kind of prolonged reversal, unable to go forward, face to face with what he does not know or understand, able only to surrender to a greater fate which cannot be known. His patience will be tested, his surrender perfected. He will have to let go of the last vestiges of self-will. His faith will be rewarded, and his destiny realized.*

*The passing away of the old must precede the birth of the new. For him, **Death** has no fear. He knew long ago that he would die to self at some point on this journey. He is willing to release whatever has outgrown its time. He moves with ease from the known to the unknown, through sweeping changes that would unsettle an untested soul. He knows that the end of the old is the start of the new. He must face his own death, and the passing of all he cherishes with calm faith.*

*Because he has always moved in the world, and never lost his compassion and sympathy for all life, his greatest victory will be the balancing of opposites in his own heart. **Temperance** is now innately his. He has achieved synthesis of polarities, perfect equality and equilibrium. He is ever centred and composed, not it a static way, but in a dynamic interaction with all life as he goes forward* on his path. He is able to mix, to match, to combine, to foster and restrain as he builds up the harmonies of his inner experience.

That which binds and tempts must come and face the seeker one more time. The **Devil**, the darkness and confusion, the temptation to despair, the pull of the material life, the paralysis of fear – all this will test him to the full before he emerges into a permanent state of grace. All that he has built may be shattered. The image of a crumbling **Tower** poignantly shows how you will see all you have built destroyed. To be above and beyond his own ego was always his true goal. This perfect detachment encompasses even the loss of his most cherished possessions, because he knows that a greater perfection lies ahead. True letting go is something he achieves in its fullness and depth. Can the destruction of the great Tower bring about any further catharsis in his heart? If he cherished any final attachments, delusions or false concepts, they are finally smashed. Then, he comes fully into the life of grace. The guiding **Star** of divine light becomes his sole refuge. He is raised to a higher level of inspiration and understanding. He achieves serenity, inner peace, a synthesis of heaven and earth in his heart of hearts.

The way before him is cleared. He now lives every moment of his life in a state of Grace.

Then, he achieves full mastery of the lesser light of the **Moon**. All that is transitory, all that is illusory, even the thoughts and stories of his own mind, stand no more as an obstacle. He has mastered the shifting appearances of life. What is impermanent can bind his heart no more. He has plumbed the depths of the unconscious, he has seen through its enchantment. He has achieved his own fullness of visionary insight. He has perfected his inner knowing of the way and how to walk it. The shadows of life, the demons and phobias hold no further terror for him. The wizardry of all things sublunar comes under his mantle of power.

He achieves the pinnacle of his journey, the radiance of Sol Invictus, the unconquered **Sun**. The enlightenment of his mind and heart become for him a source of great joy. He is now a true Gnostic Being, sure of his power, energized by his inner vision. His awareness of truth is absolute. The light in him is so strong that he has consciously lived his own rebirth. Some may call this experience Judgement, but he embraces it as the transformation and *resurrection of his life into the fullness of the Divine life. He has lived the fulfillment of **Prophecy**. This is the true apotheosis, the rebirth that follows from dying to self. It is a fresh start on the very highest stages of the spiritual journey, and beyond this point, there is no map. Beyond the fulfilled prophecy, there is a new opening, a new possibility, but it cannot be grasped by the mind or expressed in language.*

*All that can be said is : the wholeness and fullness of creation, represented by the symbol of the **World**, are now centered in the seeker's heart of spiritual realization. He has become the channel joining heaven to earth by which the World realizes its high destiny. His life and the world's are one, and their fulfilment is forever intertwined. His consciousness has expanded. His mind, heart and soul have become universal He is the light of love which has embraced the whole of creation. He has taken everything which the Empress offered to him, and returned with it to the Source. He is one with Creation."*

One by one, the Tarot archetypes had appeared before my inner eye, in the light of the crystal sphere, in the moonlight, and each of them had communicated to my mind a testimony of their significance. They had revealed their roles in the history of the soul's unfoldment.

This Tarot is the language of the soul, I realized. These primal images are the story of the soul's journey through the stages of life toward full mastery. They are parts of a single story, the story of the inner pilgrim. In this vision-quest, I began by donning the robes of a Fool. I was willing to begin my adventures knowing that I knew nothing, that I was a 'babe in the woods'. Although the spirit was whole, I did not know how to reveal and express its light in a world where chaos, ignorance, deception and ill will reign supreme. Each figure of the Arcanum was a teaching and a teacher. As their images had emerged in my meditation, they had communicated lessons of immense worth. Thus, I had been empowered to push on through many ups and downs, through many lifetimes of experience, to this stage of insight. And yet the insight was vaguely familiar, like an awakened memory.

I knew about many of my past lives, sufficient to see that I had indeed covered this terrain of challenge and progressive achievement in many lifetimes of alternating fortune. I had once been a rebellious slave who was beaten to death, and in other times I had been a shaman, a spiritual teacher, a prophet, a monk. I had been a poor shepherd, and then, in a different life, I had been a czar. I had been a general in Napoleon's army, and an adept working with crystals in the halls of Atlantis, a teacher in the temples of Egypt, and in the stone temples of the Incas and pre-Incas, high in the Andes. I had been a Celtic bard, master of music and the spoken word, a druid teacher, and a Greek philosopher. And I had been a settler and homesteader in the New World. I had been a crusader who shed blood in the name of truth, and I had been an alchemist and an occultist learning about the forces of light and dark and their synthesis and harmony in a greater wholeness. I had been a Renaissance painter, and a dancer in the French court in the seventeenth century. I had attained power and misused it. I had suffered and I had learned. I had been blessed by the company of spiritual masters, and at one point had consecrated my existence the path of enlightenment. My soul had learned to value wisdom above all else, and to serve others in the role of teacher. I had pledged to serve spiritual seekers from all walks of life, and to be a perpetual student in the voyage of self discovery.

All this I had done, all this had I experienced and known, but now the "pattern of the whole", the stages of the journey, my own journey, had come back to me in an archetypal pattern of wholeness. I could see it from the perspective of the eagle on high, from beginning to end, simultaneously, in an overview beyond time. The Tarot images of the Major Arcanum were catalysts, releasing the memories of the journey's events.

At the end of my meditation, when my visions and audition had moved to a point of completion, I returned to the wellspring of my heart and opened it up in gratitude to the Divine Mother. I thanked Her in Her aspect as the wise woman of great age and experience, the Sibyl. Then I placed my two hands over my eyes and wiped away the consciousness of introversion and mystical vision. I stood up from the tripod, averted my gaze from the crystal orb in the moonlight, retraced my steps and exited the inner temple.

With my meditation concluded, I placed the crystal sphere which I had been holding in its normal resting place, turned off the gentle music which had been playing, and then I returned to my room to write down the account of the experience and add it to what had already been revealed.

On my desk, in a clear plastic cover, I have a page on which all the Tarot images are printed in full colour. They look at me as my fingers move over the keyboard. They continue to speak to me and to abide with me in spirit as I set down this account of how they spoke to me in contemplation.

Now I know the **Magician**, the **High Priestess**, the **Empress** and the **Emperor** more intimately. I know that the **High Priest** and the **Lovers** are not at odds, they are part of myself, aspects of my own experience. I have been and I eternally am the master of the **Chariot**. I hold control of the reins of power which unite my senses and desires to the work my soul must do.

I now know that I am pre-eminently in this life the **Hermit** who is guided by the light of contemplation. The revolutions of the **Wheel of Fortune** do not dismay me, for I profit by their every change. If I depart from **Justice**, I know that it is I who will suffer. I know that the **Prisoner** does not suffer, for he is able to accept reversal. Nor is **Death** the great evil to be feared, nor is the **Devil**. They are my teachers, and I am grateful for their lessons. I have at times acted under the Devil's influence. I have at times succumbed to temptation. I know what that is about, I needed to know in order to embrace **Temperance**. I have known Shiva and Rudra the destroyers, and when I see the **Tower** of my life's so-called achievements falling apart, I am not dismayed. A **Star** in the sky is now, for me, a symbol of Divine Grace, my own inner guiding light. The **Moon**'s beauty and mystical fascination will never prove too fascinating to my curious mind, nor will magic and enchantment delay me from entering the **Solar Liberation**. The **Prophecy,** the judgement of the Divine upon my **Fool**'s journey, is fulfilled. I have nothing to fear. Each failure has been a learning experience, and each success has become a Tower that needed to be dismantled. I have been liberated even from the prison of my fondest successes; no more can they bind me.

Time has taught me well. I have not become the prisoner of experiences, but rather their bard. I celebrate the residual wisdom that is there when success and failure have danced their way through the rhythms and harmonies of many lifetimes. The World and all in it are mine, because they are all Divine in their essence, and so am I.

These Tarot images are a story, and it is my tale, my own experiences of a soul's pilgrimage in time, and the harvest of the pilgrim-wisdom. This wisdom is so much more than mere abstract philosophy. It has been tested by adversity, honed by suffering, refined by unpredictable swings of fate. It is a wisdom which has found its own voice and which speaks to those who will hear, not for the purpose of winning fame or riches, but because the very nature of light is to shine.

The Hermit, who is my own Tarot counterpart in this life, holds a lantern before him, and it lights his way. He moves forward as the light reveals the path, and he holds his precious lantern firmly in the grip of his hard won self-mastery. This I know. The crystal sphere in the temple of my visions and the crystal orb which I hold when I meditate are now not merely objects or possessions or symbols of something abstract and remote. They are living expressions of an infinite potential to unfold and evolve. Archetypes of my soul, I have claimed each of them as my own and incorporated them into the story of my heart. Each card, each image will now be richer in my understanding because I have seen the wholeness of their story, and I know it to be the tale of my very own soul's pilgrimage.

As I complete these words, I glance at an email which has come in from a dear friend, Bonny, who has been reading the drafts of this manuscript as they take shape, chapter by chapter. Her email letter reads in part :

I can't thank you enough for sending me the first drafts of the book. Throughout the whole time I was reading them, I was

*"remembering" seeing you at the entrance of the building in Egypt
as I told you at your country place. I firmly believe you taught the
very same subject then and reading it again had such a familiar
feeling to me, just as it would if I were reading it again after only a
very short time. Now I know for sure that I attended your lectures
then and I believe you attended some of mine ...*

*I am learning as I read and remembering and waiting anxiously
for further excerpts! Each card comes alive in my understanding
as I read.*

Bonny, your words express what I would wish to say to the Mother, the
Sibyl who guides me in this discovery. To her, always and ever, I look
for wisdom and for the blessing of the Muse to give it beautiful
expression. Now I know why the Hermit is pictured as the Goddess
Vesta in my Spiral deck of the Tarot. It is because She, the Mother
guides his seeking every step of the way. We are in her loving hands
forever.

The Language of the Soul

For some time I had felt that the Wheel of Fortune could be a symbol of
the goddess Fortuna. I did not have a personal familiarity with the
goddess of destiny, but I knew from my studies in ancient history that
she was very important to the Greeks and Romans. The shape of
destiny has always been of interest to human beings, and "fortune
telling" is simply finding out what the Goddess Fortuna has to say to
us. Fortune means destiny, and telling is narrative. One's fortune is the
unfolding story of one's soul and its experience in its path to liberation.

As one unfolds one's core being, an individualized psychic being takes
form (The Fool) and a destiny unfolds in the plotline of a story. The
stories we believe shape our destiny. This is the role of myth and of
religious belief systems. The meaning of a life becomes clear in the
course of that life's events, based on one's personal choices. Credence
shapes our choices, and we experience both successes and failures as
we learn the consequences of our actions. But it is above all in our

dreams and ideals that we cherish in our heart of hearts that the guiding spirit of our soul's journey can be found.

In the course of thirty years of daily meditation, I had come to feel that finding the soul and becoming one with its wisdom was of central importance. The essence of the soul's wisdom consisted for me in trying to be sincere in my aspiration and to live my life on spiritual principles. The core of my aspiration has for many years been to find and follow the Divine Will, to surrender to the Absolute and be at one with my Higher Self.

To ponder the revelations of Fortuna is to participate in divination. The Tarot is one means of evoking stories about the unfolding of our soul's earthly destiny. But the perspective we have on the stories we hear, whether the hearing takes place in churches, in the reading of scriptures, in studies of mythology, courses of philosophy, in dreams, in contemplative visions, or in Tarot readings, will have much to do with the eyes through which we see. What the Goddess reveals to us depends on the sincerity of our intent and the level of our aspiration, as well as the maturity of our spiritual development. The seeing of symbols and higher patterns is one gift of the spirit, but the wisdom of correct interpretation is quite another. Happy are those who have been gifted in both ways! For them, divination is likely to be most meaningful, either in their own quest, or in service to others.

The different levels of human seeking are a fact of life. Our notions about how to find happiness vary with our inner maturity. Fortune telling often revolves around people's need to know more about a budding romance, an unfaithful spouse, or about job prospects, or financial investments, or possibly about the causes of stress and unhappiness on the home front or the work place. It is about "gold and women" as Sri Ramakrishna would say, about the desires we cherish and our fond hope that we will find happiness by fulfilling these desires. This level of consciousness is what the Buddha called "samsara" or suffering.

Lasting happiness, in the spiritual sense of liberation, comes with the transcendence of such concerns, not their successful gratification according to the ego's wish list. The ego and the soul see life differently, and the achievement of inner freedom takes a long time.

It was clear to me that in my dream-vision experience with Sibyl that I had entered a place of revelation and sacred wisdom, Sophia. I had been brought to an inner temple which was structured in such a way as to communicate deeper understanding from my soul to my mind. I knew that whereas the symbols and the archetypal personages of the Major Arcanum are part of the universal soul's language, the thinking and writing I would do about this inner experience constitute my mind's efforts to parse and comprehend the grammar and the syntax of the revelation.

There is an unusual word which is relevant to this discussion, but which is not used very often in the English language : *hierophany*. This word means an experience of something from a plane of reality beyond our world, a glimpse of a reality of a higher order, but mediated by objects which are normal to our experience in this earthly time-space continuum of normal waking consciousness. When the poet Tennyson saw "eternity in a grain of sand", this was *hierophany*. In all such experiences there is a sense of the sacred. Although all hierophany is divination, not all divination is hierophany. Hierophany takes place on a plane of awareness which is deeper and higher than the "marketplace" milieu. It is part of the quest for self-understanding and right relation to the Divine. Because western religion has become increasingly bureaucratic and dogmatic, it has a diminished ability to offer its adherents glimpses of the archetypal beyond. Thus, seekers of revelation have in many cases turned to eastern spirituality, holistic forms of exercise (like yoga or Tai Chi), and meditation, as well as astrology and Tarot for answers. Any exercise by which we hear the words of Fortuna, (the Divine Mother in her aspect as oracle), speaking to us about our destiny, is essentially an experience of the sacred. But it is our own heart-opening, and our own need for higher understanding that establishes the level and degree of our connection to the Divine.

The rituals of fortune telling, such as lighting a candle, burning incense, becoming inwardly focused, or shuffling a Tarot deck, serve a very important function. They help us to place our consciousness in the dimension of the numinous. They help us set aside the secular mind and open to the guidance of our spiritual heart, the portal through which we hear the voice of the soul.

It is part of our soul's work to become fully conscious of negative patterns in our life so that they can be healed, and also to recognize positive patterns so that they can be reinforced. In this way, we realize our full potential. Tarot is a tool by means of which the soul can get on with its work. Tarot is revelation. Revelation takes place when we enter into sacred space: "Intro ibo ad altare Dei," as the Sibyl had pronounced. Sacred space is a place where we go within our own consciousness when we are inwardly at peace, open-hearted, sincere and aspiring. Sacred art and architecture are meant to attune us to be open to the presence and the revelation of the Divine. Sacred music and poetry work in this way also. Tarot, if it is understood as part of the soul's sacred discourse, connects us directly and deeply with an understanding of our ultimate destiny.

Infinite consciousness is beyond form and time. But human consciousness tells stories which play out across the white screen of infinity, like coloured reels of film in a movie-house. When we read the stories of our lives rightly, especially the stories told to us by Goddess Fortuna, we see a deeper level of meaning. This deeper meaning gradually liberates us from the suffering that comes from being in a state of ignorance, and true oracles when rightly heard orient us to an alignment with the wisdom of our soul.

The wisdom of the soul is not communicated to us in the same way that universities teach dogmatic theology. It is not by reading books, writing essays and passing courses or collecting degrees after our name that we acquire such wisdom. Often, it comes rather to the simple and the pure.

It comes as insight, as revelation, as a will to change and widen one's awareness. Intellectual sophistication, and the educational systems which foster it, have nothing to do with the cultivation of inner wisdom.

Those who have progressed in the inner journey of self-awakening tell us that there is an invisible unity which underlies the multiplicity of the phenomenal world we see with the five senses. They say that they have seen how man is a microcosm, having within him all the qualities of the great Universal Being (the macrocosm) that transcends our human limitations. There are inner worlds invisible to us inhabited by great beings who live by different principles than those of our world. In the Judeo-Christian tradition, for example, angels are the messengers of God, and they may visit us in our dreams. We can experience these higher planes of reality and see and feel and learn from our inner experiences. Symbols, as we have seen, can serve as portals for making the inner connection between our normal outwardly-focused mind and our contemplative and intuitive mind. Certain kinds of art and music and inspired speech can also connect us with higher planes of consciousness.

Once we see the higher realities for ourselves, our awareness is widened. Then, we identify more fully with our soul and its work. If we approach Tarot with the expectation that we can transcend our mental conditioning and connect with something larger than ourselves, then the doorway that makes this possible is open. We will be able to develop the relaxed trust and intuitive openness necessary to access the oracular consciousness.

The twenty two images of the Major Arcanum and the Court cards are excellent subjects for visualization. By concentrating on a card like the Priestess in the right way, we can achieve an altered state of consciousness which is more than simply a relaxed state of mind. To go deeper, we must let go of any effort at actively imagining a landscape, or character or symbol and simply open up psychically to receive images from the plane of being associated with the card. There are certain adepts who can project themselves into the plane they contact, move about and encounter its inhabitants. These astral planes are considered realms of illusion, relative to the higher levels beyond them. This does not mean that what we learn there is "untrue", it only means that it is an incomplete or partial truth. It is still part of the relative truth of duality. The truth of universal oneness is to be experienced on higher planes of consciousness, but these too are our birthright and destiny.

When we entertain archetypal images in our mind repeatedly, their scope of influence expands. They begin to become more real to us. Their stories and powers and dispositions and personalities are communicated to us in a variety of ways. We develop an awareness of how they act, where they go, with whom they like to associate and their areas of concern. Each of us has the potential to explore the power and symbolic depth of images. It begins with allowing our own imagination to work, and remaining open to whatever arises as we feel our way forward.

I remember that I was quite good at this when I was six years old. I had quite a few toy soldiers, and many of them had their individual characters and stories. I would play with them by making stories in which they were the main actors, and over several years I developed an imaginative world peopled with these characters. I still have some of those toys, forty years later, and when I pick them up I can still feel those imaginative associations. The unencumbered soul of a child has this natural inclination to play with images in the fields of imagination, to create stories and discover a world of inner experience that is meaningful. Slowly, we are educated away from this by our formal schooling. I remember that on the day I had to go to school for the first time, I wept. This happened at the tender age of five years, but already I sensed that my beautiful world of imagination was being overshadowed by a public educational system that would obscure my soul. Later on in life, when I was once again free, this spiritual damage would take years to undo. I knew that social conditioning was going to shape my mind and draw me away from my soulful instincts, and there was no one who understood my dilemma. Years later, to express this experience, I composed this poem:

> There was a time when I was still.
> I knew how to feel,
> I knew how to move.
> I heard the music in my heart.
> I saw the dance of life with the eyes of my feelings.
> I was a part of the world-life,
> And it was a part of me.
> I was free and happy.
> I saw as I was, and it was good.

There was a time when I had to go to school.
On that day, I cried and cried.
My heart knew that I would be made to forget
the music inside me.
I would be made to forget my heart's way of seeing.
I would be made to study
the words and the ways of clever men.
I would learn to use words as one who valued power.
I began to study and study.

A sleep entered into my heart, and I forgot.
I forgot the sound of my heart's music.
I forgot the feeling of my life's dance.
I learned the ways I was taught, and I became clever.
I developed power, and I became successful.
My life became fixed in success.

Pain became my teacher then.
When I could no longer feel, pain awakened me.
Pain took me by the hand, and led me to the door of my heart,
the sealed door I had turned from when I fell asleep
I told pain that I was not a clever man.
I told pain that I was not a lover of power.
I told pain that I had not been successful.
Pain held me closer, and the mask fell from her face.

I saw that she was love.
Love stirred my heart, and from behind the sealed door,
I heard music.
Love touched my body,
And I knew that I could again move and feel.
Love touched my head,
And I understood that I knew nothing.
Love held me in her embrace,
And I felt that I was everything.

There was a time when I was still
It was the best of times,
For I knew how to feel, how to move, and how to hear
The music in my heart.
In stillness and in movement,
In pain and in love,
That time is being born once more.
I have begun to unlearn
So that I may feel what I do not know.

Tarot is a field of play for the resurrected imagination. And this imagination is the doorway into true intuition, which in turn puts us in touch with the powers and principles of the inner world. The Tarot cards can help us to express our intention to re-connect with the invisible world of archetypes. The fact that we can study and shuffle and lay out on a table cards with images of the mythic figures of an inner pantheon makes it possible to connect our physical world of reality, and our physical mind, with a dimension far beyond it. Communication with dimensions of the beyond is facilitated by the medium of symbols. We can conduct a conversation of sorts, or read a story of sorts by means of these images on the Tarot cards. I was probably much closer to being able to do this at the tender age of five, before going to kindergarten, than I was when I graduated from University and walked away with a diploma of "higher learning."

When we begin to respond in a living way to the Tarot images, a spread of Tarot cards becomes an interactive space in which the personalities and events of our life can be re-interpreted in light of their inner pattern, the meaning they have for our soul. A reversed card is a very good example of what we mean by pattern. It tends to indicate some kind of blocked energy in the field represented by the card. To give you an example: not long ago, I had a dream in which I was visiting with an Empress. She was not exactly like the Empress pictured in the Rider-Waite deck, she was more like a grandmother or aunt. I knew from the dream that she was an influential relative of mine, and that she could help me a lot if I were on good terms with her. She was sitting down, and there was some social interaction, but what I mostly remember was, I could be greatly helped by having this connection with her. Now, a reversed card might mean, for example, that we were not on good terms, that there was some disruption. I would have to reflect what role she plays in my life and how she relates to my personality. I would try to understand how and why we were not on good terms, and how this could be corrected. I know that if I lived in South America, I could ask to have a shaman make an offering to Mother Earth. He would prepare a bundle of special foods and precious things that she likes, and these would be taken to a holy place and buried. This would be one way, in one culture, that the bond could be re-established. But in my own case, living in a different culture, I would have to approach the question in a different way of my own creative devising.

For example, I could concentrate on the Empress by using her image onthe Tarot Card. I could try to build a bridge between us, and then from that identification, I could speak to her, or she could speak through me. I could begin to utter what her concerns were as I felt them, to the extent that I identified with her consciousness. That would be one way. Or, I could place the card in a position of elevation and offer a crystal, a flower, some incense and a vigil-light candle to her, to express my desire for reconciliation. This is the approach of ritual, which has value if it comes as an expression of heartfelt sincerity. In every case, through all the different ways in which we may use Tarot, the ever-present reality that shapes the results is our *intention*. When we intend to heal, or to learn, or to foresee, this intent bears fruit in the world of consciousness. This is how karma works. The events of our outer life are assembled by threads of intentionality woven in and out of our time-use by the loom of our every thought, act and deed. The weavers of the loom, in ancient mythology, were known as the Fates, and they had places of honour in quite a few ancient temples.

Imagery has great power to bring forward the soul and to place it at the centre of our awareness. When our attention and our intention are connected to soul, the patterns of our karma begin to change. In ways that cannot be fully explained, the Tarot arouses and summons the powers of the soul to come foreword and contribute its guidance as we move forward in our life journey. As a creative tool, Tarot images stimulate our capacities for visualisation. They assist us to see beyond the limits of the present - which is the prophetic capacity, the art of divination. As something that can be used ritually, as a magical tool, they help us to alter karma, and as a field of imaginative association, they raise our consciousness from the physical mind to the visionary mind. In these ways, Tarot can provide openings through which soul can operate more freely and powerfully.

In these matters, success depends on personalizing our activities. This is what I was doing, unconsciously, when I took my toy soldiers and put them in various situations, and developed an understanding of their different personalities. If we take the cards of the Arcanum and just sit down to play with them, to let them live in our imagination, we will find our own way of building up the personal connection. The Charioteer and the Hermit and the Hierophant then become real people that we know. The messages they might communicate to us could then be different from the official script assigned to them in various books. We must find our own personal variations of the Tarot tradition, and we do this by creating our own sense of play as we entertain fantasies, affections, stories, interactions that are meaningful to us. Just remember the way you used to play with your doll or teddy bear. This can be a key to re-discovering the language of the soul in Tarot.

If we are not bound by a need for serious answers to impending problems, we will likely get farther in creating our own world of imaginative associations. When we play, we experience a kind of liberation. We are not working at something in any serious way in order to arrive at "answers" or "solutions" to anyone's personal problems. We are enjoying a deepening of our own awareness when we open the gateways of imagination. We are taking time to allow the soul to pass on to us its communications and its visions of possibility. We are giving our soul some time and some tools of play so that it will become our playmate in a game of revelation. Just as children never complicate their childhood games with toy soldiers or dolls, so it works best not to bring our needs and expectations into this play. Divination comes later, when we have developed right relation to the archetypes, the elements and the energies of number.

When we begin to work with our Tarot cards in this way, they become an ideal tool for opening up our intuitive, synthesizing potentials, and thus for changing our lives. By inviting us to make connections between our mind, our sense of play, our instincts, intuitions, feelings, story-lines, and our love of imagery, Tarot helps us to step beyond the confines of our mind's limits. We change our way of seeing the world when we reactivate the child in our own heart. And when we see the world in a new light, we also change our way of being in that world.

The process by which we acquire understanding and information is often more important in shaping our consciousness than the information itself. When we play with the archetypal images of Tarot, we are setting up a situation where the soul can communicate to us in its own language. We are developing a new way to learn and think, beyond what we learned in school, and this is possibly the most important part of our interactions. Tarot is a medium, a language, a space where mind connects with soul and is transfigured.

The Grammar of the Goddess

Tarot has its origins in a distant past when the rites of the Goddess held sway. During the fourth millenium BC, in Europe and the Mediterranean world, as well as the Middle East and large parts of India, patriarchal influences began to take precedence over the older religion, and thereafter they progressively suppressed or degraded the importance of the Goddess and her cult. But still, in most forms of ancient religion, we find that the matriarchal deity presides over creativity and its symbols, and over homes of all kinds, including temples.

Hers are the sacred alphabets, and in the form of the Muses, she inspires the poets who use them. Hers are the sacred arts as well as the powers of intuition by which the bard and the prophet master them. She retains her influence in all things lunar, and in most forms of healing, as well as birthing, sowing and reaping, nurturing and mothering. It is in this ancient domain of associations, in the world view that prevailed at the very dawn of the world's sacred alphabets, that we find the origins of Tarot.

Symbols have their origin not in the featureless Absolute which is formless and incapable of being seized by the mind of duality, but rather in the sublunar world of form where the Goddess rules the processes of cyclical change. One of the most difficult points in

61

philosophy has been to explain how and why the Supreme Being entered into manifestation or brought about creation in the first place. Somehow, it is posited, there arose this Absolute Being a need for experience, and from this resulted the birth of the universe.

The first spark of creation is often pictured in traditional wisdom as a point of light which arose from the darkness of the void. This is the cosmic seed or primal Word from which all creation subsequently came into being. This seed then expressed its oneness as duality. It became bi-polar. The polarities of yin and yang, positive and negative, light and dark, male and female come into being by this division of the One into Two. When the two poles had differentiated their existence from the Primal Light, and emerged from their common matrix, time and space came into existence. Then, there took place a devolution of spirit into many gradations and planes of expression, the most dense and inert being matter. In the space which arose from their separation, the two polarities of yin and yang exerted a mutual attraction on each other, and from this arose a column of light and energy, a pathway linking heaven to earth.

This was the Third stage in the sequence of original creation. All around this primal pillar of light, a field of energy came into being, a living force and consciousness extending outward in the four directions. Within this field the entire creation took form. This primal pillar has itself often been taken as a form of the divine, as in the Shiva lingam which we find in the most ancient temples of India. It is the symbol of the world axis, a great pillar extending from earth to heaven having opposite poles at each end. This pillar is a pathway of ascent from this world of multiplicity and ignorance into the solar regions of light and truth. All early religions concern themselves with sacred space at the centre of which is the 'axis mundi' which unites heaven to earth and constitutes a pathway of self-transcendence for mankind.

In the early cosmologies of pre-recorded history, the universe or macrocosm is believed to the body of the Divine. The body of man, the microcosm, is also considered to be a temple which houses the Sacred Presence. Mother Earth is a divine being with her own axis, twin poles, and a magnetic energy field that supports life. When humanity lives in right relation to the indwelling divinity, as well as to the divinity in the outer world, which includes other people, and also in right relation to the transcendental Divine, the souls move forward the great journey of return to the Eternal Home.

The function of sacred tradition is to properly orient humanity so that we can ascend the primal pillar, the axis of the worlds, and realize progressively the transcendental states of being. The centre around which all creation turns is this bipolar divine beam of light which radiates consciousness, energy and matter into manifestation. All the worlds have been created so that the Divine might be revealed to Itself. The Divine Ray emanates downwards from Its Absolute Transcendence through the realms of the gods, the angels, and the spirits into the earthly material creation, and then it further descends into the hells and the chaotic manifestations of darkness and disorder. The hero goes on a quest and re-discovers his true home, his hidden divinity, and he comes eventually to the world axis which helps him to accomplish his ascent to the heights, which in the ancient traditions of Greece is called *apotheosis*. One who has returned home to his innate divinity has been regenerated, he has experienced a 'second birth'. Such a being has passed through the 'sun-door', transcended all the degrees of existence, and achieved divinisation.

The Magician, which is the second card in the Major Arcanum of the Tarot, represents the necessities of the quest. This is the destiny which confronts the Fool at the beginning of his journey. In the Rider-Waite deck and its many derivatives, which is the best known tradition of Tarot in North America, The Magician has the symbols of earth, air, fire and water on the table before him. These stand for the physical, emotional, mental and spiritual levels of his own being. Above his head is the lemniscate, symbol of infinity, the infinite consciousness of divine attainment and he holds aloft a scepter or wand, which stands for the pillar of light uniting heaven and earth. Such a scepter is a symbol of power and mastery. His left hand points downward towards the earth. He mediates between the higher and lower spheres of creation and harmonizes them in his own being. Flowers blossom at his feet, for he establishes beauty and harmony in the world by virtue of his self-mastery.

In all forms of ancient tradition, the symbolism of the axis, the journey, and the eventual divinisation of human consciousness are present. For traditional cultures, a mountain can suggest or represent the sacred pillar or the world-axis, and sacred rituals were frequently performed on a high place, such as a ziggurat. Esoterically, to ascend the mountain means to move up the world axis and attain higher degrees of consciousness, to become more concentrated and centred until one attains the pinnacle, or high point of the climb. This mythic journey carries the hero through form into the formless. It is a journey beyond the shifting vagaries of lunar influence, even the highest lunar wisdom, into the solar transcendence. Here-below, on earth, the changing cycles of the moon govern everything, but there-above, in the highest heavens, the infinite light of the solar Source exists in perfect, unconditioned freedom. It is the state of Pure Being that is man's true home.

The world axis is also identified in many traditions as the cosmic Tree whose roots, trunk and branches form the three worlds. It holds down and restrains the infernal powers below, and stabilizes the cosmos so that the drama of existence may be played out. The tree is a way for man to re-ascend into Paradise. The true hero turns away from attachment to this world and goes up through the Gate of Life, leaving behind the earthly mind and body, receiving in their place a new mind and body, mastering thereby the four elements and attaining identity with the One. The axis symbolism is basic to cosmologies from all times and places. Even children who have no education in cosmology have the spontaneous sense that "up" moves in the direction of heaven, and "down" moves towards hell. This is a racial memory, an archetypal pattern that is imprinted in the human psyche from the dawn of creation. The mystic also experiences the contemplative journey as an ascent into the heights, and a liberation from the heaviness and darkness of matter.

It helps to remember that in early times there was no division between religion and science, no separation of secular from profane. All life was centered on the essentially sacred reality of the Earth Goddess. Her forests, streams, oceans and mountains were filled with the mystery of sacred presence. Every home was a temple of sorts with a small altar where appropriate rites were performed, as they still are among the Brahmins of India, and every family was joined to the community in sacred rituals whose timing was written in the stars. The mind of early man saw correspondences between certain herbs and the Solar or Lunar or Venusian or Martian energies. A shape or a taste would suggest where a tree or a plant or a stone might fit in the cosmic pattern. These correspondences were worked out in great detail, and the study of how all parts harmonize into a single whole, and the art of preserving universal harmony was at the heart of the Mystery School teachings. Long before writing was developed, this tradition was passed on orally, and preserved by memory, as the Vedas still are in India. When writing was first developed, it took birth in this web of cosmological interconnectedness. Every letter of the alphabet was a sacred symbol, and every symbol spoke forth an aspect of the original Word by which the goddess created the World and continued to manifest Her presence therein.

Cabala is the science of alphabetic letters, their relation to universal principles and the language of number which describes the cosmic harmonies and proportions. Some religions have a different name for this field of study. In India and Tibet, for example, it is called "tantra". Pythagoras knew it as the science of numbers. In all ancient spiritual traditions, sound was understood to be a sacred power, and writing was full of magical possibilities. A letter or a word, when scribed or uttered correctly could have the value of a talisman or mantra. These could give protection, they could heal, and they could change a person's destiny.

The Magician is one who understands universal laws and is able to apply them in the physical world. By means of the Word, God created everything that has name and form. One who masters the sacred powers of the Word will know the universal language, and will thus be able to apply the universal laws. A true magician has been initiated into an understanding of the laws of vibration. He commands powers which correspond to the different energies represented in the letters of the sacred alphabet. In whatever sphere he wants his language to materialize, it will. At the highest level, such a magician will understand the power of the Word, and can use it as a force for order in the microcosm and in the macrocosm. He is able to bring about true harmony within himself and around him by the application of his knowledge. He becomes in his own physical body a representative of the macrocosmic Divinity on our earthly plane of existence. Whenever he speaks the original language as a representative of the Divine, what he expresses is actualized, for he wields the power of connectedness to Source. This is the future destiny of the Fool. He will become a great magician as he moves forward on his journey of experience in the Major Arcanum.

Tarot is linked to Cabala by matching each of the cards of the Major Arcanum with one letter of the alphabet, and its corresponding number. The Hebrews maintain that the Cabala is of Hebrew origin, but in reality the Hebrews drew their understanding of Cabala from the old Egyptian religion. Even the 22 letters of the Hebrew alphabet are taken from the more ancient letters, 22 in number, of the Phoenician alphabet. Cabala is only one example of the sacred science of vibration which was developed in the temples of the Goddess. How far back sacred alphabets go in their origins, and how widely they are distributed has been a subject of debate for some time. Scholars keep moving timeframe farther and farther back into the dim recesses of prehistory.

In the 1920's, in Glozel, France, tablets were found with written symbols similar in many ways to Phoenician, but older by millennia than any examples of Phoenician writing. These tablets have been dated to over 4,000 years of age, and they are one of the earliest sacred alphabets yet to be discovered, (not excluding the Sumerian or early Egyptian). It now seems that there was a widespread proto-alphabet in use far earlier than we had imagined, and that it flourished in Europe

even before the earliest examples of Mesopotamian writing. The origins
of early religion, sacred alphabets, and the esoteric teachings of various
schools of pre-Hebrew Cabala are lost in the mists of time. But the
remaining hints are tantalizing. We know, for example, that the ancient
Celts and Druids had their genuine Cabala and runic magic, and that it
has many similarities to the Aryan traditions about which we can still
read in the Vedas and Upanishads, India's most ancient scriptures. We
know that Egypt developed a supremely sophisticated system of high
magic in an ongoing variant of the Goddess tradition, which lasted
with minor breaks for over two millennia. Wherever the cult of the
Goddess flourished, we find the unified primal vision of harmony and
power, and the presence of a set of symbols through which this power
was mediated. At such points of history, if we look for the roots of
Tarot, we shall not be disappointed. In researching this aspect of Tarot,
it might help to keep some of the following points in mind :

1. In the Major Arcana, each card has a corresponding letter from
    the 22 letters of the Hebrew alphabet. It would be worth
    looking into the 22 letters of the Phoenician alphabet, which
    parented the Hebrew, to determine the sacred traditional
    significance, and associations of each letter. Still further back,
    the rudiments of the alphabet discovered on the Glozel and
    Tartaria tablets speak to us of a time when the Goddess reigned
    supreme in Europe, and the primary symbols of a unified
    vision still held their power. The symbolism and meaning of
    this earliest of all alphabets, overlapping as it largely does, the
    Phoenician and Hebrew, deserves careful attention.

2. The true vibration of each letter of any alphabet, esoterically
    speaking, is to be found in its corresponding colour. If a user of
    Tarot gives importance to the vibration of the Hebrew or Runic
    correspondences, then colour should be considered as a means
    of attunement to that consciousness. Franz Bardon in *The Key to
    the True Quabbalah* explains for each of the letters of our
    alphabet what is the corresponding colour, and how that letter
    affects the physical, astral, mental and spiritual bodies when it
    is vibrated there. There are tables of correspondence matching

the runic alphabet with colours and the cards of the Major Arcanum as well.

3. Many alphabets used letters to signify numbers at a period of time when Arabic numerals had not been invented. In the Phoenician alphabet, for example, aleph (A) signifies one; beth (B) signifies two; gimel (G) signifies 3; daleth (D) signifies 4, and so on. The correspondences are carried over into the Hebrew alphabet, and should be read into any Tarot card carrying letters of a cabalistic nature. The Pythagorean and Hermetic understanding of what each number means may help us to see new levels of meaning in any given Tarot card.

4. New deck designs based on ever deepening insights into cosmology will be developed in the future, and they may supercede the dominance of the symbols used by Waite, whose ideas have had an important influence on the evolution of Tarot art. Glimpses of Primal Truth are available to adepts in all walks of life, from all periods of history. Especially valid are the visions of true spiritual masters. The cosmic language and the images of the Tarot Cards can be used for all levels of divination and spiritual study, from the most mundane to the most exalted, but it helps to realize that there is a primal pattern in creation that pre-exists any of its cultural expressions, and that many cultures since the decline of the Goddess period of history have been severely imbalanced and deficient in their connectedness to the Divine and its cosmic language.

5. The Grammar of the Goddess can be learned most directly in the school of the heart, from the inner teacher. But for many students, it helps to use Tarot images to get the process started, to visualize the sacred presence with the help of art and design that truly express the primal energy. The images in *Ancient Mysteries Tarot* have been drawn from the art of the early Mystery Schools, and they epitomize the ancient vision of a cosmos filled with spiritual life.

6) The self-communication of the Goddess through her symbols is an oracular event. It occurs when a receptive human

consciousness is attuned to the sacred presence. When we do serious work with Tarot, or even when we play with it in a sense of openness, our interface with sacred presence may be enhanced if we: a) burn a candle b) burn incense c) take tea of anise, thyme and camomile (which opens the centres of higher awareness) d) quiet the mind and open the heart e) play peaceful music.

The remnants of Tarot Art from the earliest Renaissance decks are interesting, but we must remember that ecclesiastical censorship severely limited what the seers and sages of that time were permitted to express. A patriarchal and unsympathetic male hierarchy of priests and bishops threatened people who crossed the official line with being burned alive in the fires of the Inquisition. How much of the Primal Cosmic Language can we expect to find being depicted in such a period of history? The tension between Patriarchal and Matriarchal religion has been a cultural fact for at least three millennia, but the Goddess has found ways to continue extending Her guidance to those who seek.

In this regard, it may help to recall to mind the shrine of Delphi, the most famous of all Greek oracular temples, a place of guidance for almost a thousand years. Here the priestess known as the Pythoness sat on a tripod and uttered pronouncements in answer to questions put to her by the supplicants. The temple had originally been a Goddess oracle, but it was seized by the priests of Apollo at a very early period of Greek history and was under patriarchal control from a point prior to recorded Greek history. Still, feminine intuition and the need for sacred guidance continued under the shadow of the male god, because these qualities have always been necessary to souls seeking their way. Thus it remains even to this day.

In order to grow into the fullness of his soul's possibilities, the Fool's first encounter on the Tarot Path had to be the Magician. The Magician demonstrates the central activity of the entire soul journey, which is progressive mastery of all parts of one's being, the physical, emotional, intellectual and spiritual, which are symbolized by the implements on the table before him. The Magician is one who devotes himself unreservedly to the mastery of the Grammar of the Goddess. His approach is masculine, for it combines will, disciplined action, courage and decisiveness. But soon the Fool will meet the High Priestess, and here he will learn the art of intuitive attunement. Happy are those who learn Tarot from the Goddess Herself! For it is only in right relationship to the personified Divine that true surrender of heart is possible, and only if he can be opened to the depths of his own heart's capacity to feel and sense can the Tarot pilgrim attain the final goal.

In the temple of my dream vision, the circular walls were broken by four alcoves, equally spaced. Pictures of the major arcana lined the stone walls between the alcoves. The crystal ball at the centre of the room symbolizing The World was the culmination of a progressive experience. The seeker himself stood in the place of the Fool, whose image hung over the doorway to the stone steps, in the antechamber. There were thus four stretches of wall containing five images each. The first set of images were The Magician, The High Priestess, The Empress, The Emperor and the Hierophant. Then, in the northernmost point of the curved wall was the alcove of Earth. The Lovers, The Charioteer, Strength, The Hermit and Wheel of Destiny followed, with the alcove Water facing west. The court cards occupied the uppermost part of each alcove, and the numbered cards, from ace to ten, were in rows beneath. Justice, The Prisoner, Death, Temperance and The Devil followed the alcove of Water until one came to the alcove of Fire which faced south. The Tower, The Star, The Moon, The Sun and Prophecy led to the final alcove of Air facing east. The stone steps which ascended into the temple came through the floor partway between the alcove of cups and the square altar with the crystal sphere bathed in moonlight. Between the top of the steps and the altar was a tripod on which to sit. The only light came as a pale shaft descending from the ceiling onto the crystal.

In my mind, I now enter this place regularly and move from picture to picture. I repeat the names of the images in their order as I see them in my mind's eye and pause to feel their presence and their significance in my deeper consciousness. From time spent in this inner temple, a revelation emerges, a vision of the truths of the mystery school tradition which lie at the very heart of Tarot symbolism.

The Path of Serapis

Iamblichus was a Neo-Platonic mystic who lived and died in Syria in the latter part of the third, and the early part of the fourth century AD. He passed away just as Constantine was making Christianity the official religion of the Roman Empire. The writings of Iamblichus are sometimes referred to with reference to the origins of Tarot. For example, in his book *Earth Under Fire*, Paul La Violette writes :

...according to the ancient Greek philosopher Iamblichus, a series of 22 frescoes identical to the Tarot Major Arcana once adorned the walls of a secret underground gallery accessed through labyrinthine passages. Priests wishing to be indoctrinated into the meaning of these frescoes entered the subterranean passage through a door in the breast of the great Sphinx. The novice priest would then repeatedly encounter the sphinx motif within this secret gallery. The frescoes lining each wall were said to be flanked by sphinx-like caryatids, 24 in all, and to be lit by 11 crystal oil lamps shaped in the form of sphinxes. A sphinx was also prominently displayed in Fresco 10 (Arcanum 10 of the Tarot), the last fresco in the sequence 0 through 10 which together depicted the science of creation ... Also, Arcanum 21 depicted the four zodiac signs of the sphinx (bull, lion, eagle and water-bearer) distributed symmetrically around a large wreath.

La Violette may or may not have known that the originator of these descriptions was Paul Christian. His book *L'Homme Rouge des Toileries* (1863) described a number of Egyptian temple frescos that corresponded to the titles of the Major Arcana, but there is no evidence at all that these originated in any ancient source. A similar "Egyptianized" set of Tarot images originated in the 1990's with Michael Poe, who described the interior of a Serapis temple based on archaeological records from the early part of the 20th century, now conveniently lost.

Poe researched Egyptian history rather carefully, and claimed that he could not find any references to the 22 images of the Major Arcanum in Iamblichus, but he did claim to have come up with something even more wonderful. He was reading a book by Bernard Bromage, who remarked that Tarot originated from the Temple of Serapis in Naples Italy. The temple unfortunately has been under water for much of this century, and was severely damaged in World War II. Thus there was little to see at the actual site, and more problematic still, contemporary archaeologists say the site was a set of market stalls, not a temple. It had been excavated in the early part of the century, and detailed notes had been made of the frescos that were found on the walls. Michael Poe claims that he obtained a copy of the excavation report from the French Institute of Archaeology in Cairo. This he posted on the internet, and then disappeared. No one has been able to find any evidence of the same report or to reach him, leading most to conclude that it is a scam. The information which Poe gives about the report can be summarized as follows:

1. Just inside the entrance to the Temple was a statue of the God Khnemu, and in front of it an altar. The god had one hand pointed towards the sky, and the other towards the earth. He is the Nile God, and flowing water represents the flow of consciousness. The altar might well have supported ritual symbolic implements such as we find on the Tarot card, The Magician.
2. To the left of this was the first illustration, a veiled portrait of Isis. seated between two pillars, one a lotus pillar and one a papyrus pillar. The goddess is holding a lotus and wears a crown that combines the sun and the crescent moon. (High Priestess)
3. The second illustration again shows Isis holding the baby Horus. She is crowned, and seated on a throne. (Empress)
4. The third illustration is of a Roman emperor in Egyptian garb holding the traditional scepter and flail of a Pharaoh. (Emperor)
5. The fourth illustration shows an Egyptian priest dressed in leopard garb, making an offering on an altar. (Hierophant)
6. Next we find an illustration of a lotus and sedge plants

intertwining, and Hapi Gods of both male and female traits. This is symbolic of the unification of Northern and Southern Egypt. (Lovers)

7. The next illustration is a shrine procession with two sphinxes in front of the shrine. They are being dragged by four priests of Anubis and four priests of Horus. (The Charioteer)

8. The next illustration portrays the Goddess Sekhmet, the Lioness Goddess who is an Egyptian symbol of strength. In this scene there is a priestess offering to the goddess a heart-symbol. (Strength)

9. This illustration is one of Imhotep, the perfected man, the Sage, holding a scroll in one hand. (Hermit)

10. An illustration of the seven Hathors, which were understood to be the seven fates in ancient Egypt, and represented man's relationship to time. (Wheel of Fortune)

11. A judgement scene where the deceased is having his heart weighed against the truth. (Justice)

12. This illustration was badly damaged, but it showed the god Osiris. He was killed, cut into bits and re-assembled. (The Prisoner)

13. This picture, also damaged showed the god Set (Chaos and Destruction)with Anubis (guardian of the soul and guide of initiates). (Death)

14. An illustration of Horus and Set, emblematic of the balancing of good and bad traits within an individual (Temperance)

15. An illustration of the solar god Ra fighting Apophis. Included is a scene of priests making offerings. The Dweller of the Threshold confronts the soul who wants to cross over. (The Devil)

16. This is an illustration of two obelisks, traditional guardians of a temple entrance. They represent the first ray of light striking earth. It may suggest that the initiate is passing the perilous threshold and entering the temple. (The Tower)

17. This illustration os of the goddess Seshat. It is a libation scene. There is a priestess with two bowls, one holding water and the other earth, facing the goddess, and there is a bennu bird in the water. The goddess wears a star as a crown. She is the

presiding deity of Higher Knowledge, and she illumines the understanding of those who approach her. (Star)

18. The Moon is shown as Khonsu, god of the Moon along with another god, possibly Thoth, who is also associated with the Moon. (Moon)

19. A painting of the Sun God Ra, flanked by hawks and the sign of eternity. (Sun)

20. Here we see the initiate hand in hand with the God Thoth, being led away from the weighing-of-the-heart scene. His found has been found true and just. (Prophecy, which Waite called Judgement)

21. The final illustration shows the Goddess of Heaven, Nut over the God of Earth, Geb, with the God of space, Shu, in between. This represents heaven, earth and all things between, and symbolizes completeness. (The World)

In this sequence of images within the Serapis temple, it is clear that we are seeing the stages of initiation into a condition of higher wisdom, something which could have lasted for the duration of single ceremony, meaning hours, days or weeks, or which might have involved a complete lifetime, or even many lifetimes of soul-seeking. These illustrations tell the story of the soul's ascent into the light of truth. What is not clear is whether divination was associated with such a temple, and whether the sequence of images had anything at all to do with divination. The image of the god Serapis is not found in the interior of this temple at all, but there are illustrations of him on the outside. There are other temples of Serapis in Egypt, Alexandria, Rome, Ament, and a place called Pithom, (mentioned in the Bible) although time has by no means left a complete and totally intact legacy in this regard.

The cult of Serapis dates back the first dynasty (3,100 BC) and continued into late Roman times. Egyptian temples and mystery teachings spread throughout the entire Roman Empire, with Alexandria being a centre of study and dispersion of the Mystery School teachings.

Michael Poe's studies of Ancient Egypt led him to conclude that there were fourteen paths of self-unfoldment that developed in the long history of that ancient kingdom. For example, the Path of Ra, the Sun, centred on Heliopolis. In the main complex, a full size tree of life stood in the temple courtyard, including a pantheon of ten divine archetypes, a 21 step path, and buildings with a complex cabalistic structure.

Another example is the Path of Osiris, the journey of Resurrection. This mystery tradition has survived in many writings and translations including the Book of the Dead. The initiation centre was at Abydos where the tomb of Osiris was secretly located. Some believe that the trinity of Isis, Osiris and Horus was a precursor of the Christian Trinity.

Then, the topic of our present discussion, we have the Path of Serapis, which is the symbolic initiation of Tarot. Some scholars have interpreted the two syllables "Ta" and "Ro" to mean "the royal road". The fact that Serapis temples had illustrations corresponding to the major Arcana is highly significant. The most important centres were in Memphis, Alexandria and Southern Italy. The cult seems to give importance to meditation, esoteric symbolism, including the stages of initiation in the soul's development, and a possibility of complete self-transcendence.

A clue about the way symbols and images were used in ancient temples can be found in the famous classical writer Plotinus :

> *The Egyptians, either by exact science or spontaneously, had arrived at a method by means of which they could write with distinct pictures of material objects, instead of ordinary letters expressing sounds and phrases. These pictures were not ordinary images of the things they represented, but were endowed with certain symbolic qualities (Sophia), by means of which they revealed to the initiated contemplator a profound insight into the very essence of substances of things, and an intuitive understanding of their transcendental origins, an insight which was not the result of reasoning or mental reflection, but was acquired spontaneously by means of divine inspiration and*

illumination. As artistic representations of the phenomenal world,
they revealed, in fact, the ideal world of the soul.

One of the most eloquent testimonies of the ancient path to
enlightenment comes from ancient Egypt. Inscribed on the walls of the
Temple of Horus at Edfu, we find the following words:

The Summit is the Mountain Peak,
But there exist both Mountain and Valley,
And Something Else which causes them both.
Also, within you is that which wants to rise above itself
In spite of the animal instincts.
And there is also that which wants to remain earthbound.
Summit and Valley, these are two manifest powers
If these two did not exist, there would be only the One.
But since there are these two,
There exist also all the others which spring from them
The other Gods and Goddesses.
One should pass through complexity
In order to exhaust all its various possibilities
Until one achieves awakening of consciousness,
Which gives rise to perfect simplicity.
This is the state between dream and reality.
If you perceive the essence and the perfection of all good
In the forms of the Gods and Goddesses,
And if you adhere to a more excellent nature,
You will attain union with them,
You will contemplate the Truth,
And you will possess illumined intellect.
True knowledge of the Gods
Accompanies conversion to, and knowledge of, ourselves.

This eloquent testimony from ancient Egyptian times summarizes very
well the inner teaching of the Tarot. The twenty two images of the
Major Arcanum were added to those of Minor Arcanum, and used for
purposes of divination. Although removed from their true place in
temples of initiation, the inner teaching of Tarot is still accessible to
those who develop the eyes to see. Tarot speaks the language of the
soul, using the creative symbols which are the grammar of the

Goddess. Serapis is a god of strength. Tarot is the strength of Truth and its ancient images still speak to those who seek.

By the year 332 BC, Alexander The Great's conquests had taken him to Egypt, where he founded the city of Alexandria on the Mediterranean at the mouth of the Nile River. The greatest library of the ancient world came into being there. Documents and artwork from every known source were collected and studied in its halls of learning. Here many of the Mystery Schools sent their students and wise men to learn the ancient traditions from the original manuscripts, and here the sacred art of the entire Mediterranean world was collected and displayed. If the Ancient Mysteries Tarot has its origin anywhere, it is in the great library of Alexandria. We know that the Egyptians traded with India and with the natives of South America, so it is not too difficult to picture halls and galleries where the art and culture of these civilizations were on display, as well as that of Greece, Mesopotamia and Egypt itself. The library lasted until the time of Julius Caesar, when it was burned with the loss of much of the ancient collection. Therefore, if we want to picture a time and place on earth where art such as that of the *Ancient Mysteries Tarot* might have been assembled, it would be the library of Alexandria between the lifetimes of Alexander The Great and Julius Caesar.

For much of this period spanning the better part of three hundred years, there would have been wise men versed in various traditions of divination who would have understood the primary sources which we refer to as Tarot, and who would have been familiar with the oldest manuscripts which explain its archetypal principals both in terms of divination and initiation. They might not have used images on cards, and they might not have used our modern term "Tarot", but they would have grasped all the essential elements of symbolism, imagery, number, the powers of the four elements, attunement to them, and intuitive discernment of hidden patterns which we pull together under that name. This knowledge was widely dispersed over the entire ancient world, but it was never so richly unified under one roof as it was in the great library of Alexandria. Its loss was a monumental loss to history. Yet in the images of the *Ancient Mysteries Tarot*, we have a reminder of that long lost time when primal realities were strongly anchored in human understanding and practice.

An Ancient Temple

It is interesting to reflect that King Solomon's Temple, built a thousand years before the birth of Christ, was a creation of Phoenician craftsmanship. The Phoenicians are also known to history as the Canaanites. They were a people who built stone circles in high places across what is now Israel, to enact mystical rites and to measure the shifting patterns of the stars. They lived in Palestine before the Hebrews arrived and fought with them until they were driven away. After the Hebrews had dislodged the Canaanites from the so-called "promised land", and confined them to the coasts of modern Lebanon, they became known to history as the Phoenicians.

From the time of Joshua until the Babylonian Captivity (595 BC), the Jewish religion encompassed two streams of tradition, that of Moses, and that of the Canaanites, in which the writings of Enoch figure prominently. The Temple of Solomon was a triumph of Canaanite sacred architecture. After it was built, Solomon favoured the Canaanite traditions and moved away from exclusive allegiance to Yahweh. The rites of Solomon's temple likely represented some uneasy balance between these two competing traditions.

Two pillars stood in front of the eastern entrance to Solomon's Temple. They were known by the Canaanites as the 'messelbhoth'. One of the pillars, Jachin, marked the northern extremity of the rising sun at the summer solstice (viewed from the centre of the Temple) and Boaz, the other pillar, marked the southern extremity of the rising sun at the winter solstice. This means that on the day of the winter solstice, the Boaz stone would cast a shadow that would align perfectly with the centre of the temple, and similarly the Jachin stone would cast a shadow at summer solstice that would point to the centre of the temple). If an astronomer or astrologer were standing at the centre of the temple he would be able to know these two important dates by the observance of the shadows from these two pillars. Bases of similar pillars have been found in a temple of Baal in Cyprus, (in Tyre, (capital city of the Phoenicians) and in various Palestinian towns such as Samaria, Hazor and Megiddo. Of course in many Tarot decks based on the thinking of Arthur Edward Waite (1857-1942) and the art of Pamela Colman Smith (1878-1951) who painted what we now know as the Rider-Waite deck, we find twin pillars illustrated in several places. In the Major Arcanum, for example, they show up in the images of The Priestess, The High Priest (or Hierophant), Justice, and The Moon. They attest to a tradition in which the relationship of earth and humanity to the stars was of central importance. The pillars of The Priestess card are actually labelled "J" and "B" to indicate that they are part of the Phoenician or Canaanite temple tradition, which was expressed in the temple built for Solomon.

The first century historian of the Jews, Josephus, is believed to have studied with the Essenes at Qumran. The Essenes were the guardians of what we now know as the Dead Sea Scrolls. Josephus writes that Enoch recorded astronomical data on two pillars. The term "pillar of wisdom" has overtones that link Tarot and history and the Enochian traditions in surprising ways.

The Phonenician alphabet had twenty two characters, identical to the number of cards in the Major Arcanum. The Hebrew alphabet is modeled on the Phoenician alphabet, and the esoteric lore of Cabala is based on this same pattern as well. Quabbalah is a Jewish esoteric tradition that draws on ancient Egyptian and Phoenician sources. It would seem to be a relic of the Enochian rather than the Moses tradition within the world of Hebrew religious thought.

In fact, sacred alphabets, sacred geometry, the science of sacred numbers, sacred architecture and sacred music are all part of a widespread culture that encompassed most of Europe (and the Middle East) for thousands of years, and which disappeared only because it was vigorously suppressed by the Romans beginning under the emperor Vespasian. It includes the lore of the pre-Celtic peoples who built Stonehenge, Avebury, Newgrange, and other great megolithic monuments that frequently predate the pyramids by hundreds or even thousands of years. Recent research has confirmed that a single unit of measurement, the megolithic yard, (82.9 centimeters), was used across the whole of Europe in prehistoric times in the construction of the great megalithic structures.

The Goddess and divination were centrally important in this tradition, and indeed they also figured prominently in the Hebrew religious experience up until the Babylonian Captivity, during which time religious exclusivity grew, leading to an intolerant focus on the tribal god Yahweh. The texts that comprise the Old Testament were edited and selected after the Yahweh cult had taken precedence over the Enochian traditions, and they still form the basis of modern orthodox Judaism, as well as a substantial portion of the Christian bible. Not until the discovery of the Dead Sea Scrolls did we know how important the Enochian tradition had been in historical Judaism. The most prominent subject in these scrolls is astronomy, the observation of the stars by means of sacred circles of standing stones, and the fixing of important religious festivals according to the movements of the stars. Tarot has quite a few hints of this tradition which predates Moses by thousands of years. The twin pillars are only one instance of this.

Even within the Old Testament, from time to time, we find hints of the Canaanite (Enochian) tradition. For example, in Kings 18 : 30 – 35 we read of how Elijah repaired a stone circle :

And Elijah said unto all the people, Come near unto me. And all the people came near unto him. And he repaired the altar of the Lord that was broken down. And Elijah took 12 stones ... And with the stones he built an altar in the name of the Lord; and he made a trench (henge) about the altar, as great as would contain two measures of seed ... and he filled the trench also with water.

Although the stone circles and henges of the British Isles are well known, those of the Middle East are less so. In fact the land of the Canaanites had many circles of standing stones in high places, and these were used for centuries by the Hebrews until the followers of Yahweh gained the upper hand. They selected what would become biblical scripture from their own point of view, leading eventually as history unfolded to the monotheistic religions of the book (Judaism, Christianity and Islam).

A very interesting example of one ancient tradition embedded in Tarot has to do with Venus. After the Sun and the Moon, Venus was the most important planet to the ancient mystics. In fact to the wise men of ancient times, in the millennia preceding the Christian era, if one were to say "The Sun, the Moon, the Star", the term star would generally be understood to mean Venus. We call Venus a planet rather than a star, but traditionally Venus was known as the "morning star". It is the third brightest object in the sky, casting a discernable shadow when the Moon has not risen, or has set. For the ancients, Venus governed fertility, creativity, and material abundance. She was known as Astarte, Ishtar, Aphrodite and Ashtar in the ancient Near East.

The movement of Venus is an eight year cycle. Every forty years it returns to its exact beginning point. Five Venus cycles form a kind of cosmic completion every forty years. Of course the number forty is a recurring theme in the Bible; it is used over and over in many contexts. The Jews, for example, wandered for forty years in the desert before coming to the land of milk and honey. If the movement of Venus through the zodiac is traced through its forty-year period of return, we find that it describes a perfect pentacle pattern. The pentacle has been a symbol of Venus from the very earliest times. For the Egyptians, the five pointed star was used in their heiroglyphic writing and it stood for knowledge, because anyone who understood the movements of Venus grasped the most important knowledge of the day, a detailed understanding of the seasons. One very good reason why Venus was so important is that its movements provide the most accurate indicator of the time of year. By understanding the position of Venus, it is possible to determine a time and a date to a precision of seconds over hundreds of years.

The five-petalled rose has from ancient times been a symbol of Venus as well as a resurrection symbol. If you connect the points between the petals, you get a pentagram. Also, the five-petalled dog rose does not need a mate to produce a rose hip. It can therefore die and be born again identical to its former self. In the symbolic journey of initiation, this meaning was and is quite important. For example in English Freemason lodges, the ceiling is decorated with a five petalled rose, and of course we find roses being pictured frequently in the cards of the Major Arcana.

Close study of Newgrange, a megalithic mound in the Boyne valley near Dublin has revealed just how important Venus was to the early builders. The mound has a corridor which is designed in such a way that once every eight years the light from Venus shines down its length past 22 massive stones and strikes a special place on the innermost sanctum. The symbols carved on stones found inside the chamber suggest that this was a place where mothers came to give birth on special dates when the light of Venus would bless the offspring. When we understand the great depth and complexity of this tradition, the meaning of the pentacle symbol takes on a whole new meaning.

The Tarot symbol of Venus stamped on a clay disc represents a whole set of concerns whose true meaning is embedded in a very ancient culture. This ancient tradition gives the goddess a prominent or even a centrally important place of honour, and from this arose the world's greatest prehistoric temples, both outdoor stone circles, and underground mound-temples. Although much of the lore has been buried, lost, or distorted, we can trace a thread of continuity from distant times to the modern day through the symbolism of Tarot. Another example may be cited to illustrate the range of possible connections between Tarot and the earliest traditions of Europe and the Near East. The rituals of Freemasonry claim to date from very ancient times. One of the most important ceremonies of this secret society involves a symbolic death in which the candidate for initiation into the order is covered with a shroud and made to lie 'lifeless' on the floor. Part of the ritual continues in darkness until the time comes for the candidate to be raised from his 'tomb' and complete his initiation. At the moment of resurrection a light in the shape of a five-pointed star (Venus) is directed from the east into the symbolic tomb and at this point the candidate is called back to life. One of the offices within Freemasonry is that of the Deacon. He carries a wand which historically was used to assess the angle of a shadow cast by the sun in order to align a building correctly. The wand-symbolism is, of course, also prominent in Tarot. It is interesting that the original prototype of a god who faced severe ordeals, then death, then resurrection, was the Phoenician god Baal. Along with Osiris, Tammuz and Adonis, he is one of the most ancient instances of such a pattern. This triumph over death is the story that is re-enacted by anyone seeking initiation. In contrast to the distant and stern Yahweh, Baal was close to the earth. He suffered, he experienced tragedy, he was reborn in flowers and plants. The pomegranate motif can be found in The Empress and also The Priestess. This tree was said to have sprung from the blood of Baal, which links it as well to the theme of death and resurrection. The story of Baal, then as now, offers food for the imagination it is easy to understand why the Hebrews were attracted to his cult.

For the same reasons, the Greeks were attracted to the hero Heracles, also an export of the Phoenicians. He is the archetypal hero who struggles against adversity and reveals the presence of the divine in the human. Similarly, the rites of Dionysus have their roots in fertility festivals of the ancient Canaanites. The rite was a spring festival with dancing and ecstatic worship. It was passed on to the Jews as 'Pesach' and to us as 'Easter', Dionysus being one of the gods who (like Jesus) died and was then reborn. Wine is central to the rites of Dionysus, just as it is central to the Catholic mass.

The ancient gods of the Near East established the divine pattern of quest, struggle, death and rebirth, and it was enacted symbolically and experientially among humans in temples and mystery schools for thousands of years. Up until the destruction of Jerusalem by the Roman Emperor Titus, a powerful tradition of this sort co-existed with the Moses traditions of Judaism in an uneasy alliance. The story which unfolds in twenty one stages in the Grand Arcanum of Tarot is one rendition of this archetypal and most ancient tale.

When the wisdom of Tarot is linked to the mystical teachings of Cabala, and the Sephiroth, it is worth keeping in mind the following : the Hebrews borrowed from virtually all their neighbours. Their cosmology comes from the Babylonians, as does their account of the great flood which Noah survived. Nimrud of the Biblical account is in fact Gilgamesh of the older Sumerian sources. Abraham came from Ur; he was part of the ancient Mesopotamian culture. The winged bulls and celestial beings of Assyria became the Jewish cherubim. The word Elohim comes from the root word El, which is the Phoenician supreme god, equivalent to the Greeks' Zeus or the Romans' Jupiter. From the Phoenicians also the Hebrews borrowed the pastoral feast of Mazzoth, at the beginning of the barley harvest, the Sukkoth or Feast of the Tabernacles. The Hebrew image of the kingdom of heaven and a number of hymns, (changed into psalms), and their temple architecture all came from Canaanite sources. Many other psalms were Egyptian in origin. King Saul named his son Esh-baal, and Jonathan's son was Meri-baal, names which honoured Yahweh's Phoenician rival, Baal. Many of the wives of David, Solomon and other Hebrew kings kept and practiced their own religious rituals in the palace. Jezebel's husband, king Ahab, allowed temples to be built for Baal and Asherat, much to the anger of the prophets. There is no complete separation possible between the traditions of the Mystery Schools in the Middle East and the early stages of the Hebrew Yahweh cult. For most of its history, Palestine, Israel and Lebanon were home to many threads of co-existing religious experience. Cabala, the Sephiroth (and their contribution to our understanding of Tarot) have their origins in this ancient melting pot of religion and myth.

The fundamentals of this ancient cosmology are also found in Europe, even its most northerly reaches. What we know of the people who lived in the British Isles prior to Stonehenge all points to this. It is not too much of a stretch of imagination to visualize a re-birth ceremony taking place at Newgrange, perhaps 5,000 years ago or more. A dead king or high priest is placed in the perpetual darkness of the inner chamber. Then, through the specially carved slot in the eastern entrance, at the appointed time, the light of the rising Venus floods the darkness. Just as the light of the morning star stabs the obscurity of the darkened chamber, the soul of the dead one is resurrected. This visitation of Venus happens once every eight years, but the bodies of the dead may have been brought into the sacred underground temple for just this purpose, at this special time, to be awakened from the slumber of death and raised into the divine light before taking rebirth. In this way, the soul of the dead person is blessed and clothed with immortality. One who was so fortunate as to be born at the sacred hour when Venus sent out her blessing would also be marked by divinity, and it is very likely that the sacred underground temples and caves of prehistoric times were places where the mysteries of death and rebirth were re-enacted for thousands of years until the cult was crushed by Rome.

In Tarot, the penultimate card is Judgement, or as it is termed in the *Ancient Mysteries Tarot deck*, Prophecy. In the Tarot art which is based on the original Rider-Waite paintings by Pamela Smith, we see the souls of the dead being called up out of the grave into the light. This is a Christian concept. If we were basing our Tarot deck on the most ancient traditions, the art would make reference to prophecies of the coming together of heaven and earth both in the microcosm of the initiate and in the macrocosm of the outer world. In fact the card which we know as The World stands for the macrocosm after Prophecy's fulfilment. The more we learn about ancient traditions, the more we will come to understand the timeless archetypes of the major Arcanum. But at the same time, we will become more discerning and demanding in our expectations of what a good Tarot deck should be.

A very fruitful line of research might involve the study of the Phoenician alphabet, and its precursors. Can it be mere co-incidence that Newgrange has 22 great stones leading down the hallway to the great inner chamber? (actually 22 on the left side and 21 on the right) Can it be coincidence that the Phoenician alphabet has 22 letters and the Major Arcana 22 archetypes? What are the meanings of these letters in the Canaanite tradition and in European traditions that predate it? We know that the letters of the alphabet also stood for numbers. Thus the letter corresponding to our "A" was a number one. Letter "B" was a two, and so on. The meanings that numbers have been assigned is a tradition that predates Pythagoras by thousands of years, but it is being used in Tarot divination even today. While visiting ancient Inca and Pre-Inca ruins in Peru, I discovered to my dismay that the most important remaining temple at the centre of the Inca sanctuary of Pisac has twenty-one niches in its walls. Each of these would have held a sacred image. In their totality, they would have been elements of a cosmological story. The hints are intriguing.

Less well known is the meaning assigned to sounds and to letters of the alphabet in ancient times. It is important to remember that every letter of an ancient sacred alphabet began life as a sacred symbol. Many or most symbols were related to the gods, goddesses and stars. For example the seven vowels corresponded to the heavenly bodies of greatest importance in astrology. The sound AO referred to the Sun; the letter I represented the Moon; A corresponded to Mars; E matched with Mercury; O was Jupiter, AW was Venus and the sound OO was Saturn. Of course Venus was Aphrodite to the Greeks and Ishtar to the Babylonians and she had many other names and forms in other cultures. When we go back in time we find that various cave sites in France and Spain dated to about 8,000 to 10,000 years ago have artifacts with letters, writing and symbols that constitute a written script. In 1896 a large number of inscribed pebbles were found dating to the Magdalenian Age and the marks on the pebbles closely resembled the symbols of the alphabet. For example eleven symbols corresponded to Phoenician letters (Encyclopedia Britannica, 11th ed., 28:853). At Glozel were found incised tablets with signs and letters similar to Phoenician and Greek alphabetical letters, but thousands of years older than the earliest examples of alphabetic writing in the Middle East, including even the oldest Sumerian examples.

It becomes clear that the Phoenicians were not the originators of the alphabet, but merely its most famous popularizers in the region of the Mediterranean. This suggests also that the symbolic significance of the various alphabetic symbols dates to the earliest periods of human history. Any effort to match the cards of the Major Arcanum with the Hebrew letters of the Sephiroth must take into account that the true symbolic correspondences are much more ancient than anything in Jewish tradition. The Jews were relative newcomers to the scene.

Letter, number, geometric pattern, starlight, all were part of a grand cosmology which was at the very heart of sacred learning and religion for ancient man. It is in this world that the roots of Tarot are to be found. When we become fixated in Egyptian or Hebrew or Renaissance history, we are merely pausing in one historical expression of this most ancient and universal wisdom. The rites of initiation and the teachings of the Mystery Schools in ancient times, along with certain libraries like that of Alexandria, had the keys to the understanding of this tradition.

Recovery of ancient documents like the Dead Sea Scrolls and the Book of Enoch in particular gives hope that eventually we will be able to piece together the entire picture. When we do, we will understand Tarot and in particular the Major Arcanum much better.

This ancient wisdom was severely restricted by Rome, and after Christianity became the dominant religion of the Roman Empire, the Mystery School tradition virtually died out or went underground. The transmission of these traditions into Christianity was facilitated by a famous Phoenician, a philosopher from Tyre known as Malchus, or Porphyurius ("the man from the purple land"). A pupil of the Neo-platonist Plotinus, he developed a view of heaven in which western and eastern gods could be effortlessly brought together and related to one another. In his day, he influenced generations of religious and secular thinkers. Christians in particular drew on his ideas of a great father god who commanded saints, angels and lesser divine beings among whom Baal, Lucifer, and others had a place.

It is a fact that Phoenician temples and religious ideas flourished in Pre-Christian Rome for hundreds of years, perhaps as far back as the fall of Carthage. Phoenicia was an amazing transmitter of religious traditions for hundreds of years, and it influenced cultural history in the Mediterranean basin in ways we are only beginning to appreciate. We find evidence of this on Roman coins, in newly discovered remains of temples, in place names, and in historical accounts. From Rome, many doorways opened into Europe not only in classical times, but later in the waning years of the middle ages and at the time of the Renaissance, when the first Tarot cards were developed.

In the earliest Renaissance Tarot decks, we see the medieval European mind renewing its memories of an ancient spiritual tradition. Given the religious restrictions and the ever present threat of punishment by the Inquisition, the Tarot illustrations from Italy and France of that period express what is possible. But today we have much more extensive understandings of history, the evolution of language, systems of ancient symbolism, archaeology, and early religion, and we have the freedom to express what we learn as we understand it, without fear of being burned at the stake. A number of modern Tarot decks make very good use of this freedom.

Our newfound liberty to explore and modify the symbols of Tarot works best when it is based on a sound knowledge of the traditions of the ancient Mystery Schools where the higher learning of historic and even prehistoric times was gathered and studied and refined. In this perspective, we could suggest that a greater depth of understanding of The Star from the Major Arcanum could come from reading into it the traditional meanings of Venus in ancient Europe and Mesopotamia. Whether the Egyptian goddess Nut or the goddess Ashtara of the Middle East is the key to the card's esoteric significance is an interesting and still open question.

Another open question that comes from understanding the tradition of Enoch has to do with the hanging man (or angel) which in the Ancient Mysteries Tarot is called The Prisoner. In the story of the Flood in the Book of Enoch (found at Qumran, home of the Essenes) we read that the people who lived on earth prior to the flood had committed many sins. Their story runs as follows : Two angels, Shemhazai and Azazel received permission to come down to earth and try to redeem mankind. But Shemhazai fell in love with the beautiful Ishtar (Babylonian goddess of love). She would take him as a lover only on condition that he would reveal to her the secret name of God. This he did. She then used the power of the Word to ascend into heaven and shine forever. After being duped in this way, the two angels chose wives and had children. They each had two daughters who led men into sin. Then God told Shemhazai that he would send a great flood to destroy the world. Shemhazai repented his sins but feared to face God. He suspended himself between heaven and earth, hanging by a rope head downwards because he was afraid to appear before the Lord. Azazel did not repent. He continued to lead humans into greater and greater sins until the flood came.

It is clear that this angel looked and acted like a human being. In the Tarot image of The Hanged Man it is quite possible to see an image of Shemhazai; certainly the story of his deeds and his repentance is relevant to the meaning of the Tarot image. But The Book of Enoch was not available to Medieval or Renaissance hermetic masters, as far as we know, and so it is all the more intriguing to speculate on how the image of The Hanged Man came down to us through time.

In 1440, William St. Clair was concerned for the safety of ancient Jewish scrolls which had come to him via the Knights Templar. He built a replica of the ruined Jerusalem Temple to house them near his castle at Roslin. In this chapel, we find a carved image of Shemhazai, the hanged man. This raised intriguing questions as to whether the Templars had uncovered parts of the Book of Enoch when they excavated under Soloman's temple in Jerusalem, and whether this material could have circulated secretly at the time that Tarot images were being popularized.

One useful line of inquiry has to do with the Knights Templar. When Jerusalem was conquered on July 15, 1099, this order of knights took possession of the land on which the Temple of Solomon had been built. They began digging in search of a cache of hidden documents which they believed held the secret teachings of Judaism. The story of what they found and where it was taken is shrouded in mystery. But it is believed that they did find significant materials which were brought back to Europe, specifically to Scotland. Whether the Book of Enoch was among these materials, and whether understandings which relate to Tarot were conveyed into the European consciousness in this way is a very good question. *The Hiram Key* by Christopher Knight and Robert Lomas is a book that explores this and other related subjects. It opens an interesting line of research that is provoking as many valid questions as it suggests answers, all of which may prove fruitful in the not too distant future for students of Tarot.

When we trace certain Tarot themes and images back to their pre-Hebrew roots, using the Book of Enoch and other sources, we begin to open doors into hidden dimensions of meaning that situate us in the world-view of the initiates of the ancient Mystery Schools. If the great library of Alexandria had not been destroyed, it would have provided answers to our questions. But even to be able to define the important questions is a step forward in our exploration of Tarot and its meaning, because armed with the right questions, we can focus our study and our research more precisely.

The Twenty One Gates

The Magician, as we have seen, represents the soul's need for mastery of all parts of its being. At some point before a human being is born, the soul descends into a physical world and takes on a physical, emotional and mental body as well as several other energy fields in order to give creative expression to its latent divine potential. When we have evolved to a certain level of awareness, we remember our soul's mission and begin to seek our spiritual destiny. In Tarot decks which follow in the Waite pattern, the pentacle on the table in front of The Magician represents the physical dimension, the cup represents the astral or emotional world, the sword represents intellect, and the wand represents the creative and spiritual possibilities of a human being, especially as they are expressed on the vital plane.

The statue of The Magician in the Waite deck, and many later decks modeled on it, have one hand pointing to heaven and another towards earth.   This indicates that the work which must be done at The Magician stage of the soul's journey is to focus on bringing together Heaven and Earth, which means to bring down the power of spirit and give it expression in physical form. The question posed by The Magician to the would-be seeker is : "Am I honouring my soul's duty to work with concentrated will to master all parts of my being and realize my full potential according to inner guidance from on high?"

The High Priestess stands for inner spiritual guidance which we access by intuitive attunement. The fact that she is veiled suggests that the gaze is inward-looking, as opposed to seeking light and guidance from some external tradition. In some Egyptian decks we find Isis is seated on a throne, like the Priestess image in the Waite illustration. A crown with emblems of the sun and moon is often present. This suggests a harmonizing of lunar and solar energies, a synthesis of mind and heart. Their position between two pillars suggests that the High Priestess gives us entry into the inner sanctum of a temple, which is the sacred space of spiritual presence. The question that arises when we come into the domain of the High Priestess is, "Am I receptive to my intuitive guidance as I go forward in my journey of discovery?" The High Priestess is fond of silence and solitude. She listens to the heart, studies sacred literature, and cultivates an awareness of deep inner sources of wisdom and inspiration.

In the Waite deck, whose symbolism has set the standard for the better part of a century, the Empress is outdoors, surrounded by lush trees, ripening grain and flowing water. All of this suggests fertility and renewal, areas of concern presided over by many forms of Mediterranean Mother Goddesses such as Demeter. The *Ancient Mysteries Tarot Deck* uses the image of the Great Goddess found at Catal Huyuk, one of the most ancient such ever found. The question that arises is : "In my relation to the archetypal Mother, and to Nature, and in questions of supply and abundance, does my life harmonize with Truth?"

The Emperor in the *Ancient Mysteries Tarot Deck* is taken from a Greek statue of Poseidon, god of the vast sea. In the domain of The Emperor, we face this question : "Concerning responsibility, the use of power and all things related to authority, is my soul in balance?"

The High Priest in the Waite illustration sits between two pillars similar to those we have seen previously in the High Priestess illustration, and he wears all the trappings of socially-sanctioned religious authority. Yet we infer that he has some higher knowledge of deeper mysteries. In the *Ancient Mysteries Tarot* the ancient statue is a Buddha-like figure with Greek influence. The question that occurs with regard to the Hierophant, in any of his forms is : "In my pursuit of sacred wisdom, in my relation to the authority of the tradition, and in honouring the precepts of the path, is my life harmonizing with Truth?"

In most modern Tarot decks, the Lovers card usually pictures a pair of human lovers, occasionally a man facing a choice between two females. But the same question underpins both sets of symbols : "Is my soul living in right relationship, creating balance and harmony in the midst of this duality-bound earthly experience?" Prior to Waite, the sixth card of the Major Arcanum was called "The Lover". A young man was depicted trying to decide between his mother and his beloved, that is between his parental roots and his own path. Cupid was there, with an arrow aimed at the young man's heart. The meaning of the card was the necessity of making a decision about love from the depths of the heart. Waite changed the card to "The Lovers" which somewhat shifts the meaning toward the question of relationship. The original Egyptian symbolism seems to be more about choice. This is one example of how Tarot meanings evolve with the art that depicts them.

The Charioteer in the Waite deck is anchored in concrete, suggesting that he exercises full control over the two sphinxes and the world around him by means of mind-power. The crown he wears, and his wand of authority (also anchored in cement) suggest that he has conquered both the material and mental planes. He is a fully developed individual who has been empowered by virtue of his disciplined will. The *Ancient Mysteries Tarot Deck* shows an Assyrian warrior or king hunting lions. The question that faces the initiate at this stage is : "Am I maintaining my soul alignment as I succeed in moving my mastery forward by means of my mental will?" In the Waite illustration, which has become the norm in recent times, it seems to be a question of whether the ego's positive, self-assured successes, and the victorious mental control which have been achieved are being held in balance with other parts of the being, in particular the ego-transcending spirit.

In Michael Poe's putative Serapis Temple, the image of Strength is the Lioness Goddess Sekhmet, who represented both destruction and healing. A priestess offers the goddess a heart symbol. In later Tarot decks, it is common to see a female mastering a lion by holding its mouth open, which suggests the gentle strength of the heart mastering the animal instincts. There seems to be a heart connection in both ancient and modern iconography. The question at this stage could be expressed : "Am I fully dedicated, in my heart, to move beyond the love of power and grow into the power of love?"

The Hermit, the ninth card in modern Tarot decks, is usually pictured holding a lantern, and standing on the snowy mountaintop of lonely spiritual attainment, clutching a yellow staff of mastery. Both the ancient and modern images seem to suggest this question : "Am I fully surrendered to go alone, if necessary, beyond all traditions and structures to strive for the highest attainment?" The *Ancient Mysteries Tarot Deck* shows the Hermit as an ascetic contemplative in the Indian spiritual tradition.

The Wheel of Fortune, and also the sphere, are symbols of the goddess Fortuna, who is the classical, Greco-Roman equivalent of the Hathors. We do well to envisage or feel the presence of the goddess Fortuna behind the symbol of the wheel in the modern Tarot decks. The question which arises at this stage is : "Am I correctly navigating the ups and downs of fate in quest of my final goal?" To endure the cycles of change and to hold fast while good luck alternates with adversity is indispensable if the soul is to attain liberation.

The figure of Justice is well known to us from our legal system. She holds an evenly balanced weighing scale to indicate the impartiality with which judgement must be rendered under the law. Justice in *The Ancient Mysteries Tarot Deck* is a wise old man from the Mesopotamian tradition. The question which faces the seeker at this point is : "How am I living the principles of integrity, balance, or right order in any domain of my life?" Justice demands of us that we develop a clear, incisive seeing along with impartiality and moral resolve. Where any of these qualities are lacking, we may be found deficient in the scales by which she measures our soul's progress.

The question posed by The Prisoner in the *Ancient Mysteries Tarot Deck* is "Am I fulfilling the law of sacrifice, which is complete self-giving to the guidance of Truth?" This human figure carved in stone is being strangled and held down by vines and tree roots, suggesting a kind of imprisonment and bondage to the earth plane. He must surrender his self-will to some higher power which now rules his fate. He must face the unknown with courage and be prepared for any sacrifice. Only this degree of total commitment proves him worthy of final attainment.

93

In modern Tarot, images of Death, the "grim reaper" suggest the fearful aspect of death, but in *The Ancient Mysteries Tarot*, the emphasis is on *"sic transit gloria mundi"* (thus passes the earth's glory). A once great pharaoh, a god-king, is reduced to a dry husk of his former glory. The question which determines whether the initiate has succeeded at this stage is : "Have I conquered the fear of death, and am I reconciled to the passing away of the old?" Because death is the greatest of all fears, victory here is a major triumph for the soul over fear itself.

The Tarot card known as Temperance stands for a harmonious balance of opposites by means of which we attain equilibrium, and it includes the themes of moderation, self restraint and control. Thus, the question which arises at this stage is :   "Am I finding the true balance that harmonizes, synthesizes, and sublimates the opposing elements of my life into a single whole?" The *Ancient Mysteries Tarot* gives us an illustration of the Sormugh, an ancient image of divinity in bird-form, best known in more recent history as Garuda in the Indian tradition.

Where our modern Tarot cards place The Devil, the ancient temples of the Mystery schools sometimes pictured Apophis who presided over the soul's transition to the other world. Each soul who crosses from this life to the next must confront the guardian of the threshold, who embodies all the shadows which one has not yet conquered and all the fears that have not been faced. Apophis is an embodiment of all these cherished destructive energies on a cosmic scale. He is thus an ancient Egyptian equivalent of the Judeo-Christian Devil. The question at this point arises : "Am I where I should be with regard to my struggle against darkness and limitation?" The Devil in the *Ancient Mysteries Tarot Deck* reveals a note of sardonic humour, which is often missing in modern illustrations.

When the would-be initiate arrives at The Tower, the question comes : "Am I willing to pass through and beyond the world of duality, and release all that I have built up by all my previous work to attain the Sacred Oneness of the Source?" In the *Ancient Mysteries Tarot Deck*, The Tower, a crack is seen to be opening up in the foundation of the building, as if from an earthquake that strikes from below. Far more buildings have fallen in this way than have ever been victims of lightening from the skies above.

The Star in many modern Tarot illustrations is often a woman pouring water from two vessels. One vessel empties into a pool of water, and the other is poured out into the earth. For the spiritual seeker who encounters The Star, the question is : "How is my receptivity in relation to the divine grace that comes from on high?" *Ancient Mysteries Tarot* shows a figure from ancient India bathed in the light of a radiant star on high.

In some Egyptian decks, The Moon is shown as Khonsu, Egyptian Moon God, and he is sometimes accompanied by Thoth, the embodied form of knowledge and understanding. In modern decks, we often see the moon placed between two pillars. The question is : "Have I mastered the cyclically changing appearances of this sublunar creation, both the illusion and the wisdom therein, to prepare my understanding for the attainment of Sophia, the highest wisdom?"

The Sun image in the Waite deck shows a child riding a white horse in the foreground. The image of the child is symbolic of our return to innocence. The fact that he can control a horse stands for his full mastery. The solar stage in the initiate's journey places the seeker on the verge of final spiritual attainment. This stage is sometimes called "apotheosis" which means divine attainment. The question here is : "Where do I stand in relation to the question of attaining enlightenment?"

When we come to the second-to-last card in the Major Arcana, the question is : "What considerations arise as to my worthiness to be admitted to the Highest Truth?" The *Ancient Mysteries Tarot* calls this stage of the soul's journey Prophecy. This is based on the prophecy that all souls will attain liberation in the fullness of time. The faith that this is our ultimate destiny empowers us to go forward on the eternal quest.

The World is usually pictured in modern Tarot decks as a nude female figure draped with the purple scarf of divinity, dancing freely. She is surrounded by a wreath of green leaves bound at the top and bottom by the lemniscate of eternity which we have seen already in the Magician and Strength images. This clearly is a card of final full attainment and supreme completeness, thus there is no question that needs to be asked or answered. The World represents completion, wholeness, and return to the Source.

When we consider that the Fool is the seeker who passes through these stages of quest and initiation, and the World is the image of final attainment, we are left with twenty questions (which like Tarot, is also a modern form of a game) that delineate areas of testing and progress for the would-be initiate.

There is no exclusivity attached to the questions suggested above. Other questions equally valid could be developed to mark the stages of the journey to full self mastery. What is important is that Tarot can now be understood in both its senses, as a symbolic journey of divination and as a pilgrimage of initiation. Indeed, these two can be merged into one process, a "divination concerning the soul's progress through the stages of initiation". From this we can envisage a new spread which reflects the internal logic of the Major Arcanum itself.

This would be a spread of 21 cards, three levels of seven cards each. Or, the cards could be placed in a circle, as if lining the walls of a circular temple, with "The World" position occupying the centre. The questions which relate to each position have been indicated above. It remains only to:

1) enter into a consciousness of sacred focus by whatever method works best;
2) shuffle ALL the cards of the deck (not just the cards of the Major Arcanum) with full concentration;
3) lay them out in either form of the 21-position spread, and lastly,
4) ponder the indications we receive regarding each of the questions.

As is normal, any card which comes in from the Major Arcanum can be considered an important indication from "on high".

All the learning we have done and all our previous experience can be used in this spread. If we appreciate that we are looking for insight from a very high level of understanding on the deepest questions of our spiritual journey, then we will approach the reading in the correct spirit. It may help to envision an inner temple and to visualize oneself entering its sacred space. We will get the best result by approaching this spread with all the seriousness that we would accord a true oracle. It is no exaggeration to say that the guidance of the Divine, in whatever form we can accept that guidance, should be recognized as the primal energy at work as we attempt to bridge the mysteries of true initiation with our own limited capacities for mental understanding.

The Blessingful Path

The number four is supremely important in the process by which spirit takes on the properties of matter. The highest reality, the Supreme Source, is unknowable and unspeakable. But it enters into a phase of self-expression as the knowable universe. That aspect of the Source which presides over creation and guides it to its destiny is called The Mother, or the Divine Mother.

The Divine Mother emanates the consciousness and force of the Supreme in four primal aspects. In the tradition of India, these are known as Maheshwari, Maha Kali, Maha Lakshmi and Maha Saraswati. But the fourfold primal structuring has many forms and names in different cultures and periods of history. In all early religions, the four directions were sacred, and each had its presiding deities and its unique field of energy and influence. The four elements, earth, air, fire and water are also basic to cosmology and early religion. Patterns of four may be seen as well in the four blood types, the four stages of evolution (mineral, vegetable, animal, human), the four seasons, the four ages of man (gold, silver, bronze, iron), the four components of DNA (nucleotides), etc. The four suits of Tarot are a part of this pattern. They are an expression of the fourfold manifestation, the four faces of the goddess. They are often understood to refer to man's fourfold nature as : body, emotion, mind and spirit.

In sacred architecture, the design of temples is based on the origin and evolution of human consciousness. True temples are living portals between dimensions of Being. They make it easier to attain altered states of consciousness in which Primal Reality can be accessed. The Tarot images present us with a language of Primal Reality. They can be matched to the basic building blocks of sound and spoken communication, the 22 letters of the earliest alphabets, and they can also be related to the inner meaning and vibration of numbers, as well as the houses and planets of astrology. These different systems of knowledge were all studied in the ancient temples of Egypt, Chaldea and India. They were part of a single, unified body of higher knowledge. Imhotep, and other great adepts, attained excellence in many of these fields, but less mature souls might master a limited number of them.

Tarot in its original meaning is a system of training which opens doorways in our awareness by means of which we can interact with the primal archetypes of creation, including numbers. The vibrations of three and of four are constantly recurring in all systems of ancient learning. Each of these vibrations is a world of experience complete within itself, inviting mastery by human consciousness. When, as a result of many lifetimes of experience, the soul learns the harmonics of the different vibrations, it gains a progressive control over itself and over creation. This progressive mastery is in essence the path of the hero.

Giordano Bruno, the famous Renaissance philosopher and magus, was part of a tradition which had its roots in ancient Egypt, Greece and Chaldea. Key elements in the 'perennial philosophy' which he championed were: the concept that the cosmos is a system of corresponding hierarchies; the centrally important relation of microcosm to macrocosm; the belief that the cosmos is animated by a world-soul which links all its parts into one; the belief that the human soul is an individual manifestation of the world-soul; the conviction that the chief faculty of the soul is imagination, and finally the faith that personal transformation and attainment of supreme knowledge is the central goal of our earthly pilgrimage. It is perhaps not surprising that a man who thought like this would end up being burned at the stake by the Inquisition.

For Bruno, the arcane knowledge of the ancient Mystery Schools was very much a living reality. He could have written volumes about each of the figures of the Major Arcanum.

According to Giordano Bruno, if we want full access to supersensible reality, such elements as love, meditation, and imagination are immensely important. Bruno believed that for divination, the ancient fundamentals of ritual and mastery of the laws of correspondence are invaluable. Unlike his contemporary Dee, Bruno's preferred procedure when making contact with the archetypes was to condition the imagination to receive their spiritual influence through magical images. These were deeply impressed on the memory by concentration. Tarot cards, especially the Major Arcanum, would be quite suitable for this purpose. What he called a "magically animated imagination" was the key to accessing the archetypal realities behind the images. If the imagination could be galvanized and awakened, the spiritual forces would unlock their powers and make them available. Giordano Bruno recommended intense meditation, visualization, and ritual magic in combination for those who wanted to release the visions, revelations and supernatural powers of the arcane beings. In our own day and age, each individual must develop his or her own unique approach in these matters, but some clues as to how to proceed can be tremendously useful, and in the current literature on Tarot this is what is so hard to find. Having made good use of our capacity to study and understand the traditional meanings of the cards, how do we then get beyond the left-brain, logical intellect and into the right-brain, intuitive attunement? Is there a way to re-structure our consciousness so that it becomes a more responsive instrument for divination?

This question leads to consideration of a most important ancient institution, the temple. Temples create and define sacred space. In the mystery school traditions, divination meant consulting higher, spiritual sources of guidance, often referred to as the gods (or in more modern parlance possibly the archetypes). Temples facilitated divination and sacred attunement in ways that are still not fully understood. But some understanding of their workings could be very helpful for the would-be Tarot user. Let us for a few minutes consider the relevance of ancient temples to the question of how we can make fullest use of Tarot. A temple is a space created in our three-dimensional world where higher order and harmony prevail. A temple is a manifestation of Wisdom, revealing the correspondence between the mundane and the cosmic, or the human and the divine. Nothing in a temple is random, all is purposeful. Even the selection and placement of building materials can reflect a conscious use of the energies of earth, water, fire and air. A temple is a supremely symbolic structure. It is a microcosm where the proportions, colours, symbols, inscriptions and building materials are combined to generate a space where consciousness can transcend its normal limits. A temple's images, colours, shapes, numbers, proportions and architectural form all join together like a symphony to express a wisdom teaching.

It is of immense relevance that Tarot is structured in just this way. All its components and the pattern of their organisation combine to present a vision of reality. An ancient temple and a Tarot deck are both designed to be living books that reveal the secret workings of the cosmos. They both testify to the interconnectedness of the microcosm and the macrocosm. The uninitiated eye will not see this. The closed heart will not feel it. Hence the requirement of instruction leading to progressive stages of initiation. Clearance to enter the inner sanctum of a temple and capacity to read true revelations from Tarot symbols have this common requirement : right preparation leading to right attitude. One who has been properly trained establishes in his or her heart the relationship of a sincere truth-seeker to the light of Truth. This entails a commitment to seek the progressive unfoldment of truth through the course of a lifetime, and to live what has been learned. Not every user of Tarot becomes a dedicated seeker in this sense. It is easy to buy a deck and read some books and do one's best to make sense of the subject. Here we come to an important difference between conventions of modern Tarot usage and ancient temple traditions. In the temple tradition, only the real initiates were given access to the higher teachings and the inner sanctum where true power and wisdom resided.

This is what we find illustrated in the mythologies of the various races of ancient times, and it is what they celebrate in their rituals and religious customs. The ancient traditions embodied in the mystery schools were proficient in giving expressive form to the movement of the individual soul through time and its evolution in consciousness. Tarot illustrates the journey of the hero-initiate as he (or she) achieves victories over the adverse forces and climbs to a higher destiny in the world of consciousness. In our Tarot story, The Fool is the protagonist (his number is 0), and his encounters with the twenty-one archetypes of the Major Arcana represent a journey of spiritual awakening.

The Magician's pathworking is, as we have seen, primarily *active* (yang), while that of the High Priestess is by contrast a more *passive* (yin) approach. The Empress is one of the *dynamic* (but balanced) aspects of the Goddess. In actuality, each of the twenty-one images in the Major Arcanum represents an opportunity and a challenge, a blessing and a test. Every blessing requires testing, just as every coin has two sides and every quartz crystal has two polarities.

A spiritual seeker who is on good terms with the Empress has a full measure of earthly supply, for her distinctive blessing to those of her children who care about her is abundance. And what she supplies is not only material abundance, such as good crops, fertile herds, healthy children, and prosperous enterprises, but also creativity, a capacity for nurturing, an attunement to nature, a spirit of generosity, a sense of fullness, joy, beauty, aesthetic style, emotional depth and growth potential, both inner and outer. The Empress is able to extend and to receive love. She helps us to develop a trusting and balanced heart, which is the essence of nurturing and healing. She has much in common with Venus, and something with Jupiter too. She is a kind of Imperial Venus who multiplies our sources of supply and nurtures our relation to the principles of abundance.

101

But just as power can corrupt, so can wealth. The temptation of riches is that we will enjoy them for their own sake and not use them according to the guidance which we receive from a higher level, from the soul or from the Goddess. Therefore, the Empress challenges us to be wise in our experience of her fullness and not to become addicted to earthly pleasures, the joys of the senses, sensuality and excess. She tests whether we have faith in the infinite supply which is available to all who come to her and offer themselves to her as her children, to do her work in the world. She places probing questions before us : Are we in right relation to the inner instincts of nurturing which she awakens in our heart? Are we attuned to nature? Do we replenish our exhaustion at her wellsprings of abundance when we need to be re-balanced? Do we linger too long in her courtyards in a selfish or lazy way? These questions or tests are always woven into the fabric of the blessings of the Empress.

She loves the Fool because he is innocent. His delight in her gifts may be wanting in wisdom, because he has not yet learned to handle abundance in a responsible way. If he is to progress, he will have to acquire the maturity of her consort, the Emperor, and indeed The Emperor will soon begin to tutor the candidate who has pleased the Empress. More than any other pair of Tarot images, the Empress and the Emperor are matched. They balance each other, and if a seeker encounters the one, then there is likely to be an encounter with the other coming up very soon.

The Goddess in all her forms is concerned with the manifestion of the Divine potential in matter. She cares about human souls because they do her work, which is to make earth into heaven. Some human souls, however, take an austere path which puts them into a state of imbalance with regard to their inner goddess. Some souls feel that earth is entirely a field of darkness, ignorance, maya and illusion, and that spiritual wisdom consists in closing down the five senses, and turning inward exclusively to find Nirvana and to escape *samsara*. This is not the path of the Mother. This approach to spirituality is something She may permit as one stage of spirituality's evolution on earth, but She sees it as an incomplete phase which we will surpass in time, based on an imperfect understanding of the purpose of creation and the destiny of the soul.

The path which The Mother approves and blesses is one which recognizes that matter is spirit, crystallized into form. Therefore, to create higher levels of order in matter is to work ritualistically and such work brings about a progressive manifestation of spiritual energy on earth. Life is not primarily about escape and the avoidance of suffering. It is about transcendence and victory over the very sources of suffering. Action can be a form of spiritual progress equally as useful as contemplation. To the Mother, karma yoga (union with the divine through work) is vitally important. She knows that total withdrawal into contemplation can lead to imbalance.

When the Goddess in the form of the High Priestess meets The Fool, it will be necessary to teach him the importance of turning inward. But when The Fool has assumed the discipline of turning inward, She must then teach him the balance which acknowledges the rightful, and indeed, the *sacred* character of right relationship with the world and its abundance.

The soul incarnates into a living human form for a reason. The body of humankind, the body of planet earth, and the field of interaction which arises between them, afford many experiences for the soul's growth and mastery. Suffering is necessary only when we cherish ignorance, but this is not what the Mother wishes for her children. Those souls who open to Her Presence in their hearts, and who learn to renew their inner childhood in Her compassionate embrace will discover that the world is a field of play, not a vale of tears. Extreme forms of penance, guilt, shame, retribution, punishment, and religions based on the fear of hell are not part of the way that the Goddess teaches. She opens the portals of the spiritual heart and brings bliss to those who will dedicate themselves to Her cause. The reason that She blesses some souls with abundance becomes clear in the fullness of time.

The Fool may not know, when he enjoys Her riches, that She will require him to become a benefactor to other souls at a later stage in his journey. The lesson She teaches when She gives abundantly is not merely that we must be wise and responsible in managing wealth (that is what the Emperor teaches). No, She is showing us the very spirit of giving in its essence. She moulds Her children so that they become capable of total self-giving. Her gifts to humanity are part of the ritual sacrifice by which creation is renewed, and so are our gifts to Her. There is a reciprocal circle in the primal ritual that unites human consciousness to the Divine, in whatever form we choose to approach it. All forms of the Divine are acceptable to the Mother, she created them. But when, in the fullness of time, the ritual achieves its purpose, the soul will have become a fully opened conduit, a pillar of spiritual strength, a channel of supply by which everything that heaven has and is flows to earth.

We know from all ancient traditions that there is an abundant and unimpeded action of grace which cascades down the primal pillar of creation and radiates outward into all four fields of manifestation to make matter into a dance of spirit. The river Ganges was pictured thus in the mythology of ancient India, but there are parallels in many other traditions. It helps to remember that the Gypsies, who are closely identified with Tarot, came to Europe from India in the early Middle Ages. The understanding of the Goddess was never completely eclipsed in India, despite the incursions of patriarchal religions such as Aryan Vedanta and Islam. Whether Tarot was first brought to Europe by the peoples of India known as the Gypsies, history is still unclear. What we do know is that for most Christian Europeans in the late Middle Ages and the Renaissance, the Gypsies were outsiders who were suspected of heresy and witchcraft. They were ideal caretakers of arcane traditions which the official church disallowed.

The Empress plays a most significant role in the initiation of any seeker who comes to her as The Fool. If we let go of our personality masks, and our self-possessed ego, if we return to the childlike nature of the open heart, and the willingness to embrace new adventures, then the

Divine Mother will bestow on us Her unconditional affection and blessings. One who has become Her Fool learns what it is to love and to give unconditionally. His heart widens. He is then ready to assume the burdens of discipline which are required by the Emperor. He becomes a prince as he experiences the uses, and the possible abuses, of power. Finally, the Star, the Moon and the Sun bestow their initiations, and the prince becomes an initiate of the highest mysteries. He passes the final judgement and attains The World. In this, the journey is complete.

In the next part of our exploration, we will trace The Fool's journey from the point when he meets The High Priestess until, under the tutelage of The Hermit, he comes to understand the deeper meaning of his adventure.

PART TWO: THE FOOL'S JOURNEY

The Matriarchs

When we look closely into the associations connected with The Magician, we find an approach to self mastery which is essentially a path of mental will. The Magician is a specialist in concentration, will power, mind power, occult power, control, and discernment. But the High Priestess opens the doorways of a very different path, and it counterbalances that of the Magician. If The Magician represents the path of the mind, The High Priestess connects a seeker to the path of the heart. If the magician is will, the priestess is intuition.

Many or most people who find value in Tarot are moving forward in their spiritual quest in a gradual and tentative way. They are covering basic lessons in their self-integration and development. They are not ready to enter the inner sanctum of the temple, nor would they be comfortable there because, simply put, they have not prepared themselves. They have not fully embraced a vision of their soul's ultimate destiny.

But slowly, the inner teaching of Tarot is loosening some of the veils that cloud their spiritual understanding, and their spiritual intensity will grow. The High Priestess is willing to work with people like this, who are not yet fully committed to a spiritual life in its purest sense, but who want to learn and progress at their own rate.

A true priestess has practiced and assimilated what she teaches. She has become the wisdom of her deep contemplation. She can show a sincere seeker a pathway beyond ignorance, but he must be prepared to see with the eyes of his heart and feel and know with the full sincerity of his soul. To speak with The Priestess is to be afforded an opportunity to embrace her teaching. This is what The Priestess is willing to offer those who approach her in the right spirit.

Picture, if you will, The Fool approaching the entrance of a secluded temple where the High Priestess is seated. He has been restless and eager to begin a new adventure. Although the High Priestess looks very dignified and solemn, seated in absolute stillness, he has the courage to approach her and to ask her the questions that are on his mind. She sees that he is immature. But she recognizes also that he is sincere, and so she responds to his questions.

Priestess: For a true priestess, all life becomes an offering and a dedication to the Divine. In this life in the precincts of the temple, we are trained to serve. We aspire to receive inner guidance from a higher source and to share it with all those who sincerely seek the way beyond suffering. We are constantly focused on the beyond, attuned to the Mother of Creation. We practice surrender so that there is no difference between our human, personal will and Her Divine Will, no motive except Her impulsion, no action that is not Her conscious action in all we do and think and say. This is why we practice stillness and introversion, so that we may be constantly attuned to the Mother and Her guidance.

Fool: It is a very high spiritual standard that you live. I am eager to learn, but I am not sure that I can embrace this life of dedication that you describe.

Priestess: In the world's eyes you are a Fool, because you do not conform to the expectations of the crowd. But in my eyes, you are the eternal child of the Mother. You do not conform to the expectations of those around you, not because you are a fool, but because you have begun to awaken to your own inner guidance. You have experienced the awakening of a spiritual spark in your heart. You are responding to a call which will take you on a long journey of inner discovery. You have come to see me because you seek the way to yourself. "Who am I?" you ask. You have come here to find the answer to this question.

The Fool: Your robes tell me that you are an initiate. You are different from worldly-minded people, but that difference is one that they respect. If I had robes like yours, perhaps my worth would be appreciated?

Priestess: The robes I wear signify the path I follow and the progress I have made. Are you ready to live as I do? Have you chosen to walk the way that leads beyond all suffering, and to follow it to the very end?

The Fool: I have little practical experience in the world. I do not know my own strengths and weaknesses. I do not see or feel my full potential. What I want and how much I am willing to sacrifice are still a mystery to me. The best that I can say of myself is that I am open and ready to learn. But I am not yet wise. I do not feel that I am in a position to choose or to follow a way that is difficult.

Priestess: You imagine that the short direct path which leads straight to the summit of the mountain is hard. And you think that the long wandering path which moves upward by slow degrees is easy. You are content to wander along the byways of the royal road and to take your time. You risk losing your way because you have not yet discovered a deep enough hunger for light and truth. But to make a good beginning, you must be radically honest with yourself. Consider whether the short, direct route is truly more demanding than the long, wandering approach.

The Fool: Teach me. You have wisdom in abundance, and I value what you have to say.

Priestess: Give yourself. Give yourself fully to the guidance of your heart. What I say is an echo of what your soul is constantly whispering to you through the lips of your own spiritual heart. Listen. Look within. Be quiet. Hear what is being revealed to you by your own soul. Turn inward. Discover the guidance there.

The Fool: Take me into the temple. Let me live hear and learn from you.

Priestess: A candidate for temple life and initiation must be tested and found worthy. Your mind is curious, true. You want to know many things. But I teach only one thing. You must walk the wandering path for a while longer until your mind tires of its hunger for variety and novelty. Then you may be ready to enter the temple of initiation. When you are ready, I will help you.

The Fool: Where will I go? If you do not accept me into the sanctuary of the temple, to whom shall I turn for guidance?

Priestess: I will introduce you to The Empress. She will bless you with her abundance, for she is very rich. I am poor. I cling only to one thing, holy wisdom. But she can give you the full experience of what this world has to offer. When you have tasted prosperity, you will be able to learn something about responsibility. And for this further teaching, she will take you to the Emperor. Who knows? Perhaps by that time you will begin to tire of the worldly round. If so, by all means come and speak to me again.

The Fool: I feel that you are like a spiritual mother to me. Promise that you will be with me inwardly, in spirit. I mean, if I turn to you in need some time, do answer my call. Promise me this, even as you send me away.

Priestess: You will always remain my child, my spiritual child, even when you wander in the pathways of distraction. I will be with you. In time, you will learn to hear the inner voice. When you listen to the whispering spirit within you, and follow its guidance, you will know I am with you. When you are ready, the doors of the temple will open. Go now, but remember always : Be true to your heart!

Fool: But how will I be able to meet The Empress? Surely she does not have time for common folk like me!

Priestess: Take this signet. Show it to the guard at the palace gate. Tell him I have sent you, that it is my wish that you should have a private audience with the Empress. You will have no difficulty. Go in Peace.

Hearing this, slowly and sadly, The Fool withdrew. This first encounter with a deeply spiritual being had made a profound impression on him. He tried to remember every word of their conversation.

He had won her blessing. Her good will and inner help would now be with him. This was the most important thing. The Fool felt both joy and apprehension. What lay ahead? Where would his journey lead?

When he came to the palace, all turned out as The Priestess had said. On presenting the signet to the guard at the gate, he was ushered into an audience hall. After a short time, surrounded by ladies in waiting, The Empress appeared. She took her seat on an elaborate throne and dismissed her entourage. Then, she sat facing the fool. Their eyes met.

The silence continued for several minutes. This was something entirely new, something that The Fool had never before experienced in his life. He had no wish to avert his gaze. Rather, and much to his surprise, he felt that The Empress welcomed this meeting of eyes. In fact, he could feel that her awareness was reaching deep inside his mind and heart, probing, blessing, enlivening. By the time she spoke, he felt full of peace, whole in spirit, light and happy.

The Empress: It is a joy to meet you again. It has been a long time. We have traveled far since last our paths crossed, you and I. But your quest is close to fulfillment. I want you to know that my love and blessings go with you on the next stage of your adventure, which will be the most perilous and the most rewarding.

The Fool: Surely I would have remembered meeting you. This meeting is a great privilege for me. I am very grateful that you have taken the time, and I appreciate the encouragement that you are giving me. To be very honest, I am not altogether clear about where I should go next, what I should do, or really what I am searching for.

The Empress: In your heart you are very clear. This is what counts most. The mind often lags behind in its grasp of what is important.

The Fool: Please, will you explain to me what is important? What did you mean when you said that?

A faint smile crept across the Empress's lips. Again their eyes met, and their inner beings melded. Again came the silent sense of being deeply known and nurtured. The Fool waited. He could feel that what he needed to know was being given to him, but on some level deeper than his mind could fathom, or higher than his understanding could reach.

The Empress: What is most important? You have always known it in your heart. You are seeking what you already have within yourself, reaching for what you know in your inmost being. Words cannot adequately explain or define it. How then shall I be able to express what the prophets and philosophers have failed to explain?

The Fool: I thought... I mean...

The Empress: Each step you take in this journey of yours arises from an intention, a wish, a dream that you harbour in your heart of hearts. It matters not that you cannot explain or describe your dream to others. They fail to understand you, because they have not yet awakened to their own vision-quest. Spiritually, they are still asleep. But you have awakened. You have heard the inner call. This sets you apart. And in the end, when you have found what you seek, duty will bring you back.

112

You suffer because in the eyes of the world you are considered a fool. You would like to be accepted and appreciated by all and sundry. But I tell you, the only validation you require is your own soul's blessing. This you have. I see it clearly. The High Priestess also saw it. You may proceed with every confidence that you are well sustained and loved and supported, and you are also embraced by the powers that lend support from within. And I predict that you will make new friends who will see you for who you really are, and share their wisdom with you, to enable you to continue on and to find that which you seek. Thus it is written in the stars. And so it must come to pass.

The Fool: There is much that I cannot understand, it is true. And this makes me feel uncertain. I feel unequal to my dreams. But from you I feel only love and acceptance. This makes me strong. I am ready to face the world. I am ready to pursue my goal. I have faith in my dream, even though I cannot explain or foresee what I am called to. Being with you helps me to find this courage, a strength such as I never felt before.

The Empress: I am the Mother of Abundance for all who approach me with openness and sincerity. Those who are hungry, I feed. Those who are broken, I heal. I *am* and I *have* the nurture that hungry hearts crave. But very few have opened their hearts to me in receptivity. And so, sadly, of the rich treasures at my disposal, I am able to give only a little. But it is my wish to bless and to empower all the sincere seekers who approach me to and to give them the very utmost that they can take away.

I am the dispenser of all that your dreams envisioned. I have the key to a treasure that is already there deep inside you. I will show you how to place the key in the keyhole, and my hand will be on yours as you turn it. You have always felt akin to the beauty of Nature. The trees, the birds, the wide skies, the pools and rivers in the forest glades, the ancient rocks and the wayside flowers all speak to you, and you hear their whispers. You will feel me near you. Only remember: remember my words, the light in my eyes, the love in my voice, my form, my presence. I will enable you to spring the lock and open the door to your hidden treasure-chamber. I will be with you in spirit for the duration of your journey. You need have no doubts or worries.

113

The Fool: I am overwhelmed by what you say. I cannot claim to understand it all, but deep down inside, I feel blessed, truly blessed.

The Empress: I want to arrange for you to spend some time in the presence of the Emperor. He is a very busy man, much taken up with the affairs of state. But you will learn something by being near him, observing him, listening to him.

The Fool: It would be a privilege.

The Empress: I am returning to you this signet from the High Priestess. It will be your pass, should anyone question you. Explain to them that I gave you permission to be present at the imperial audience. Then, when you have taken in as much as you wish, go your way. You will be ready for the next stage of your journey.

The Fool: Thank you from the bottom of my heart.

The Empress: My lady in waiting will take you to The Emperor's reception hall. Observe what takes place there as carefully as you are able. When you leave and begin your quest anew, remember me. My love is with you.

She summoned a lady in waiting and passed the signet to her. Then, she folded her hands, stood and exited. The lady in waiting came up to The Fool and passed him the signet. Silently, she nodded her head, indicating that he should follow.

They passed through several chambers and hallways, richly decorated with gold trim and polished mirrors. Finally, they came to a large reception room hung with purple curtains. The lady again nodded her head, and then she too made her exit.

Somewhat uncertain of where he was, or what kind of dress and etiquette was expected of him, The Fool looked around.

The Patriarchs

The Fool's encounters with the High Priestess and the Empress helped him to realize that his adventure was turning out to be far more interesting than he had ever imagined it could be. He felt his perspective on life and his mental horizons widening to such an extent that he wondered what could possibly happen next. The Empress's suggestion that he might like to see The Emperor had come as a complete surprise.

When the Emperor and his followers entered the room, The Fool had a sense that the occasion was serious and solemn. The Emperor was plainly a man with many responsibilities. A number of courtiers and members of the public were seated in the audience chamber in a semi-circle around the imperial throne.

The Fool was shown to one of the seats. As to whether he should look the Emperor in the eye, or avert his gaze, The Fool was not uncertain, so he decided that discretion was best, and he tried to be as inconspicuous as he could. He also had a concern that he might not be dressed appropriately.

Soon, a second distinguished person of considerable importance, The High Priest, accompanied by several richly robed ecclesiastics, entered the audience hall and took his seat on a chair almost as splendid as The Emperor's. The chairs of The Emperor and The High Priest faced each other at such an angle as to encourage conversation. There was a brief pause, which added to the atmosphere of expectancy as everyone waited for someone to speak. Then, The Emperor began his address.

Emperor: Our esteemed brother, High Pontiff, supreme authority of sacred tradition and all priesthoods in the land, master of the mysteries, master of sacred learning, has joined us today to discuss several things of importance. Our imperial authority is vested in him, and like us he is anointed from on high. Thus we venerate his wisdom and we give careful attention to his words.

High Priest: Our sister the High Priestess joins with me in greeting you. We wish you all peace and well being in both your earthly and your spiritual concerns. It is recorded that in ancient Egypt, Pharaoh and High Priest were once one and the same, as the traditions recount. Today, you see these two kinds of power divided into two offices, that of Emperor and Hierophant. But in heaven, the sacred and the profane spheres of concern have never truly been separated. From the Divine perspective, a profane world is a creation of human ignorance, not an enduring reality.

His Highness, The Emperor, is invested with a heavenly mandate that invests him with absolute power and dominion on earth. The teaching authority that comes from Heaven is delegated by him to my sacred office and to my person. Together, we carry and discharge these responsibilities. We are responsible to God for your well being in both the sacred and the secular dimensions of life.

Emperor: Our most ancient teachings are to be found in the temples and schools of higher learning. In these the High Priest is well versed, and in such matters his authority is absolute. My concern, on the other hand, lies with matters of law, social order, the protection of all citizens from those who might harm us, both within and from outside our borders. This duty came to rest on my shoulders the day I was crowned. Upon me rests the duty to maintain the peace, to regulate our customs, to plan and create wise laws, to exercise leadership with foresight and self control, to adapt our knowledge and experience and traditions to the needs of the present time, while preserving continuity with the past.

Above all, it behooves me to be strong and to exemplify the virtues of the heavenly code. Because I honour the laws and institutions which come down to us from the past, because I do not indulge any personal ambitions, I can act confidently to preserve and protect what is right. My concern for all of you is fatherly, but I would defend our kingdom with my life, if that were necessary, to protect your lives from danger.

High Priest: My duty complements that of my Imperial Brother, The

Emperor. All the secrets of heaven and earth have been passed down to our venerable priesthood from ancient times in an unbroken tradition.

In our sacred schools, the great sages and seers, the bards and healers, the mystics and the initiates have been trained to do their noble work of sanctifying, teaching and healing. Upon the authority of tradition they have relied, and in this way, they achieved excellence in their respective fields. As it was in the beginning is now, and ever shall be. This we know from the prophets. This we teach in seamless continuity with the revered fathers of long ago. No man is above the law, but by living by the law and by observing the law in all you say and do, each of you may find peace of heart and wisdom and joy that passes all understanding. This we teach and uphold.

The Emperor: My spiritual brother speaks words of wisdom. I enjoin you to listen carefully. Continue.

High Priest: We promulgate Holy Scripture by the authority of the Supreme Being who reigns on high. He has spoken to us through the revelations of the holy ones. We have recorded their words and deeds and preserved them in our temples. He, the Eternal Being On High empowers us to guide and teach and judge and punish. What we approve on earth is sealed also in heaven. All power comes from on high, but on earth we two, Emperor and High Priest exercise it in these two domains, the sacred and the profane. And in each of these spheres the mantle of power and responsibility we carry is absolute. In the same way that the wife honours and obeys her husband, so society must humbly receive the mandate of heaven from our hands, for we have been anointed and called and elected, indeed destined for this sacred work.

Emperor: When a man seeks to advance himself in the world, he must first become worthy of the station in life to which he aspires. He must acquire experience, and he must be tested. There is a hierarchy of authority, a pyramid of power, whose capstone is the imperial throne. All earthly power proceeds downward from that throne, which is like the throne of the Supreme Deity above. Round this throne the various orders of angels and the heavenly hierarchies are arranged. My dukes, my earls, my barons and knights, my merchants and my serfs are part of a heavenly mandate which orders all things to be in harmony, both there on high and here below. To me falls the duty of preserving that harmony.

When you are truly bonded to me, and when my authority and power are honoured by you above any temptation to bend the rules or profit by some unlawful means, then my mandate will be yours. My power comes to me from on High, and I mediate that power to those who serve me well. There is no power beyond that which comes from on High to which any citizen should give importance. In matters earthly, my word is absolute and final. In matters spiritual, the most holy Hierophant, the High Priest of all temples and sacred orders, is to be believed implicitly and obeyed unconditionally.

High Priest: If the voice you hear inside your mind or the guidance you imagine in your spirit contradicts the laws we promulgate, bring your case to the temple. There the teaching authority of the priesthood will enlighten you concerning the truth. If oracles and visions and voices from hidden places give you counsel that contradicts the words of wisdom in our sacred scripture, seek repentance and forgiveness, and if you are sincere, you will be pardoned. We know that the human mind and heart are feeble and prone to error. We are inclined to be merciful to those who lay bare and unburden their conscience to our priesthood. But we counsel against anything which departs from tradition, any form of worship or teaching or belief which lacks sanction and precedent.

As the authority of The Emperor is absolute in matters secular, so the authority of the temple, the priesthood and the High Priest are final in all things concerning sacred tradition. Look within, listen to your heart, as the High Priestess teaches, but reconcile what you find revealed there with tradition and with the teaching authority of the temple. Enjoy the material abundance of Mother Earth, but follow the law in every detail when you buy and sell and trade with the wealth that comes to you. In this way, order and harmony will be preserved, and you will live in peace and happiness.

By this time, The Fool was beginning to feel restless, and somewhat out of place. As he looked around, he sensed the solemn respect which everyone was giving to the words from these two great patriarchs, but he could not tell whether in all cases it was completely sincere, or whether it was just a well-rehearsed act, a matter of polite convention. The atmosphere of formality, control and inflexibility made him squirm, but he knew he had to suppress his urge to go for a stroll and get a breath of fresh air.

In the matter of belief systems, dogma, theology and higher learning, The Fool knew full well that he was altogether uninformed. He did not have any special predilection for religious orthodoxy and political correctness. Nor was he enamoured of rhetoric. Rules and codes of law left him quite bored. He felt that the need to conform to the norms of some large institution would have stifled his instinctive spontaneity. Within him there was a struggle, a need to be playful and free while living in a world of collectively sanctioned tradition. He found its rituals and high-sounding phrases sanctimonious. He did not want to appear to be a rebel or to draw undue attention to himself, but he felt uncomfortable in the presence of rigid authority. Perhaps all authority was rigid, and all laws had to be inflexible. Perhaps this was part of the divine plan. He could not say. What he knew was that he felt more at home with the High Priestess than with the High Priest, and he felt closer to the Empress than to the Emperor. But he realized he had much to learn from all of them, and that their teachings were complementary parts of a single body of wisdom which his understanding could not yet encompass.

Somehow, The Empress had succeeded in being just herself, and she had a charming, gracious and affectionate personality which was always worthy of respect, while never forcing deference from others. Everyone knew that she was at the pinnacle of the social hierarchy, but she never made anyone feel that they owed her subservience on that account. People respected her spontaneously, because she won their hearts. These questions of power and social order, religious authority and the weight of tradition were things that The Fool found tedious. He longed for the simplicity of the open road, and his mind began to wander to images of green fields and bubbling streams.

A great bell was rung. The Emperor and the High Priest stood, and everyone else took the cue and rose up as one body. Together, the anointed pair and their personal attendants left the room, followed by the majority of the well-dressed audience.

The Fool was one of the last to leave the audience hall. When he came to the door, he caught the eye of the guard who was on duty, and winked. The guard, just for a moment, looked puzzled. Then his face revealed that he was totally confused.   Finally, he averted his eyes with no a hint of acknowledgement. He put on that mask of official oblivion which The Fool had seen many times already at court. It meant: "Although I know you are there, you are not worthy of my recognition." It did not matter. The Fool knew in his heart that he had the blessings of The Empress. That was enough.

The Fool left the audience hall and set out to find the fields and streams he had been longing for. It was with a sense of relief that he took a deep breath of fresh air and headed for the open road.

"This feeling of freedom and joy that I have in this moment, is this what it means to follow my heart?" he asked himself as he stepped out into the sunlight.

All he knew was that he felt good. To be where he was, to be going forward and pursuing his adventure felt completely right. The sunlight and the fresh air and the beckoning fields and forests were there calling to him.

The Lovers

The Fool passed out of the city gates and into the hills and vales of the surrounding countryside. Before long, he found himself on a trail that wound through a thickly wooded canyon. In time, the trail became so faint that he was following no way at all, but moving forward completely on instinct. After a while, the narrow canyon broadened out into a valley, and he came to a clearing in the woods. It was, in fact, a ring of twelve massive oak trees. And there, standing behind an altar of white marble stood The Magician.

Magician: Welcome to this sacred glade. What brings you here?

Fool: I have had enough of the city life, and the royal court. I need fresh air and freedom. I have just followed my own feelings and wandered here by chance, not by design. I am a looking for adventure.

Magician: If you were at court, you might have spent time with The Emperor and The Hierophant. They are very wise and powerful. You must have learned something from them.
Fool: They are wise, yes, and powerful no doubt. But power is not as important to me as freedom. I find the trappings of power oppressive, even the power of a priestly tradition. But I have still much to learn, this I admit.

Magician: You have arrived at the valley of The Lovers. There is much to learn here.

Fool: What are you doing here in this lonely place? Where are all the lovers?

Magician: Like you, I am a student of life. I come here to deepen my understanding. If you like, I can show you something of what I study and how I profit by being in this place.

Fool: I would like that.

Magician: Then step up, come over here. You see this silver scrying bowl in front of you on the altar? You will observe something quite interesting if you gaze on the surface of the water which is inside it.

The Fool approached the altar and stood gazing onto the surface of the water inside the silver bowl. At first, nothing happened. Then, he began to detect a change taking place. He saw first a faint mist on the water's surface, and then a light from below the mist. Then, within the light he saw shapes moving, and as he gazed, these insubstantial forms became clearer. In this vision, he was looking down on a clearing in the woods where he could discern a number of cottages, with people coming and going. These were beautiful people, young men and women in the prime of life, and the setting was full of charm.

Magician: This is the abode of The Lovers. They are a community. They have a peaceful and harmonious life together. They come together to learn the ways of love.

The mist on the water's surface clouded over and the light within it faded. Then the mist cleared away, and a different colour of light, a reddish light, began to glow from within the water, and a new scene appeared. It was a moss-covered bank in the woods, surrounded by ferns and violets in bloom. And there he could make out a man and woman together on the ground holding each other tightly.

The Fool: Is this the study of love they for which they come together?

Magician: This is the first rung of the ladder of love. These are new arrivals to the valley. If you find this form of love meaningful, there is a place for you here. They are close by. There are many like them, and some would be ready to be your lovers. You have only to wish for it, and they will find you. This is how it goes in the valley of love.

The Fool: So this is what one can learn here?

Again the mist clouded over the vision, and the reddish light faded. Then, a pink light appeared below the water's surface, and the mist cleared. He saw the inside of a cottage, and an elderly couple sitting before their fireplace. The wife stood up and approached the man from behind his rocking chair and began to brush his hair. Then she began to sing to him. It was only a simple lullaby, but he smiled and closed his eyes. Their contentment seemed complete.

The Magician: These lovers have achieved the second rung of the ladder of learning. They have tasted passionate love, but beyond this, they have discovered how to live together with integrity. This has taken them much time. They are old now. They are patient, kindly, peaceful, and full of affection for each other. They are loyal, unselfish, and forgiving. They will be together until they pass on to the next life. Some learn these things quickly, and some take more time. A whole life is not too much to attain the second rung in the ladder of love.

Fool: It is very beautiful. This must be a life full of satisfaction.

Magician: It is yours if you wish. The valley of love welcomes all who would wish to spend their days in this way. If you truly want a life of love like this, then you will be able to have this experience. You have come to the right place. There is much maturity and integrity required to live loyally in a committed relationship. These are good people. They would welcome you into their community.

Fool: Is this all that I can learn here in this valley of lovers?

Magician: No, there is another, a higher rung on the ladder of love. It requires even greater resources of heart and soul for the living of it, and not all are called. For this deeper love you must feel the call. You must have the willingness to sacrifice. Whatever you have, and whatever you are will be plunged into the fires of transmutation if you choose this love. Only the worthy are reborn in these fires. The others are destroyed.

Fool: I may not be ready. But I would wish to glimpse at least the possibility, or understand in some measure the nature of this love of which you speak. It would be a shame to come here and miss the experience of such a marvel.

Magician: Listen then. Listen carefully. I will explain.

In the beginning, only the Great Mystery existed. It was One. There was no other to know it. It has been called the Source, but in truth it cannot be named because it has no form, and is not separate from all that is. This sublime unknowable Source existed beyond time and beyond our capacity for understanding. It simply was and is. Before any names and forms came into existence, this has always been. It precedes time and space but holds them both within itself as a tiny fragment of its infinite life.

Somehow, mysteriously, in the secret heart of the original One, a need was born, a hunger for experience. You have felt it in your own heart, you can understand what it is. Your spiritual hunger is a spark of that original need for expression and experience. From this came creation, the 'he' of it and the 'she' of it, the light of it, and the dark, the over and the under, heaven and earth.

Heaven and earth between them brought forth life, which is the dance of their eternal love. Although they are now two, they want to join as One. From their desire to join, they beget the many, and this is the dance of creation. Hence come all the stories that have ever been, and all the languages to tell them. Of this the poets sing. For this we laugh and weep and dance and procreate. We become lovers because of this memory we have, and this need in our hearts to be re-united with the Source. Even in our forgetfulness of the Source and the true way of return, we have this need to embrace the dance of life and love.

Your journey is a quest. You seek to embrace and be embraced in a way you do not yet fully understand. Today, your understanding of this will deepen.

All that was to be known and felt and seen and lived between heaven and earth, the glory of it, the agony, the mystery, lies hidden in the heart of humanity, to be brought forth and given birth in form. The stories of our lives are chapters in the love-epic of heaven and earth. When you experience within your heart the cry that earth has for heaven, and the smile that heaven has for earth, you will feel a need to be alone in a clear space in order to cherish the memory in your mind and heart, because nothing else can give you such bliss. You will know when this happiness steals into you that you are ready to experience something new and precious.

This valley, and this grove are that clear space of awareness. Those sacred oaks are planted in, this square marble altar in their centre, this silver scrying bowl and the water it holds and the eye that beholds the water and the soul that sees through the eye, and the visions seen and the intelligence that knows their meaning, they are all part of the ritual of return. By this ritual, you embrace the Source and become One again.

If you love in that way, as the sun loves the moon, as fire loves the fuel it consumes, as the trees love sunlight, then you are ready to study in the third realm of love.

Do you feel you are ready? Do you feel that it is this need which has brought you here? Or will you be satisfied with something less than this?

Fool: Yes, I know something of what you describe. There is a princess in my heart, and a prince too. They both love me. I cannot choose between them. Somehow, when I choose, I lose. I want to learn true love. I made this choice long ago. If it were not so, then it would be a mistake for me to be here. Yet it feels so right! I feel the happiness you touch upon.

Magician: I also am here because of such a choice. And it is, as you say, a destiny and a deep call rather than a predilection of the curious intellect. Perhaps if I tell you how it was with me, you will understand better.

Fool: Please tell me, for indeed I do wish to understand.

Magician: One day, my wanderings took me to a grassy hillock deep in the forest glades not far from here. I fell asleep and dreamed that I had found a doorway into the centre of that hill, and on passing through the door, I entered a great hall where harp music played, and an assembled throng was gathered. People of all sorts mixed and mingled there, dressed in styles both ancient and modern, the simple and the richly attired all together, all talking as if they knew each other and were wonderful friends. And there was the beauty of the harp music too – that I shall never forget. But the noise of their talk died down, and before long the notes of the harp stopped too. Then, the High Priestess entered and took her seat in the place of honour at the head of the assembly, and everyone present sat down on chairs in a great circle, but the youngest among them simply sat on the floor. A table was placed in the centre of the circle, between the Priestess and the crowds, and on it was a silver cup. Within the cup was placed a gold coin bearing the mark of a pentacle. Then, on one side of the cup was laid a wand of rowanwood and on the other they set down a very old sword. "Come forth" the High Priestess said to me, and I stood up from my seat in the circle and came before her with the table between us.

"These," she said, "are the implements of the craft of love. If you are wise, you will master their use. If by this mastery you learn to love truly, you will exercise the law of One in all four kingdoms of your being, represented here by these signs of the craft. If you master the law of One in all four realms, yours will be the world and all that is in it. The way of mastery is yours to choose. The paths are many. But in their endings, mark well, all the paths are One. That One is seated on the throne of your own heart. Go there. Learn. Awake!

With this, she waved her hand in a motion of banishing, and I awoke. I was no longer in the hall beneath the hillock. I was alone in the forest. But I knew that I had been called to pursue a quest. This was the way the call came to me. It is not so for everyone, this I well understand. The call comes to each in its own way.

I must ask you now, have you also been called?

Fool: Between the prince and the princess in my heart, as I have said, I cannot choose. Between the longing to know which is there in my mind, and the aspiration to simply be, which I feel in my heart, I cannot choose. Between the glory of the sun and the peace of the moon, I cannot choose. But if there is a secret truth beyond the splitting up of all things in creation into opposites, as you say there is, then this is something I must find out for myself. I do not need the throes of passion; I do not need domestic bliss. What I need is the knowing of who I am and why I roam the world with such a hunger for adventure. I need the slaking of this hunger and this endless thirst that makes me restless to keep seeking and seeking. I need to come home to a place in my heart where the many roads end in sanctuary and peace.

Magician: You speak as one who has been chosen. You do not need a dream vision, your ideal is pure. You are ready to discover the way of love that unites all things in their secret oneness. By coming here, you have clarified your intent. True love is clear like the water in this silver scrying bowl. Allow it to be your teacher. Find a space within you where there is stillness without even a single ripple. There you will find what you are seeking. Then, The Magician moved his arm in a gesture of banishing, and disappeared. And the altar and the scrying bowl disappeared too. The Fool was alone, at the centre of the circle of oak trees. But in some deep corner of his being, there was a difference, something he could feel, but was unable to express in words.

At this point he heard the distant sound of horses' hooves. It drew nearer and nearer, while he savoured the meaning of the Magician's words, and all he felt within himself. Soon, from one point in the clearing there appeared four white steeds drawing a chariot and inside it a magnificent charioteer. They rushed toward him, and then when it seemed he might be trampled, abruptly they stopped.

"Come aboard," The Charioteer called. "I will take you on the next stage of your journey. I know where you must go. I will make your way easy." The Fool climbed up onto the chariot, and held fast to its side. The Charioteer snapped the reins, and the four horses pulled away from the spot in the direction from which they had come.

Soon, The Fool was speeding through the woods on a well marked trail to an unknown destination. The wind whistled in his ears and his hair rippled in the breeze. He could feel the power of the four horses as they surged forward, and yet the master of the reins exerted complete control over all their forward momentum. The Fool could feel his confidence and power. He radiated this impression of strength, being tall and powerfully built.

Gazing ahead, The Fool saw the trees of the forest fly by at an incredible rate as the chariot sped forward. Where this new adventure would take him, he could only guess. The thrill of forward movement was exciting.

The Lady and the Lion

As the chariot rolled relentlessly forward along the open track under the canopy of forest trees, The Fool was in admiration of The Charioteer's mastery of his team of horses. The Charioteer turned to The Fool and with a bold gesture offered him the reins. For a moment, The Fool hesitated for he had never before taken command of a team of horses. But his sense of adventure instantly replaced his doubt, and he took the place of The Charioteer at the helm.

As soon as he grasped the reins of the chariot, a new feeling of decisiveness and control surged over him. It was like nothing he had ever experienced before. In that moment of empowerment he had a realization of the fullness of his own capacity for self-control, and his self-understanding was profoundly altered.

He felt firstly that it was by no means through the reins in his hands that he guided the four white horses, rather it was the focus of his will and his intent, his one-pointed attention that mastered their energy and commanded their obedience. This sense of being completely centered, this ability to communicate his will to a team of powerful horses – this was an altogether new experience. By stepping into The Charioteer's place, and accepting control of the reins, The Fool had instantly gained extraordinary powers.

The Fool knew in that moment what it was to be supremely self-confident and absolutely self-sufficient. Nothing could stand in the way of this inner decisiveness and conviction by which he felt possessed. The Fool knew in that moment that he was a victor, a destined success, a master of himself and equal to anything which life could throw across his path. His emotions were steady and self-assured. They flowed forward like a dynamic current of energy, enveloping the team of horses who surged eagerly ahead.

He could feel that these vibrant steeds were an extension of his own cohesive intent. He knew and understood that they were living projections of his own fourfold power-base, his body, feelings, mind and spirit. Grasping the reins of control, The Fool became master of his destiny, hero of his life's script, author of his triumph. All of this he knew, not by thinking, but in an instant of lived experience, in a clear space of altered consciousness. Thereafter, he would never again doubt. In the world's eyes, he might be considered a fool, but never again would he allow the opinions of others to limit his potential.

The chariot had not gone far when rounding a bend the horses suddenly came to a halt and reared up in dismay. There before them on the path was a lion. He snarled and raked the air with one of his huge paws. This giant lion was not going to move. Indeed, it seemed like he was getting ready to attack.

Immediately, without a moment's hesitation or thought, The Fool seized one of the three spears which were attached to the side of the chariot and leaped down to the ground. Yet, by the time he had positioned himself between the lion and the horses, someone else had appeared on the scene.

From the woods to the right of the lion, a lady robed in white linen stepped forward. Immediately, the lion's attention was drawn to her, but he did not attack. He merely paused to stare. Slowly and with great deliberation, the lady in linen robes approached the lion, and wonder of wonders, he became as meek as a kitten in her presence. She bent down over his massive head and placed her hand on his snout. He lifted his jaws up to lick her hand, and it would have been very clear to any observer that they were friends.

Then the lady looked up at The Fool and motioned to him to drop his spear. This he did, again without thought or hesitation. He continued to gaze in amazement as the lady beckoned him to approach. To his surprise, The Fool felt no fear, only immense confidence and self-assurance. He knew that no harm would befall him. When he had come near, the lady reached out and took his hand. She placed it on the lion's mane, with her own soft palm on top. For a few moments, the three of them stood like this. What The Fool felt in those moments was like nothing he had ever known.

He felt a new kind of power flowing through his body from his heart to his hand, and thence into the head and the heart of the lion. It was a gentle power, a power that knit together fragments of energy, a power of deep, peaceful love. He could feel that this power was in essence a sense of inseparable oneness. Invisibly, it spoke heart-to-heart and revealed a hidden bond of unity which he had forgotten. The Fool knew that he, the lion and the lady in white were at one with each other in a deep bond of peaceful accord. Only a moment before, he had been ready to kill the lion with his spear. Now, through his hand, he was extending the power of his heart's love in an unconditional outpouring and it conquered the lion's aggression.

But really, it was the lady who was revealing this hidden heart-power by her touch and her presence. Her presence revealed to him his own latent capacities of harmony. In this moment, he saw the difference between the power he had felt when he commanded the horses, the chariot, and the spear, and a different kind of power that could deeply identify itself with any living thing, even an angry lion, by reaching out and touching its very essence. This indeed was supreme power.

Meekly, the lion withdrew from his touch and bounded off into the woods where he quickly disappeared from sight. The lady released The Fool's hand and stepped away from him.

Fool: Who are you?

Lady: Some call me Strength. Men and women feel my power when it touches their hearts in moments of grace, but they do not understand its source. Those who love power for its own sake never know me by my true name, for they have closed their hearts and cannot hear my voice. I tell you who I am, because your heart is open and you are free from guile. I am love. The power of love is my strength. If you have this power, you conquer. You conquer not by destroying, but by unifying. In the valley of love, you will find much of this power. This is the power that drew you here.

Fool: How can I thank you for revealing this to me? What can I do to show you how very grateful I am?

Lady: Carry this power with you wherever you go. Give it expression in all you do and say. There will be times when you must demonstrate this power by exercising patience, by being resolved to persevere, by enduring what you find intolerable. Then, when you are tested, remember my words. There will be occasions when your composure and forbearance are greatly challenged. Remember me then, and call to mind what I am telling you now.

This power which I have awakened in your heart is full of kindness and acceptance. It is forgiving and compassionate, gentle and sympathetic. Some see this as weakness. They are ignorant. Only those who conquer ego with the power of spirit will be able to see that the power of love is greater than the love of power. The feeling of oneness with all creation is true strength, true love, and true magic. Carry this power with you. Express it at all times and in all places. Claim it now and forever as your very own. This is how you will best be able to say "Thank you". I shall be happy if you will do this.

Having spoken, the lady turned and departed.

The Fool stood there for some while after the white of her robes had disappeared into the deep shadows of the forest. When the experience had settled into his nerves and into his understanding, and when he had assimilated it as much as he could, he turned round to rejoin The Charioteer. But lo and behold, The Charioteer, the horses and the chariot had all disappeared. He had not heard them withdraw. They had slipped away noiselessly. And again, he was alone.

Alone, yes, but the solitude was different than before, different from the loneliness he had felt at the journey's beginning. He felt somehow less separate from the trees, the birds, the sky overhead and the earth beneath his feet. He felt more himself, and somehow not vulnerable as before. And it was good, this feeling of wholeness. In the midst of many uncertainties, he was strangely at peace.

The Wheel of Fate

In that dark wood, as dusk began to descend on hushed wings, finding a bed of moss and ferns, The Fool lay down to rest. He closed his eyes and slept.

In that sleep, in his own inner world of dreams, The Fool moved in a world of enchanted harmonies. He traveled far in a landscape of mystery and magic, and dreamed of an encounter with the lady in white. Long he lingered in her company, receiving instruction from her lips concerning the wisdom of the heart. How long he slept, he did not know. But the way of his waking was most curious. Gently at first, and then more insistently there came a tapping on the sole of his foot. He imagined at first that this was part of his magic dream. But then the tapping became so urgent that he could sleep no longer. Opening his eyes, he saw first a light, so bright in the darkness of the forest that it made him squint, and then, behind the light, a figure dressed in a dark robe, his head covered in a cowl. He was holding a staff, and it was with this that he had tapped The Fool's foot and awakened him. The light from his lantern showed the great age and gravity of his features, yet there was clarity and innocence in his eyes, and The Fool felt completely at home in his company.

The ancient man spoke not a word, but turning away, he headed into the woods with only a gesture of his staff to indicate that The Fool should follow. For some time they walked in silence. The stranger's lamp gave sufficient light to show the way forward through the gnarled oaks and tall pines.

After some time, the old man paused. He had reached the entrance to a cave of some sort which he had to bend down to enter. The Fool followed closely behind, and when he looked up again, the lamplight revealed a simply furnished cell, with a plain table, a modest bed, a shelf of papyrus scrolls, and a few simple cooking implements.

The old man lit several candles. Then he offered The Fool a seat by the table, and a cup of water, while he himself sat on the edge of his simple bed.

"The life of a hermit is not lavish," he said, "but for me it is filled with joy. You must be very tired. You have come to a place of sanctuary. You will find peace in this place, humble as it seems."

Fool: I met the lady in white today. And when I slept, I dreamed that I was with her. We spoke together at length, and she explained many things to me. These woods are her home.

Hermit: She has many forms, this lady in white. She comes to you as Strength when you are ready, or sometimes when you are needy, but for long periods of your life she will be with you in other ways, perhaps as a call to pursue some quest, or as a need in your heart to find answers to an unspoken emptiness you feel within yourself. She will often be with you in your love of adventure, in your hunger for wisdom, or as delight in the beauties of nature. She is a priestess, an empress, the queen of our dreams, the muse of our inspirations, the melody of our songs, the lilt of our laughter, the salt in our tears, and the deep need that finally takes us home. She is the goddess, the guidance of our soul's divination, the wisdom we seek and the way of our seeking. Ah yes, she comes to us in many forms. These woods are dear to her heart and she often wanders here. I live here because her teaching is most accessible when her physical presence is close by. You are very blessed to have met her.

Fool: How long have you lived in this place?

Hermit: I came to this cell when I was young, not much older than you are now. I have never left these woods since that day. All my needs are met. Everything, everything is here. I have come home, you see. The Valley of Love is my home.

Fool: When I first set out on my journey, I did not know what I was seeking. But I knew that I needed freedom, freedom to be myself, and also I wished not be misunderstood. I have always had a love of adventure, and it never fails that I feel confined when I have to fit in to society and to behave in ways that I find unnatural. To me, a classroom is as good as a prison. So is a church pew for that matter. But I have come to feel that I cannot be happy until I find answers to my questions. I did not even know what my questions were - until I met the lady.

Hermit: We are all her children. She draws us to herself in different ways. Like you, I have never lost my love of adventure, but I find it fully satisfied in this simple setting. You see, I have become an explorer of the inner worlds, the domains that lie between this visible landscape that you can apprehend through your five senses and the shores of eternity. My quest and my seeking take place in the cave of my soul, in a temple that has no form.

But perhaps I am getting ahead of myself. Perhaps you find all of this rather puzzling. Does it perplex you, what I am saying?

Fool: No, oh no! I understand you. I mean... you are saying things I need to hear. I am not familiar with these ideas, because I did not finish my schooling. I dropped out. But I somehow find it reassuring to listen to you speak.

Hermit: If you feel rested, I mean if you really are not too tired, I have something to show you which will help you to understand what I have been talking about.

Fool: I feel fine. I needed the rest!

Hermit: Then follow me.

At this, he went to a far corner of the cave and pulled open a curtain which concealed a portal. The Fool followed him through the portal and down a set of stairs into an underground chamber. The air was cool, fresh and fragrant. The glow of the lantern lit the surfaces of the rock all around them as they descended deeper and deeper into the bowels of the earth. Then, they came to a vast door of bronze, curiously inscribed with many symbols.

"Push" The Hermit said.

The Fool pushed hard, and the door moved just a little.

"Push harder!" The Hermit urged.

He redoubled his efforts, and then ever so slowly, the great door began to move. Slowly it moved against the pressure of The Fool's body, and in a moment it swung wide open.

The Hermit went to the far end of this dark chamber and lit two candles, which stood on a rough altar made of granite. The light of the candles showed that they were in a richly furnished room which appeared to be a chapel of sorts. The air was fresh, but from what hidden source it came, he could not determine. The candlelight revealed that behind the altar, a vast circular carving had been made on the surface of the stone wall. In the dim light, The Fool could see that the circle was divided into segments, twelve in all, and that many figures and symbols were carved into the various spaces of this pattern. The centre of the wheel was a small, empty circle. Surrounding it was an inner circle comprised of four clover-shaped leaves; but they could as well have been the leaves of some flower, it was hard to say.

Hermit: This is the Wheel of Fate.

Fool: It is truly a wonder!

Hermit: I come here to contemplate. The wisdom of the goddess is here, inscribed in the symbols of this stone image. Your fate and mine, indeed the destiny of the entire world and all in it – all are inscribed here. You will not see all this in the beginning, of course. The eyes to see, and the heart to know are not there at the beginning of the contemplative journey. These develop from within you if you contemplate the symbol at length. It teaches the heart how to open, and it guides the soul home. It is the story of the wisdom of the goddess, the tapestry she weaves in time.

Fool: I do not understand these symbols. I have never seen anything like this before.

Hermit: Ah, with your intellect you will never gain this understanding. No, you must approach The Wheel in a different way. Did you know that your heart has eyes? Well, it does! With the eyes of your heart you can reach out and touch the essence of a mystery and come to know what it has to say by a kind of inner recognition. At the point of merging, you will have the experience: 'I am That!' This is the marvel of contemplation, we become what we contemplate. This is the path I have been following these many years. The goddess and her signs are my whole world.

Fool: I had this feeling once before, when I spoke with the High Priestess. She said I was not ready to enter the temple. That seems a lifetime ago, so much has happened in such a short time! Is it difficult to learn to contemplate? Does it require training?

Hermit: Some training, some effort, but mostly it requires a sincere dedication. It helps if you come to this work with an open heart, a need to understand, a hunger for truth at all costs. When you have this spirit, you find hidden help on all sides. Simple things become your mentors. Solitude, stillness, detachment from worldly cares, these make it easier to take up the threads of self study, and weave them into an understanding.

The goddess of the wheel is also sometimes called the weaver. She has three aspects which are often called The Fates. This Great Wheel is the creatrix of our fate. She spins it round and round as she creates the threads that she will weave into the stories of our lives. Our destinies are spun by her; she weaves our tales and our adventures. We live them out unwittingly, until we answer her call, and seek for a revelation of the way forward. Then we begin to see things as they really are.

Fool: Do you understand the meaning of this wheel?

Hermit: In time, in deep contemplation, one becomes more and more receptive to the secret teaching of the goddess. Some people think that this study of hidden truth is the most arid form of asceticism. I find it a delight. For many, the harnessing of the steeds of the mind and the mastery of the reins of attention is a burdensome and tedious chore. Many are unwilling to take it up. Yet, if it is the work you are destined to do, you will come to love it. Here, in this sanctuary, where all diversions have been stripped away, I have found a simplification of my life and I have progressed in my understanding of The Wheel and its teaching. Here there is time to be alone with the symbols that reveal the sacred mysteries of the universe. The pulls and pushes of society cannot reach so far below the surface of the earth as to disturb my contemplation. In this place, I withdraw from the distractions of the world and look deeply into the divine pattern as it unfolds, its warp and woof and its mystic beauty. The wheel of fate is the picture of our souls' journey. Even a lifetime of contemplation could not exhaust what it has to teach us.

Fool: I wish to learn. I want to know the beginning, the middle and the end of the story of my soul. Where am I on this wheel? What will happen to me in my quest? Will you teach me? Will you help me find answers to my questions?

Hermit: Life is your teacher, my child. The goddess has accepted you as her child, her very own. Gaze deeply now at the centre of the wheel, the still point round which all else moves. Gaze deeply into the centre of the wheel and tell me what you see. Gaze deeply, deeply...Fool: I had not noticed it before, but there is a crystal sphere in the wheel's centre. Now I see a mist swirling in the centre of this crystal. Ah! now there is a light in it, in the middle. Now I hear a voice. I hear the lady's voice. She is speaking!

A gentle light began to shine in The Fool's eyes, and his voice became filled with tender care. Slowly and softly, words formed on his lips:

Many are those who flee the world, but this is not your path my child. This world IS the Divine projected in space and time. If you find suffering and imperfection here, understand that they are but ripples on the water's surface, an appearance only, nothing but the fleeting shadow of a reality. Within the living waters, underneath the surface, lie moonlight and mystery waiting to be born. Every aspect of this turning Wheel of Fate, every life being whirled into existence, every blade of grass and grain of sand are THAT, only THAT, only the Divine. There will come a time, perhaps after much contemplation, when you can never be separated from this vision of the Beloved in all things. In how many ways He plays this creation into being. The world is His stage, His canvas, the clay He moulds, the jewel He facets. He plays at changing positions, changing appearances, shifting fates and destinies – it is all His play! And when you see this wholeness of all things in Him, in the Beloved, you will delight in the illimitable marvel of it all, for it equals and surpasses your highest aspirations. Then, truly you will come home, you will find comfort and sanctuary. You will attain peace. You will be the witness of the turning Wheel, not one of the threads it spins. You will know everything that is going to happen, and all that has happened as well, for it is all there, one presence, one shining light in the eye of the Beloved. The poor actors in the play do not know their parts, and so they experience the revolving wheel as an alternation of good fortune and disaster. In truth, this wheel is inside your very heart. You contain it in your wholeness and your love, you make it spin for the joy of showing yourself how many ways your divinity can be expressed in time and space. In the centre of the wheel, there is no alternation, there is only joy. And peace, such peace! Such full, radiant, complete peace in which

there are no more conflicts, no more contradictions. It is one single, luminous harmony. It eliminates nothing, rejects nothing. All are held in the single light of Oneness at the centre of the wheel, in the heart of the Beloved. Make this vision your own, my child. Come home!

Hermit: You have spoken truly. And wisely! The goddess has spoken through you.   This is her wisdom I hear on your lips. Ah how wonderful! You have glimpsed it, my child! You have glimpsed the mystery of the Wheel, and its teaching power. But can you live this wisdom? Can you preserve it in the purity of your heart when the world around you denies and tests it? Only then can you say it is truly your own. Only then will the High Priestess admit you to the inner sanctuary of the temple.

Fool: I had thought that this sanctuary could become my resting place. But I see that this is not meant to be. I cannot rest. I must push on.

Hermit: The blessing of the goddess is with you. Come. Come back to my cell and rest a while before you continue on your way.

He extinguished the light and led the way back to his cell. There The Fool slept. He slept long and deep. When he awoke, he found a meal of bread, cheese, wine and fruit on the table. But The Hermit was nowhere to be seen.

The Fool feasted on this meal, and he thought nothing had ever tasted so delicious. Then, he stepped outside into the forest clearing, and looked around. The sun was well above the horizon, just cresting the treetops and making shadows across the opening in front of the entrance to the cave. The birds were singing. The dew was sparkling on the leaves of grass and on the ferns and mosses, and a sweet smell of fresh promise was in the air.

He breathed deeply and felt truly well and whole. What would the new day bring?

The Trial

At the point where the pathway entered the clearing, there appeared a palanquin borne by four porters, all dressed in white. Within the palanquin sat a noble lady of serene composure, robed like a person of considerable authority, and leaning forward on a great sword whose tip touched the floor between her feet. The porters placed the palanquin on the ground not far from the cave's entrance, and the noble lady motioned The Fool to approach.

One of the porters came and offered The Fool, a small silver plate. But when The Fool reached for the plate, he grasped The Fool's hand and pressed his thumb onto its surface, leaving its clear imprint there on the shining silver. The lady now held a weighing scale before her, and as the porter approached to offer her this silver dish, she reached out and took it, and placed it on one arm of the scale. Another porter approached the lady with what looked like a small white feather. She took this from his hands and placed it on the dish on the left arm of the scale. Then she extended her arm and held the scale out for all to see. As The Fool watched he saw the scale with the white feather move upward, and the scale with his thumb print move down.

"The Lady Justice has measured your worth on the scales of truth," said one of the porters, "and now will pronounce her verdict."

Justice: You have been weighed in the scales and found wanting. If you have anything to say for yourself, speak now. If not, we shall pass sentence.

Fool: But of what am I guilty?

Justice: The heart of an innocent man is expressed in all the patterns of his life, and it is an energy, which is imprinted on every cell of his body, even to the tips of his fingers and thumbs. The just man shows equilibrium in all ways and at all times. But you are not just. Your heart lacks the lightness of the feather of truth. Take this last opportunity, see and admit your guilt.

Fool: But I do not understand.

Justice: Your integrity is probed, your insincerity stands revealed. The scales of truth are impartial. You stand accountable, and you have been called on to admit the truth and accept responsibility for your errant ways. Now think carefully, before I pass sentence, weigh all sides of this question, balance all factors of your life in your awareness. It is not too late to rebalance the wrong that has been revealed. Look at these scales! Your error is measured out before you in plain view for all to see. Assess your lack of integrity. Consider how or where your life lacks balance. And if you can find where the equilibrium has been disturbed, it is not too late to hope for leniency.

Fool: I must throw myself on your mercy. It may not do me any good, but I protest my innocence. If there is disorder somewhere in me, I do not see it. If right order must be re-established in my life, I am willing, but I do not see how I have been unjust with others or with myself. I try to act fairly. I have no debts to settle. I admit this to you freely, because it is the truth. I am telling you that I am innocent.

Justice: Justice is blind. I now draw down over my eyes this blindfold of impartiality as I pronounce your sentence. My sword of discernment cuts away illusion. My pronouncements never err. It is time for you to face and acknowledge your error.

You are guilty of standing before the light of absolute love as a blockage and impediment to its action. You protest the unfairness of your judgement, but in so doing you further reveal your error. You cling to the ignorance of your ways. You cherish your disorder. You are guilty of hidden pride. Your ego has blinded you and filled you with a sense of your own righteousness, which you uphold and defend even when you have been given the opportunity to see and admit your disorder.

This, then, is your sentence. You are to be taken from this place and suspended from the limb of a sacred oak tree until Death, The Reaper,

141

shall be moved by pity to put you out of your misery. From this time onward until such time as he shall release you, reflect well on how you have lived. Ponder how you have disturbed the scales of true balance. Your own choices, your own ignorance has brought you to this fate. Your punishment is just. So be it.

Immediately, all four porters seized The Fool and bound his hands behind his back. They pushed him ahead of them into the woods, and shoved him on and on, stumbling through the trees until they had traced their way back to the circle of sacred oaks. Then they tied a long rope to his ankle and suspended him upside down from the limb of a great oak tree, and left him alone.

He hung there, upside down all that day and night.

It was not the pain in his ankle, where the rope held him fast, or his immense thirst or the hunger in his belly which tormented The Fool most. It was the fear of Death, fear of the unknown Reaper who was coming to claim him. If The Fool had been guilty of pride, he knew in his secret heart that he was at least equally guilty of fear. Where, he asked himself, was the courage he had known when he leaped down from the chariot with the spear in his hand? Where was the strength he had felt when the Lady in white had placed her hand on his and directed it onto the lion's mane? Where was the peace and the joy he had felt when he heard the words of the goddess on his own lips expressing a vision of the oneness of all things? Why did he cling to this small life that he called his own?

To one side of the clearing where he was suspended, The Fool could see an ancient statue, the head of a man. It was very old, and trees had overgrown it. The head could be seen imprisoned by the roots of trees, and bound by vines and creepers. He too was a prisoner of fate, this stone face with wide, staring eyes. He too could only wait and endure the unknowable. He too was ensnared by a force greater than himself to which he could only submit. To endure. To exist. This was all that could be managed. Non-existence – this was The Fool's great fear.

Truly, when he reflected on his fate, The Fool had to admit that he cherished many fanciful and unfounded notions about himself. Now, he was ready to give up everything he had known. He was convinced that the outcome of this situation was beyond his control. The only thing he could do was to let go of every vestige of what he knew and believed about his life and his virtue and release himself totally into something greater than the importance of his own separate existence. This sacrifice had been forced upon him. He had not willed or chosen it. Face to face with the possibility that he would soon cease to exist, The Fool looked more deeply into his soul than ever before he had done. And there, he found reconciliation.

Gradually, it came to him that this was the final test of all he had learned. This was the last moment in which it was possible to honor his high dream, the vision he had been granted, the truth that he had glimpsed in his heart of hearts. Yes, he had faults and failings. His life was perhaps not blameless in the scales of absolute justice. But the vision he had pursued and the noble influence it had radiated into his being was still something he held to be real and precious. He had known the compassion of the goddess. He had glimpsed the secret oneness of all life. His heart had known the bliss of homecoming, and tasted the peace of inner union. If this final sacrifice of his body and life were to have value, it must be a voluntary release, a joyous self-giving, a victory, a choice of bravery. He could do no other. And none but himself would know the secret choice he had made.

He began to feel happy again. Uncertainty as to his fate became, in a sense, his refuge. There was no possibility of intervening on his own behalf. He was stripped naked of all resources and crutches, with only the bare bones of Truth to comfort him. And in this emptiness, he found consolation. He was ready to die.

The day wore on. The birds chirped in the trees. The breezes rustled the leaves around him. He saw and he heard the flow of life, and knew that it was good. He blessed it, sensing that this day might be his last. The ebbing and transition of life into something unknowable he could also accept and bless. He could do no other. In his heart there was acceptance.

Towards evening, he heard footsteps behind him. But he could not see who was approaching. He felt a chill in his bones, but was beyond caring. "Let it be" he said to himself. "Let this be. I have no wish or will to escape my fate. Let it be."

Then closed his eyes and waited.

There was a long silence. Within himself, The Fool felt only peace. There was no hope. There was no expectancy. There was only resignation. Only resignation and peace. He closed his eyes and sank into oblivion.

Awakening

The Fool awoke, as if from a bad dream, to feel a moist cloth mopping his forehead. He opened his eyelids and beheld two clear blue eyes gazing into his own. He was resting on an improvised bed of moss under one of the sacred oaks. Bending over him was a fair-skinned lady with a countenance of immense kindness and dignity. She smiled, and he felt a burden of anguish fall away from his heart. The memory of his sufferings seemed to dissipate in the glow of that smile. But the questions tumbled forward in his mind.

Fool: Where am I? Who are you? What happened?

The lady did not answer him immediately. Instead, she dampened the cloth and again pressed it to his forehead and cheeks.

"People call me by different names," she said. "I come to those who attain true equality in spirit, a virtue men call Temperance. My name must remain my own secret. You are safe now. Your test is over."

Fool: Test? I was sentenced by the lady with the scales. I protested at first, but as I hung there waiting to die, I gave up. I did not see his face, but towards the end I could feel the presence of Death nearby.

Temperance He came to end the old and begin the new, to close one door and to open another. What you had to experience has been experienced. It was necessary. It had to be this way. The worst is behind you.

Fool: What more can I lose? Something inside me died. Somehow, I know that I am no longer the same person. I could not avoid my fate. I had to accept it. My pride was smashed. I let go of my grasping for life, my hunger for experience. I lost the need to continue my separate existence. What more can be taken from me?

Temperance: Do not worry. From death comes rebirth. From your insight, a new life is already being nurtured. You are moving from a life you thought you understood into an existence that you have never before known. Put the past behind you now. You have no need to worry.

Fool: I have so many unanswered questions.

Temperance: You do. But you are close to finding your answers. You were able in that last moment of waking consciousness to release yourself from yourself. Things will no longer be the same. You will see.

Fool: But I still do not know who you are, how you found me. Thank you for rescuing me, for tending me. I am sure I was about to be embraced by Death.

Temperance: Death was here. He was very close. But he saw no one to claim. You had released yourself from yourself. The one he had come to claim was no longer present. But still a little remains to be done, your sufferings are almost over.

Fool: What do you mean? You say "almost". What does that mean?

Temperance: You have come so far already! But remember, in every test that may come your way, you will have the possibility from this day forward to remain centred in your own inner being. When you take refuge in the heart of your heart, as you have recently learned to do, and when you face Death and live to tell the tale, none can shake your poise, or separate you from your inner courage. This balance, this inner harmony of spirit, is a noble mastery which is always hard won, and steeply priced. From the outside, a victor appears to ordinary mortals as a man of moderation, restraint, self-control, patience. Those who have attained true equality walk a middle path free of extremes and void of disharmony. They are even-tempered, calm and deliberate. Their composure is a source of strength and inspiration to everyone they know. But few observers see how hard-won his inner victory is. Only if you die to self can you be true to your highest Self. You are close to victory now, the greatest victory, the victory over your own ego. When you surrendered, before you lost consciousness, you released your grip on life and placed yourself in readiness for the final transformation. This lies ahead. Keep going until your journey is complete.

Fool: Journey? I have hardly the will or the energy to go anywhere.

Temperance: Nevertheless, you must go on. Return to the place where lady Justice passed sentence on your life. Here you will find what you need.

She helped him to his feet, and walked a while with him in the direction of The Hermit's cave. But as they neared the clearing, she paused to say goodbye and turned to depart. The Fool continued on until he came to the cave's mouth. Then a feeling of despair swept over him. Even before he entered The Hermit's cell, his heart sank.

A smell of smoke was in the air. On the floor of the simple abode he could see broken furniture, the remnants of a fire, and shreds of papyrus. The room had been rifled. Everything had been broken up, burned or scattered in utter destruction. The simplicity and peace he had found in this cell short hours before were replaced by a feeling futility and destruction, and in his heart there arose a feeling of utter desolation.

Looking to the corner of the cave where the curtains used to hang, The

Fool could see no portal, only unbroken walls of stone. Where was this gateway into the underground chamber and the Wheel of Fate? Had it too disappeared?   And where was The Hermit? Who had done this deed? He sank to his knees and covered his face with his hands. Then, before his inward eye, a powerful vision arose.

He saw a magnificent tower stretching from earth upwards into the clouds. It was massive, on a scale far beyond his wildest imagination. Around it, dark clouds were massing. Suddenly an earthquake struck, and a large crack opened up at the base of the tower. The stones began to loosen and crumble. The Tower fell into a heap of rubble. The Fool gazed in his inner vision upon a shapeless heap of boulders that had once been a proud tower. And in that debris, he saw the remains of his own life.

In that moment of utter and final desolation, the face of Lady Temperance flashed before his inner eye. She smiled. Was this the last trial?

It was as if shackles fell away from his consciousness, and he understood something that he had never before grasped. It was an illumination, not an idea. It was a feeling, an insight, a wordless recognition of something long hidden. In later weeks and months, he would reflect on this moment of revelation and attempt to put it into words. But this was later. In this moment all he could feel was pain and loss.

He knew now that he could cling to nothing and to no one. Yet he knew also that he was not and never would be from that moment on alone. He could no longer cherish even a single small expectation about his life or the world in which he found himself alive, for he knew now with utter finality that they were not his. Everything was simply what it was, impermanent, destined for change. Nothing that existed, including his own body, could offer him refuge or satisfaction. Only the now moment was complete and perfect, no fond hope concerning its outcome or its result, or even its ultimate meaning. He released a final, obscure attachment and felt a burden being lifted from his heart and soul. At last, he was truly free.

In later years, The High Priestess would put into words some of the meaning of this moment's insight, and he would remember what she said and paraphrase his recollection. When he had occasion to try and explain the wisdom of this moment's insight, he thought to himself:

I would have worshipped The Hermit as my master, for he had the wisdom that I sought so long and hard. It was not to be. And yet I am richer for this loss, for there is within each of us something that can make us whole and complete. And it is the finding of this hidden part of my own being that will open a doorway into a new life and a freedom beyond all my dreams. I shall become that which I sought so arduously, in so many blind alleys and difficult circumstances. Suffering can no longer pierce my heart. I am one with the entire universe, and do not fear the turnings of the Wheel of Fate. The empty husk of my personality has become a magic flute. MY life has been hollowed out, emptied of illusions. The holes that pierced my heart have become spaces for notes which the Supreme Lover intends to play, for it is His plan to enchant the hearts of other fools who can be tempted to venture forth on their own quests. He journeys in them and beside them, all unseen. They too will move beyond the boundaries of what can be understood. They may be rejected by their parents and friends and even by their human lovers. Yet in losing all, they may one day find all. It may be that they will suffer. But that which suffers falls away. What remains is clear. This alone endures.

The Wisdom of the Fool

The Fool looked across the room and beyond its desolation to the place where the portal had been. To his amazement, who should be standing there but The Priestess. Her eyes were closed. It seemed that she was in a state of meditation. From some distant inner plane of deep absorption, she began to speak.

Priestess: You are growing and learning very quickly, my child!

Fool: I have been through so much. I feel as if I had lived several lifetimes since we last met.

Priestess: Only a short time back, The Devil came to you in the guise of temptation. You were tempted to despair, and had you given way, the destruction you see would have been all the greater. But you did not yield to temptation. In your heart, you held steady and preserved the equality with which you were gifted by Lady Temperance. By this, you proved worthy to pass from the lesser to the greater mysteries.

From your first meeting together, the Hermit served you as a true friend to help liberate your mind from illusion. For this he took you to his cell. For this he left you alone. For this he prepared your food. And for this, he awaits you within. Nothing is lost, and nothing gained, except the awakening of your spiritual destiny. You know now who you truly are. And this can never be taken from you. Yet there is more, and it awaits you within.

Fool: This moment of despair, this was The Devil? I had no idea...

Priestess: He is the energy from outside yourself by which you submit to obsession He is the experience of temptation, bondage, enslavement. He makes you forget your spiritual heart. His wizardry causes you to be taken in by outer appearances. He weaves a web of ignorance, and brings on clouds of depression, doubt and hopelessness. He darkens the path of those who would push forward into the light. He is the sum total of all false notions and paralyzing fears. But he has no hold on one who embraces the light.

Whenever you are obsessed by a person, an idea or a substance that is unhealthy for you, this is The Devil. He is limitation. He comes in many forms, but in all of them he seeks only to bind you. You did not yield to the temptation of despair. You proved to be the victor.

The Devil is a master of illusion. He tempts and tests those who would progress beyond his control. But he can only delay their ascension, never prevent it. Now you are ready to hear what I have waited for so long to tell you. Now you are ready to understand the meaning of your adventure.

Fool: Tell me.

Priestess: When first you came to me, I foresaw that all of this would happen. You would experience suffering. You would have to learn to look deep within, to see what lies beyond the appearances of things. When a human being can see beyond the world's superficial appearances, he has earned the right to seek initiation. At this time, the soul gives birth to an inner child, the child of the heart. This psychic being is born when you become conscious of the divine guidance in your life, and as it grows, you come closer to the truth of your being.

Your body, your emotions, your mind and its concepts, even your aspirations and dreams all move through cycles on the Wheel of Fate. Soul is the centre of that wheel, the expression of the Divine on earth. The child of your heart grows and develops into a heroic youth as you live the adventures and challenges of life.

Fool: Since meeting The Charioteer, I have experienced that this being in my heart is not only sweet, but also powerful.

Priestess: When you become aware of this inner being and claim it as your very own, you become your eternal Self, for it links the human to the Divine. When the two parts of your being are thus yoked, you will embody the Light and Wisdom of Spirit in all that you do and say, and you will be continuously anchored in its poise and power.

Fool: You are telling me the story of my future. You seem to know the biography of my inner life. No one has spoken to me in this way before.

Priestess: In the depths of your heart is the temple of the Divine. This is the centre, the axis around which all the other parts of your existence become gradually unified. Your body, mind, vital energies and emotions, your subconscious instincts, all are gradually brought into harmonious attunement to this inmost centre. When you bring forward the aspiration of your psychic child, the light of your heart, nothing can stand in the way of your final victory. The crown of attainment comes to those who have persevered. Strength, courage and endurance are needed, and for this a would-be initiate must be tested by adversity.

Fool: I see. This is why it was necessary to experience these trials and tribulations. But I never thought of myself as an initiate.

Priestess: You know it is said that cowards die a thousand deaths, and the hero dies but once. Those who prolong their suffering through many lifetimes of ignorance must somehow find or develop the courage to face life and achieve victory. Fear holds them back, and they come to cherish their limitations as a kind of false security. But fear dissipates in the light of true understanding.

Fool: The Charioteer was strong, but I know now that in his fortitude there was wisdom. And that wisdom is the greatest strength, for it is nothing but love, and it is equal to every challenge of life.

Priestess: For most people, the crust of personality and the many layers of mental conditioning are so hard and thick that they are quite unconscious of this child of light in the garden of the heart. But for a long time now, you have been making the crust of dullness and convention thinner and thinner. It will take time, but soon you will feel this harmonization of all parts of your being around the divine spark within your spiritual heart. This is the reason you were born, and took up a human form, to accomplish the great work of building a human temple. You have been busy in all your lives and through all your learning experiences building up a column of light by which spirit could pour itself into matter. This temple is an image of your own being as you have developed it by your choices and by your will to progress.

Fool: I try to listen to my heart. This has been how I have lived for a long time now. But for me it has been very lonely. No one understood me.

Priestess: Most humans go through life without knowing why they are here. They take up their bodies, live and then die without knowing the purpose of existence, and they have to begin the same cycle all over again. On and on it goes. But then, one day somehow there comes about an awakening. A small crack occurs in the armor of ignorance. A little ray of light gets inside and stirs things up. The old ways are no longer good enough. There is a creative dissatisfaction, and a need to pursue some evanescent dream. Then comes the discovery of a deeper purpose to life.

Those who are coming out of ignorance will no longer see you as a fool. They will feel that you are the child of your dreams, the possibilities inherent in your highest ideals. They too are giving birth or have given birth to the inner being, the Divine Child. Heart speaks to heart in the circle of those who have awakened. The inner child gives us eyes to see and a secret inner way of knowing things that have never been explained to the mind.

Fool: In some people I have felt this inner affinity. I could not understand until now why it was that I could meet some perfect stranger and feel that we knew each other. It is true, people who are inwardly awakened do have eyes to see, and a heart to feel. I feel I can trust people like that.

Priestess: It is the Divine which gives birth to the Child of the heart. Something of this Divine Presence is seen and felt all around us on earth. All human development, action, temperament and inclination come from the power of the unseen Source. You are ready to move on. You have come to the gate of the inner sanctum Follow me!

She turned and walked between the pillars into the darkness. The Fool followed.

The Inner Sanctum
Here again were the familiar stairs that led down to a crypt in the bowels of the earth. But whereas on the previous visit, when he had

reached the bottom of the steps he had seen a doorway leading to a room, the room of the Wheel of Fate, this time The Fool saw ahead of him another set of stairs leading upward. He counted the steps as he ascended them behind the High Priestess, and there were fifteen.

At the top of the steps, he found himself in a circular chamber lit by a shaft of light from the ceiling. The light poured down onto a crystal sphere which rested on a square stone altar. Four pillars stood round the altar like sentinel guardians. And on the walls, in equally spaced positions, there were four alcoves. Between the alcoves were hung many paintings. To his right, The Fool saw a painting of The Magician, one of The High Priestess, and still others of The Empress, The Emperor and The Hierophant. Then came the first alcove with courtly figures in the top section, and symbols of water below. There followed other paintings, including one of The Hermit, and other alcoves with symbols of earth, air and fire in turn.

Priestess: You have come to the Temple of Truth. It is a place of initiation and divination. The Mother is present here in spirit, and her power is with all who are brought here.

You see the four sides of the altar there, in the centre of the chamber, and the four petals on the floor design. These express the four primal forces of creation. Each human being embodies these powers. Each human is a living temple.

In this temple there are four alcoves. Each is placed in one of the four directions, North, South, East and West. Each of the alcoves tells a story about one of the four primal powers. Each expresses and enshrines one aspect of the Mother.

Fool: Tell me more about these powers of the Mother.

Priestess: The Absolute Supreme Being is beyond all notions of our so-called mental understanding. But the Mother reveals a new way of knowing and being and living in Her chosen children. She shows them the meaning of life and its higher possibilities.

Firstly, as you know from the tale of creation, the Mother created the polarities of being, the light and dark, electric and magnetic, called yin and yang. Then, their play of relationship was manifest as the pillar of light. Then, from the pillar of light came the four directions, each of them an expression of divine possibility. The outer forms we see in the material, earthly world are only the final crystallization into form of Her work. Hidden to our outward vision, the Mother arranges the harmony of Her forces and processes, She activates nature to reveal all that can be expressed of the divine potential in life.

Each of the four radiations from the centre is a revelation of divine power and beauty and potential. Each alcove is a special area of focus where the creative forces are working out new expressions of life.

You also are a pillar of light. You are the temple of temples. Yours are the four powers of the Divine Mother. You are Her child, Her hero. For you She took human form and became a teacher.

Fool: What are these powers? What is the meaning of these four shrines?

Priestess: By the power of Her four emanations, the Mother shapes the minds and hearts and bodies of Her future divine warriors. One day She will manifest her fullness in the physical world. In the template of a perfected human being, some complete epiphany of Her power and presence will be revealed. Because of this, She called you to set out on a great adventure of self-discovery. For this, She has brought you here.

In the East, the Mother of creation manifests harmony, beauty, sweetness, rhythm, charm, grace and an opulent fullness of satisfaction. To receive all this, the heart must open like a chalice. You see the symbolism of water engraved here in fountains one through ten.

In the West, She acts with strength, decisiveness, speed and power. Here we see Her warrior mood, Her sword of discrimination that separates truth from falsehood. The true hero must develop an overwhelming intensity, a passionate force to achieve, a strength to shatter every obstacle and win through to his final victory. Those who embody this aspect of The Mother never shrink from battle. They tolerate no imperfection, obscurity or treachery. If need be, they will suffer pain and deprivation, but they are dauntless and relentless in their pursuit of Truth. This is Air, the clear mind.

In the North, we find Her ability to execute flawless work, her intimate knowledge of processes that end in creations of perfection. She executes skilful work in all things physical to manifest the divine possibilities, and She is unfailingly exact in Her craft and precision. She is infinitely patient. She is tirelessly efficient in organizing and administrating the laborious and sometimes minute details of Her flawless work. The northern alcove shows you images of stone, one through ten. These represent Her flawless craftsmanship impressed upon earthly matter. The dolmen is a symbol of completion and perfection, the axis which reaches from earth to heaven.

Finally, in the South, we see the Mother of peace, calm and tranquility who houses infinite wisdom in Her wide and sovereign majesty of spirit. She pours it down from the heights into the receptive minds of those who seek the life of spirit, but She is forever unmoved Herself, because all wisdom is eternally Hers. She sees and knows all things, imparting light and knowledge and higher vision to those who open to Her influence. High and majestic is She. Fire is her sacred symbol and you see it here, again in arrangements of one through ten.

These four alcoves and their symbols represent four great powers of the Mother, Her harmony in the divine hero's emotions, Her strength in his mind, Her intimate perfection in his body and its works and Her wisdom in his spirit.

Fool: North, South, East and West are facets of my own being. When I become one with the child of the heart, I AM the temple of these four great powers. I am the pillar of light and the four emanations of divine power.

Priestess: This insight is the beginning of wisdom. Something of the Mother's omniscience is imparted even to those who are just coming out of the sleep of ignorance. Even at the beginning of our long journey, She often gifts us with some power of foresight and insight. In due time and by inward development, the various initiations bring with them a capacity for true divination. But for divination, you must understand number. Form evolves in matter by the power of number. To see a divine story in symbolic form is the essence of divination.

Fool: I see number in these four shrines. There is some teaching here which I do not yet understand. The various symbols are in groupings one through ten.

Priestess: There is much that you do not understand, there is much to learn. The language of number is present here, as you observe, and you can also notice four figures in the uppermost section of each alcove, a king, a queen, a knight and a page. These also are part of the teaching, the Book of Truth that opens doorways to true divination.

Fool: What is this language? Can I learn to read it?

Priestess: This is truth is sometimes called Tarot. It is one form of divination. It encompasses the language of the stars, the ancient forms of augury, the secret lore of the alphabet and the powers of mandala and mantra.

Fool: And this is divination?

Priestess: Divination is seeing the pattern of the Divine written into the story of creation. Divination speaks to us through number and pattern in such a way as to connect the timeless with the time-bound.

To the mind which has been hypnotized by outer appearances, divination means a glimpse of the future, or an understanding of the secrets of the past. In reality, divination is a vision of the hidden oneness that gives meaning to the complexity of life. It is a revelation of the pattern of wholeness and holiness that is unfolding in our souls.

Since you are a divine fool, you will understand that, in truth, the sacred never has become profane. It is only the dullness of the human mind that separates what is eternally one into the many.

Fool: The pillar of light is one. But when it takes human form, it dances, and the dancer whirls the worlds into existence! And I am that dancer!

Priestess: Those who see the pattern of wholeness in the broken fragments of the human mind are called seers. They remind us of the presence of the sacred when we have been conditioned to see only the profane.

Fool: I want to understand more about divination. For I see now that it has a place in the path of initiation. I had not seen this so clearly before.

The Priestess stood for a few moments in silence. Then, she turned toward The Fool and beckoned to him to approach.

Priestess: Gaze into the crystal sphere. Let your vision rest on the inmost point to which you can penetrate with all the powers of your attention. Let your mind be quiet, and clear like a mirror, deep as a well of pure water in the hidden glades of the forest. Gaze, gaze, gaze deeply into the crystal sphere...

The Fool saw the crystal begin to glow from within. There was a mist, but it quickly cleared. Then, he saw a face, the face of a beautiful child with a star in her forehead, and her eyes had the light of the stars in them too. The child spoke :

> I bring you Starlight and blessings. I bring you guidance so that you may always be in a state of grace. The way ahead lies clear now. The light of grace will lead you forward. Yours is the heart of giving, sharing, offering and devotion. Hold back nothing. Be at peace. You have reached the serenity of the still centre. You have become a melding of heaven and earth. They have been waiting to

come together in you for so long! My force will be with you from this day forward. You will feel guidance from your own heart whenever you look within. Starlight and blessings are yours. Hold and treasure them forever!

Her image began to fade, and in its place he saw a beautiful full Moon floating in an indigo sky. In his mind, the image spoke:

I am magic and dreamlight. To those who are not pure, I am illusion and distortion, deception and bewilderment. To the clear of heart, I am inspiration, revealed knowledge, the depths of the unknowable, the mystery of eternal cycles in time. I am enchantment and I am wonder. Few find me, and of those who do, fewer still transcend my wizardry. You have opened your heart to the triple light of higher wisdom. I will guide you through realms of meditation and insight as you grow in wisdom. I will teach you the mystic symbolism of the universal speech. I will give you creative power to weave visions and speak mysteries the like of which the world has never known. I will guide your steps safely across the flux and instability of all things sublunar until you cross into the eternal kingdom.

The Moon's image slowly faded away inside the crystal sphere. In its place, the light of the Sun began to glow. It was brilliant gold, blindingly bright, but gentle on the eyes. And from this light, a rich voice spoke to him in gentle tones:

Now is the time to let your light shine. You are victorious. Celebrate your joy within your heart and prepare yourself for a still greater life in the spirit. You have been given all the power and all the insight that you are capable of holding at this time. You have awakened your mind of gnosis, and you have energized and charged your body and your vital energy with its radiance. You have lived in such a way as to honour the truth of your being, therefore your power is sure. Know now and understand that this power will be with you for as long as your thoughts, words and actions harmonize with truth. You are heaven's gift to earth. You are the action of the goddess, the co-creator of glorious worlds to

come, beyond the vision of even the wisest of men. For you, the
moon and the stars weave their heavenly dance. In you, the sun of
truth shines. Rejoice and be at peace, for you have accomplished
that which called you to this great adventure.

The brilliant light of the Sun began to fade. Then, from within the crystal, he saw small wisps of light rising up into the beam from the ceiling and floating skywards.

Priestess: These are the souls who have been liberated by your victory today. They have been brought to their own day of judgement, which is the day of their destiny and transformation. The ancient Prophecy is being fulfilled. They are set free. Your transformation is their victory too. They were with you in spirit. They hoped and prayed for you when you were tested. They whispered their love and concern from a distant place. But they could not rise up and be freed from limitation until you attained your victory, for your fates are intertwined together in a tapestry of oneness.

Like them, you are reborn this day. You are transformed and awakened to a new life. The past and its mistakes are behind you. You will begin a new day with the dawning of new possibilities, renewed dreams and high purposes and above all, the blessings of the goddess. Send these souls your love now as they rise up into the light and pass over.

The Fool watched as the last of these glowing entities rose up like fireflies in a swirling cloud and disappeared into the pillar of light. From the aperture in the ceiling down to the crystal orb on the altar, the light glowed more radiantly. It became a shimmering luminescence of rainbow colour, swirls of pastel radiance that shimmered and flowed like water. The crystal sphere glowed with these subtle colours, and it drew his attention into itself and held it there in the inner depths of the radiance.

The Priestess: This is the world. This is the wholeness of heaven expressing itself in the perfection of earth. The crystal world you see before you is clear and pure. It has been restored to its original beauty, which is the lustre it revealed on the first day it sprang forth from the Word of the Logos. Look upon this world. Tell me what you experience.

The Fool: I hear a kind of symphony of tones. And I am seeing many crystal spheres, one within another, and as they turn they are making music, and from the music comes beautiful colour. Ah! It is so beautiful!

Priestess: Child of my heart! This world of perfection and beauty is your home. This is completion. This is wholeness. This is truth. This is what heaven has longed to express from the moment it first fell in love with earth. You have come home. You have found sanctuary.

Close your eyes now, and look within the lighted sphere of your own soul. Look to your secret heart of hearts and tell me what you see.

Fool: I see spheres, one within another turning and turning … and the dance of light and the celestial music – they are all there within my own being. I am That! Ah! Bliss!

The Fool closed his eyes and entered fully into the vision. And it was as if he entered the cradle of his sweetest dream, and there he finally found peace. He came home to himself.

Hours later, when he awoke, and found himself resting on The Hermit's cot, all was as it had been. Moreover, on the table there was a meal of fruit and bread and fragrant wine on the table, which he knew were meant for him.

But he did not break his rest so quickly as his hunger might have urged. He closed his eyes and lingered in the feeling and the memory of the experience. He rested and he remembered.

PART THREE : THE BOOK OF TRUTH

A New Beginning

Again, The Fool slept. He dreamed that he was not alone in the room. He dreamed that The Hermit had come back. Then, he began to feel a tap-tap-tapping on sole of his feet. Opening his eyes, he could hardly believe what he saw. There was The Hermit, standing at the foot of the bed and smiling at him.

Of course there was much questioning and rejoicing on The Fool's part to see the return of his friend, for whom he had feared the worst. The Hermit was not very clear or precise about the details of what had taken him away, or where he had gone, or why. And because the damage and disorder to his cell had been cleaned up as much as possible, their conversation could range to other subjects.

Hermit: I have a story to tell you, my young friend. I want you to listen very carefully, and try to remember all the details. You are going to begin the serious study of what I call The Book of Truth. It is actually a collection of five books, but taken together they are known by this name. Now this book is very important to your future studies. In order to appreciate where it comes from, and how priceless it really is, I am going to tell you a story.

There was once a wise hermit living in a lonely retreat in the high and remote mountains. He had spent a lifetime in spiritual communion with the Divine Mother. His days were numbered and he knew it. It came into his mind and heart that he should leave some gift behind when he passed away, some wonder that would speak to the world about what he treasured most. Not knowing what this legacy might be, or how to proceed, he began to pray to the Mother for guidance.

Nine days he passed in prayer, and then as he slept, a wonderful dream came to him. He saw four large books resting on the grass in front of the sacred river that flowed past his hermitage, each of a different colour, one red, one yellow, one blue and one green. As he watched, a beautiful maiden came up from the river waters carrying a golden box in her two arms. She stood behind the four books and looked deeply into his eyes. He felt the purest love radiating from her, flowing directly into his heart and filling him with bliss. And he experienced a peace that was deeper than any he had ever felt before.

The beautiful maiden placed the golden box on the grass beside the four books. Then, she opened its lid and took out a book bound in the purest white leather and placed this book on top of the other four. Turning again to gaze on the hermit, she spoke.

This is my gift to you, the best of what I have to offer. It is my love and my wisdom set down in words as a pathway that will guide the seeking souls from earth to heaven and back again. Take these five books. Guard them with your life. Share what they contain with those who will treasure the teaching and follow the way. Those who come after you, who seek with pure hearts, feed them the clear light of guidance. Nourish their spiritual hunger from the wellspring of these five sacred tomes."

At this, the hermit awoke. In his heart, he understood the meaning of the dream. The four coloured books represented the four energies of the Mother. Red was Her Fire, blue Her Water, yellow Her Air and green Her Earth, Her physical body. The fifth book, purest white, was known as the Book of Spirit. It contained Her highest wisdom, and described the stages of initiation.

The hermit pondered the meaning of his dream and reflected about how he might fulfill the Mother's order to pass on the wisdom of the books to others. Pondering and meditating thus, he fell asleep, and once more he entered into the world of dreams. A second time found himself watching by the river with the five books still piled there on the grass before his gaze. The beautiful maiden was still standing there, looking into his eyes. Again, she spoke.

I have divided myself into seventy-eight parts. All that I have and all that I am is there, to be shared with those whose hearts are true. Love my children, serve those who will come after you. Feed them the wisdom of the way so that they can climb the heights and attain the golden summit.

In earth, water, air and fire, experience grows by numbered degrees. Each number is a lesson, an energy, an event. When the soul has climbed through the life-experiences of the numbers, it develops into a young page, an apprentice. Then, the soul learns to be a warrior. Afterward, the soul learns wisdom directly from the queen, and lastly it attains the full powers of the king. But the journey does not end with this attainment, for the Book of Spirit must be lived. It is a journey of inner unfolding and initiation. To one who finishes the journey, I give myself. Such a one becomes my world. I am his universe. Teach my children the way. Open the doorway of the secret heart and let wisdom guide them home to me."

Then, she smiled. The hermit awoke. Her smile was there in his heart radiating love and affection through all his being. He understood. He knew the meaning of the books. He accepted the task that had been given to him. He was ready to fulfill the River Maiden's request.

The Hermit closed his eyes and entered into his most profound meditation. Gazing silently into the ether of his heart, he went deeper and deeper into the infinite peace. Then, gently, like the shadow of a cloud crossing a sunlit field, a question arose within him. Slowly, slowly it took form, like a ripple on the surface of his mind's mirror-stillness. Like a reflection of the moon on the deep waters, this hint of a question arose. Like a glimmer of light from a firefly in the dark forest it moved, forming itself into words and finally finding expression. "How, Mother?" he whispered. "How?"

From the deep silence within came the answer : "With love, only love."

*   *   *   *   *   *   *

The Fool watched as the hermit completed his story. As he finished speaking and closed his eyes to rest, a mood of great calm settled down over both of them. The Fool hardly dared to break the silence, for the old man's tale had worked a profound effect on his emotions. At last, he found his voice.

Fool: Where did you hear this story?

Hermit: From my master. He told me the tale himself.

Fool: Ah! Did he show you the books? Did he show you the 78 parts of the wisdom?

Hermit: He taught me. He taught me all he could, and then he passed away.

Fool: He had mastered what was in those books that he saw in his dream?

Hermit: The books were real. They were not just a part of his dream. He went to the place he had dreamed beside the river and he found them resting there on the grass, just as he had seen them. Five volumes, one each in red, blue, yellow, green and white. The lady had left them there. And the key, the key to understanding the books had become clear to him as a result of his dream. He was a great master. It was a privilege to be his disciple.

Fool: And he passed this wisdom on to you.

Hermit: I was very lucky. It was another land, and another time. the mountains, the ancient ways – a different world, really. Things have changed so much since then!

Fool: You have already taught me so much. But I want to learn more, as much as I can.

Hermit: Indeed, I have taught you so very little in comparison to what there is to know.

Fool: For me, it has meant more than you can imagine.

Hermit: It has been a preparation, only a preparation of the mind. Consider it all an introduction, a beginning, something to make you ready for the greater wisdom.

Fool: A beginning?

Hermit: A start. That is all.

Fool: And now?

Hermit: And now, I must ask you a question.

Fool: Yes?

Hermit: Are you ready to study the Book of Truth in depth?

Fool: I feel that I am. But let the Mother be the judge.

Hermit: She speaks in your heart when you listen rightly. This you know.

Fool: I know. I feel she approves. I feel that I was guided to meet you.

Hermit: Then, with Her sanction I am ready to teach you the seventy-eight parts of wisdom, the five books of Truth.

Fool: But you say that what I have learned so far is only a beginning? And I thought it was so much!

Hermit: It is a dream in the mind, not untrue, but simply incomplete. A vision of truth, no doubt, but seen through veils.

Fool: Can you explain?

Hermit: Truth is naked, like the earth and water of the Mother's own world-body. Mind creates elaborate costumes. Thus far, you have seen Truth in her costume, trappings invented to please the minds of the inventors, forms believed, perhaps, by the minds that invented them, but limited in scope. You have not seen Truth naked. There is some power in personal belief, and in cultural symbols, and what you have learned has at least this much power. But there is greater power in the womb from which these mental visions come, the light of the Mother. The mind spins patterns from the limited light it can access. Greater mind sees greater light in its purity. Now you may learn to see Truth as the mind of the Mother herself sees it, Truth without trappings.

Fool: This is revealed in the five books?

Hermit: Yes. This wisdom is not information or abstract reasoning. It is a living power. What you have been through so far is a preparation.

Your heart is open. You are ready to go farther.

Fool: Will you teach me then? Can we begin?

Hermit: The world you see outside you is only yourself writ large. Soil is flesh of the Mother's earth-body. Rocks and mountains are Her bones. Rivers and streams are Her lifeblood. The Mother is the Divine Reality behind your limited self-form, your individuality.

Fool: Air is Her sacred space. Fire is Her transmuting force.

Hermit: And the action of Her spirit. Tarot means Truth. It speaks of earth, water, air and fire, the four powers. It speaks the powers of ten numbers in each of these four fields.

Fool: Is number the power, or is each element the power? Or are there two powers?

Hermit: There is One Power. But Two, duality, is necessary for creation. Number breathes its energy through the medium of each element, and a unique expression comes about. When the power of one breathes in fire, we get a particular result, but when it breathes in water, there is something different.

Fool: The Goddess writes this story across the whole face of creation.

Hermit: Yes, and the life breath of number moves the four elements according to Her patterns. In this way, she weaves the patterns of our destiny. The Mother is often pictured as the weaver of fate, as you know.

Fool: Therefore one earth, two earth, three earth - these sacred realities - these are my own story. And this is the story of the Divine Mother's self-revelation.

Hermit: One water, two water, three water, all sacred realities, as you say. Different aspects of the creative action, a book of your own experiences. A jewel with 78 facets. It is a story that moves forward, gathering new power at each stage. It is a journey of challenge and transcendence. Difficulty and suffering arise in the mirror of mind and ego. So many people are obsessed with the small events of their personal lives, the suffering caused by their separation from Source.

Fool: And for them, Truth wears costumes. They see the costumes in their own mind's mirror, and they are content to watch the pageant.

Hermit: Those who cherish separation fear to see Truth naked, or to see themselves as they really are. Fear blinds.

Fool: And one air, two air, three air, these are aspects of myself, my mind.

Hermit: As one fire, two fires, three fires describe phases of your own vital energy in action. This becomes very clear when you approach Tarot in the right way. The revelation never stops. All we can do is open to it from the heart.

Fool: The powers of four, five and six are also playing their music in my earth, water, air and fire.

Hermit: You can watch it happening if you have the eyes of innocence. My master had such eyes. Many judged him to be a fool. You know, it is always the same old story. People misjudge what they cannot grasp. And I too was such a fool, and this is why he taught me.

Fool: He passed away?

Hermit: He left his physical body. His bones are still there in the mountains. But he himself is more present and more powerful than ever. The enlightened ones never pass away.

Fool: Then you are still in contact?

Hermit: He is here now.

Fool: These veils that people create in their minds, is there no easy way to remove them?

Hermit: Only those who weave the deception can undo it. Usually, they do not wish to be undeceived, unmasked. They fear innocence and are scandalized by nakedness. They are not ready to quit the world of their illusions, and they go on insisting to themselves and to others that their illusion is truth. Until this changes, nothing possible. They remain in their fantasies. Tarot can only give them shadowy glimpses of what is real.

Fool: But the free ones see through the veils.

Hermit: They see. They have removed the veils from the eyes and ears of the heart. They know.

Fool: Wisdom can only enter this way, yes I see it.

Hermit: So the Book of Truth – this is what I call Tarot – is not my teaching or my master's, it is a direct revelation from The Mother, Her four energies, and Her Spirit. Those who feel themselves to be Her children have already been chosen. And when the chosen ones speak, it is revelation, because they see clearly and they hear truly. The innocence of Truth flows into their words.

Fool: And when they consult the Book of Truth, they have no selfish interests.

Hermit: There is a purified ego that does not do violence to Truth. Mother's mysterious purposes are being worked out even in those who have not altogether gone beyond ego.

Fool: Can we know our progress in this matter?

Hermit: Only the ego suffers. This is your clue. Look to your suffering to teach you.

Fool: Selfishness is suffering. Absence of love is suffering.

Hermit: The wise ones call it ignorance. The words and actions of the ignorant corrupt truth. And so the students of the Book of Truth come to greatly value silence. They speak only to release energies of harmony into the world. And in their silence, they nurture the vision of Truth so that it grows stronger. This is their secret power.

"Divination" and "initiation" are only words to those who have no experience, no awakening, no inner call. Only the children who have chosen to follow the way come to know the real meaning of these words. They open the Book of Truth in their hearts. This Book must be read in the sanctuary of the heart. Only the innocent are invited to enter there.

Fool: Do you have the books which your master received? Will we use these?

Hermit: Ah, you are eager to begin. Well then, come with me.

The Fool followed the Hermit. He was reflecting on everything that had been said. A quiet excitement was growing inside him, and he wondered if his friend and mentor could feel it. It was a new beginning, indeed.

The River Maiden

They came to a place by the river which was especially beautiful. The grass was soft and fine, quite unlike other grass in the area, and it smelled very sweet. They sat down and looked out over the water. A few minutes passed in silence, and then The Hermit reached into his pouch and took out a small cloth-wrapped packet which he handed to The Fool.

Hermit: This deck of Tarot cards is something which I want to give to you. It has never been used before by anyone else. You will be the first one to open its windows into the beyond. Use it as a way of following your soul's progress in wisdom and light on the pathway to Truth.

Fool: It seems that everything I need is being supplied to me.

Hermit: These cards are crafted from my master's teaching.   The images date back to the Mystery Schools of ancient times.   It is a tradition that goes back to an age before recorded history. In those mountains, there are still stone temples from that early period, far older than people generally imagine. It was in some of those that my master explained the five books to me. If you really want to understand the Book of Truth in depth, these cards will help you immensely.

Fool: When I look at these cards I see many images in stone. And there are paintings set into alcoves, or niches in stone walls. I have never seen figures like these.   Hermit: Did you know that stone speaks? Stone is part of the body of Mother Earth, her very bones. And she stores records of her experiences there. Stone can hold great power and much knowledge.   In the ancient temples there were such wonderful carvings, full of life. I have seen them. You could speak with them, you could learn from them. These paintings set into the walls of stone will link you to that world and its mysteries and powers. You can speak to these images and they will speak back to you in turn and teach you.

Fool: I wish to meditate with these cards and sleep with them, to hold them and feel them close to me. Then, when we have bonded, I will be ready to begin. I will be ready to learn how they should be used.

Hermit: Then let us make tomorrow our beginning day.

Fool: Come and walk with me in the woods before it gets too dark. I am feeling such a deal of gratitude that I cannot sit still any longer, I have to move about before nightfall comes. At this time of day, as the shadows begin to lengthen, I always feel a special calm settling down in nature. We can come back to this place tomorrow when we begin the work.

They strolled in the forest glades talking of many things until dusk settled across the horizon and darkness began to deepen among the trees.   Then they sat down on the grass near the entrance to the

Hermit's cave and together they entered into a long and deep meditation.

Of that inner journey in spirit which The Hermit and The Fool made under the light of The Moon little can be said. Silence deepened around them and throughout the forest, as darkness covered everything in its velvet mantle.

Much later, by the light of The Moon, The Fool took out his new set of cards in their cloth wrapping and examined them. He asked his heart to tell him where his journey was leading, and what lay ahead.

He divided the deck into three piles. Then he brought the piles back together into a single pile, and turned over the top card.

He gazed at the card and felt its message speaking to him in spirit. Indeed, he thought to himself, the stones do speak. Even the images set into the stones speak. The tradition lives. It reaches across the oceans, across the centuries to communicate its power and its wisdom. One could feel the energy, of this there was no doubt.

In his mind's eye, The Fool saw an old man, high up in the mountains walking up to a moonlit stone temple and pausing. The old man looked up at the moon. Then, he looked at the dark gateway to the temple. Slowly, he moved forward and disappeared into the blackness of the entranceway.

The Fool smiled. He looked up at The Moon and marvelled at her tranquil beauty. This mystical moon had seen so many strange things in times gone by, but her light was still the same. It bathed all things in silver silence.

Whether it was in the sleep of the waking mind, or whether it was the awakened understanding of a true dream, The Fool was never afterward able to say, but in some domain of his experience, he found himself back beside the river where he had sat and talked with The Hermit earlier that day.

In this experience, which he later spoke of as a dream, The Fool saw four books resting on the grass by the riverside, one piled on the other. The top book was crimson, the next was indigo blue, the third was bright yellow and the bottom book was emerald green. As he gazed on the books, a beautiful maiden came walking up out of the river carrying a golden chest. She approached the four books and gazed lovingly at them. Then, she opened the chest and took from it another book bound in the purest white leather, which she placed on top of the crimson volume. Then, she looked up at The Fool and smiled. In that smile, he felt the whole world blossom inside his heart. He experienced the coming together of love and knowledge in such a way that they were not two, but one. They were one and the same. He knew the meaning of bliss. And he knew that the only sanctuary he would ever need was there inside the temple of his own being.

The beautiful maiden closed the lid of the golden box, turned away, and walked slowly back into the river until she was no more visible. But the five books were still there on the grass, and the Fool continued gazing on them. He knew that they held the secret tale of how the bliss in his inmost heart had forgotten itself. And he understood in that moment why it had become necessary for him to leave home and pursue a quest, to recover what he had misplaced within himself. Everything he would learn in the coming days was already known in that temple of his own spirit. It was only the mind that needed to be reminded.

The Fool understood why it had been required by Fate that a story should be created which would remind others of the way home, in later days, in times to come, when some youthful adventurer would come to him, eager to find his bearings in life. And he, The Fool, now a Hermit, or perhaps a Magus, would tell the story of this moonlit dream, and of his master, and his master's master who lived in the Andes, and the circle would come full closure. But that was the future. Now, it was time to sleep, to assimilate, and to prepare for a new day of revelations.

The Archetypes

The Hermit decided that the soft grass by the river was the best place to sit for talking about the Book of Truth, so he invited The Fool to join him there early next morning.

The Fool was delighted when the Hermit spread a finely woven linen cloth on the grass and then pulled from a bag he had been carrying a large volume bound in the purest white leather.

Hermit: This is the Book of Spirit, also called the Book of Archetypes. It tells of the twenty one great beings who teach and test you on the way to the highest initiation. As a seeker actually experiences them, some may seem more like impersonal situations than like living beings. But others are definitely real persons. You can learn from them, draw on their strengths and enlist their help. They are part of your own wider self, part of your cosmic inheritance.

The path of initiation is a journey of experience and testing in which spirit becomes the leader of all other parts of one's being. The seeker's mind, emotions, vital energy, and even his or her physical body surrender to the guidance of the soul. To put it another way, the soul gains mastery of earth, air, fire and water and it learns to apply its knowledge according to the light of spirit. This book tells the stages of experience which lead to this victory of spirit. This is why it is named The Book of Spirit.

Fool: Ah, some of these great beings I have already met on my adventures thus far.

Hermit: You have. And yet, to say that you understand them completely would be stretching the truth.

Fool: I have studied the cards you gave me, I have looked at the pictures very closely.

Hermit: The first page of the Book of Spirit, apart from The Fool, is about The Magician. In the mountains, there are many magicians, or shamans. This part of the world has always kept alive the ancient ways, and a magus is a living embodiment of the ancient spiritual traditions. We will study the archetypes, and when you have read what the book has to say about each of them, you may ask me any questions which come to mind. Are you ready?

Fool: I am ready.

Hermit: Listen carefully then while I read to you. First, the figure of

The Fool

The Doric youth's dance expresses a pattern of cosmic wholeness as he moves with spontaneous abandon. A young man of ideal beauty, he was called by the ancient Greeks "kouros". In such a physical body, harmoniously shaped and graceful in movement, the wise ones saw a touch of the divine on earth. Kouros expresses in human form some of that perfection which we aspire to in our journey of self discovery. In this picture, the he is dancing with joy because the call has come to set out on a great adventure. His heart and body feel the rhythm of an invisible drummer summoning him to quest of consciousness. We can imagine the simple music of pipes and lyre in the background as he sways to the ancient rhythms of shepherds' music. Soon he will meet the heroes and demons whose stories he has heard from earliest childhood. He will strive for the laurel of victory, and risk life and limb to accomplish his destiny. Those who know Kouros well think of him as a seeker, not a fool. He seeks fulfilment, and he is willing to follow the path to the very end and to face with courage what it brings him. As you know, his qualities include innocence, spontaneity, freshness and a carefree, un-inhibited response to adventure. His mind is relatively uncluttered and unstructured. He brings new beginnings to those who encounter him. His heart is light and he is not afraid to take risks. His openness and naivety will carry him forward and he will have many learning experiences.

The Magician

The Magician, or Magus has mastered the four elements of his own microcosm. His physical body, which is earth, his mind (air), emotions (water) and spirit (fire) have all been centred in the truth of his Highest Self. He has focused his will and his concentration on the timeless words of wisdom inscribed over the door to the mystery school : "Know Thyself"; and he has progressed considerably toward full self-mastery. In ancient times, such an adept would be a mentor and teacher of novices such as the dancing Greek youth who is setting out on life's adventure. In the world of the magus, there is no separation between science, spirituality, occultism and art. He has experience in all these fields, and in others, but he has specialised in divination and initiation. Having achieved many levels of attainment while studying the ancient mysteries, The Magus is willing to offer his help to those he finds worthy.

On the mental level you may find yourself more adept at thinking and communicating when the influence of The Magician is at work. This comes from clear seeing, which is one of his gifts, and from focused intent, which really is the essence of what he has to share with you. You will have undistracted focus in your undertakings, and you will have more sustained powers of concentration than previously if he is with you. Emotionally, you will feel increased confidence. On the practical plane, you might find you had extra initiative to manifest things in the physical world. The special possibility that The Magician brings is a challenge which has in it a hidden opportunity to grow and to master your inner powers. Remember all of these possibilities are there, but the ones you actualise will depend on your own election and determination.

The Priestess

Educated from late childhood in the sacred cloisters of a moon-temple, the priestess has developed immense sensitivity to the realities of the inner world. She is deeply versed in sacred tradition, but she has gone far beyond mere intellectual mastery and progressed far in her intuitive ability to access wisdom directly from on high. The Priestess values silence and solitude, but she lives closer to the secular world than, for example, the hermit. She is happy to assist those who approach her for guidance. She values the coolness and darkness of the night as much as the warmth and light of day, because it is a time when she can enter more deeply into the sacred depths of the beyond. The feminine, mystical aspects of her development have reached a pinnacle, and The Priestess has become an adept at divination.

Intuitive awareness of things mystical is the special talent of the High Priestess. If she is present, it indicates the dawning of wisdom concerning higher things. The mind is being invited to trust its intuitions. And the feelings are being invited to open to higher guidance. On the physical level, stillness is called for. It makes introspection possible, and this is what The Priestess encourages. The special development which The Priestess brings is insight. This insight is most often of a spiritual nature. Generally, the High Priestess communicates a mood of inwardness, introversion, withdrawal and seclusion. She encourages us to become receptive to inner guidance, passively attuned to the promptings of our own soul. She is a truly oracular being. She senses the hidden mysteries and opens us so that we too can become more aware of what lies beyond the five senses. She counsels patience, inner calm and vigilance as well as dispassion. When we connect with the High Priestess, ancient wisdom from the past may come forward so that we are infused with higher knowledge.

The Empress
The balance of inner and outer capacity has been perfected in The Empress. She stands for the Goddess in society, but her authority comes from sacred roots rather than from social consensus. She is the consort of the god-emperor, and she supports his dynamic, outward actions. The Empress embodies the fullness of feminine power in all its forms. The ancient matriarchal power radiates from her person. She is a human embodiment of the Prime Mover, in its goddess aspect, and her will is sovereign. But her power is fecund, and her inner help will assure you success if she chooses to support you.

If you connect with The Empress you will have access to the healing power of the Mother's love. Her abundance will touch you and balance you at the mental level and nurture and fulfil you at the emotional level. The ability to extend and to receive love will be enhanced, also the capacity to feel trust in your relationships. You will be able to feel more loving care and generosity of spirit, and to enjoy earthly pleasures. On the physical plane, beauty and harmony and creativity flourish as a result of her touch. The Empress promotes culture, art, aesthetics and all forms of gardening and farming. Inner and outer growth are her gift. The special opportunity which she brings is an opening to become more attuned to nature.

The Emperor

More outwardly focused and dynamic than The Empress, The Emperor shapes society and its institutions. He uses his sacred authority to impose law, justice and social order. He implements the heavenly plan for earth, drawing guidance and energy from above. His leadership may be forceful, diplomatic or practical as required by circumstances. He is the ultimate authority figure on earth, and his word carries the power of life or death.

When we draw The Emperor, the indication is that some experience of power or authority is coming our way. This strength will likely find expression and application in some practical way, since the energy of the Emperor is directed toward outer action, frequently service. In the mind, we will taste leadership, initiative, organisational ability and a sense of command and control. Emotionally, the feeling of empowerment or authority will likely be noticeable. At the physical level, we will sense that our creative powers are equal to all challenges. The special experience that may manifest from this archetype is one of shouldering responsibility. We are given an opportunity to act confidently for what we believe to be right, and we are likely to do this in some social rather than solitary setting.

The High Priest

The High Priest has duties both esoteric and administrative. Because of his position, he must be more outwardly and socially involved than the High Priestess. An adept who rose to a position of prestige in the mystery schools, The High Priest was then appointed leader of the religious hierarchy. This made him responsible for education on many levels, but with a general focus on tradition and spirituality. He understands well that the higher truths must be presented to the public in forms that can be appreciated by the more ordinary mind. Therefore, he maintains continuity of religious tradition. Seeing beyond its external forms, he understands its inmost realities by direct experience. A highly evolved spiritual being, the High Priest has the astuteness to bridge the inner and the outer worlds and hold them in balance. He can be all things to all people, but in everything he says or does, there is an inner spiritual vision of truth which he brings to bear.

The High Priest brings you a connection with spirituality. On the mental level, this may mean involvement with belief systems, theology, pursuit of knowledge or education, or even religious rituals. Sometimes, the purity of spirituality may get lost in the admixtures of social custom, this seems inevitable in religion. The High Priest represents the full spectrum of expression. There is an element of traditional formality and conservatism as well as reverence for tradition and morality which the High Priest is capable of emanating and awakening. We might experience this aspect of his presence as a need to conform to religious rules and to accept spiritual disciplines. All this being said, on the higher and purely spiritual plane, when we contact his influence, we have the chance be in touch with a spiritual consciousness. In fact the High Priest sometimes brings an opportunity for initiation under the norms and forms of tradition. On the emotional level, therefore, if the constrictions of tradition are not too heavy, you may experience a genuine movement of faith, or even an inner empowerment. At the physical level, conformity to moral codes is indicated. The special possibility that the High Priest presents is to have a genuine spiritual experience that furthers your inner development.

The Lovers
The lovers pictured in your cards lived in ancient India. In their idyllic world there was not a separation between body and spirit, and concepts like the sinfulness of sex and guilt about the physical body or

ideas concerning its impurity had never crept in. Eros was held to be a spiritual force that pulled the emotions, body and spirit into powerful relationship with something bigger than the individual ego. These lovers move in harmony with the rhythms of the cosmos, but their words and actions are shaped by an ancient and traditional code of honour. Their images were carved in stone in ancient times to create a lasting expression of a deep human ideal, the ideal of right relationship, intimate relationship.

If you draw The Lovers, it means that you will have a choice to make in your experience of relationship. It may be that you need a healing union, or a balancing of opposite energies into wholeness, or you may need the feeling of closeness, connection, intimacy and sharing. In its highest essence, love unites us to the Divine and is universal. You may wish to measure your own experience of love against this perfect standard to sense where there is an opportunity to widen and deepen. You may have to work on relationships or a particular partnership and make some ethical choice about what is right and what is wrong for you. The mental level of this experience may well be commitment, or a discernment of values, possibly a moral choice. Emotionally, there may be affection, devotion, sincerity and romance. On the physical level, you may feel passion, physical attraction and sexual desire. The special opportunity here is that you have a choice which gives you an opening to follow your heart. This may mean leaving behind something old and accepting something new.

The Chariot

The Charioteer and his Chariot are one, and we may refer to this archetype by either term. The Charioteer has been schooled as a warrior, and he has lived the hero's code of honour in its fullness. For him, obedience, discipline and intense striving have always been an utmost necessity. He has not allowed himself to fall prey to luxury or self-indulgence. In this way, he has become an obedient and reliable extension of The Emperor's will and vision. Because he has lived his code with integrity, The Charioteer is entrusted by his superiors with ever increasing responsibilities.

When this sign comes up, it means self-mastery. If the mind has not been purified of ego, which is often the case, there may be self-assertion. On the emotional level there is strong motivation, and physically, there is an inner strength which makes perseverance possible. The special possibility here is a victory of some sort. The Chariot is the symbol of an individual who has many of the attainments of The Magician, the most conspicuous being focused will and intent, one-pointed effort toward a goal, confidence, self-sufficiency, emotional mastery, self-discipline, self-assurance, firm determination and the ability to steer his own way. All of this spells success, and the sign of the Chariot indicates that success is coming your way.

Strength

The feminine archetype of Strength is firmly connected to Earth. She grasps a fruitful staff, expressing the harmonious flow of the primal connection to the Mother Power. Her force is fruitful rather than violent, poised rather than aggressive. Strength is a 'state of being' for her, not a demonstration of authority or mastery. She is centred in the connectedness of earth to heaven, sun to moon and water to fire. Balance and wholeness maintain her power, and according to the ancient Hellenic way, she embodies the living beauty and presence of all this in physical form.

When Strength comes up in your divination, it means that you are being supplied with courage from the level of spirit. In your mind this may take the form of tolerance and quiet determination, composure, forbearance and inner equality. On the emotional plane, you may given a chance to practice compassion and benevolence, because true inner strength is based on good will, which is loving-kindness. It is easier to accept, to forgive and to bless when we have this form of strength in our hearts. True strength supplies one with the power of gentleness and sympathy. True strength is constantly centred in the heart and aligned with higher inner guidance. We spend many lifetimes practising obedience and co-operation with others in order to be sufficiently developed that we are capable of receiving guidance from our inner, spiritual sources. At the physical level, quiet determination and patience may be supplied to you, or required of you in order to get you through a challenging situation. You may need physical endurance, stamina and resolve to deal calmly with frustrating circumstances. The special possibility which may arise when Strength comes your way is a test of fortitude. Tests are opportunities for growth because they show us just how far we have come in our inner development, and where we need more work.

The Hermit

The Hermit has devoted his whole life to the quest for truth. He has sought solitude, silence and freedom in order to plunge deeply into contemplation. Sometimes, The Hermit lives in a forested retreat, and at other times he wanders the mountains. Those who are fortunate enough to win his approval will experience his wise counsel. But he only helps those whom he judges to be sincere.

The spiritual level of this archetype is inviting us to contemplation and introspection. We may feel a need to understand and to look within for wisdom. We may also be called upon to give guidance, to mentor another seeker. All of this implies disciplined, focused effort and attention, the implication being that solitude is far better than society. "Go it alone" is The Hermit's advice. On the mental level, seeking and teaching are indicated. Emotionally, The Hermit is motivated by spiritual love which is centred in tremendous detachment. Physically, solitude and withdrawal are indicated. The special possibility which The Hermit may bring into your life if you draw his image in divination is a spiritual retreat. The Hermit encourages us to put the outer world aside in order to focus on spiritual issues.

The Great Wheel

Known to the Romans as Fortuna, and to the Greeks as Keres, the Fates, the Goddess of Destiny has always expressed her action through the symbolism of the wheel. Sometimes her face seems terrible, and sometimes it is beneficent, but her revolving wheel pulls humans into an encounter with destiny, the destiny they have sowed by their actions and intentions. All sentient beings reap the fruits of their actions. This immutable law forces us to face situations and learn lessons we might not have chosen. When we neglect to follow the guiding light, inevitably suffering becomes the teacher. But through all the revolutions of the Wheel of Destiny, we learn and grow and move toward wholeness. The image on your cards comes from the Mystery Schools of India where the Great Mother presides over the revolving wheel and oversees the destinies of the souls which ride it. They rise and fall, they rejoice and suffer. But in time they begin to seek liberation and when this call comes, She will be their helper. She will bless and assist them in the quest for liberation.

If this sign comes up for you, it means you have attained some realisation or insight into your own destiny and karma. Intellectually, this translates into an understanding of the patterns of your life, and possibly the larger life of the universe in which you participate. Emotionally, you may be experiencing a change of life circumstances, a turning point. Physically, there may be movement and change, and the special possibility that arises under the sign of The Great Wheel is a surprise. This brings you to a turning point, a rendezvous with destiny, possibly a stroke of good luck. The Great Wheel is usually auspicious, but it may occasionally indicate a reversal of fortune. Usually, however, when we draw this card, we are being supplied with extra understanding and insight to realize the meaning of reversals and to rise above them. Therefore, take the time to step back from the immediacy of your life and look at it from a new perspective. See how its pattern is changing and expect the unexpected.

Justice

The most ancient written codes of justice are to be found in Mesopotamia. Traditionally, the dispenser of Justice is a wise man who has achieved righteousness in his own life, and who can apply the code impartially when the need arises. He must be morally incorruptible. The Law originates in heaven, but on earth it is defended and administered by The Emperor and his appointed ministers, of whom the judge pictured here is one. Ancient tradition is an ever-present guide in the application of Justice, because wisdom arises from the lessons of the past.

When Justice comes up in a reading, its highest meaning is Truth and Balance, or some development which will restore them if they have been compromised. At the mental level, we may be challenged to evaluate and discern in an impartial way how we can re-instate right relation with ourselves and the world around us. Emotionally, we are faced with a need to re-align and restore good feelings, eliminating any excess and becoming accountable for our inner equilibrium. At the physical level, it may be necessary to assume responsibility in some area of life that we neglected. The special possibility raised by Justice is that we will face a reckoning with Truth. Whether we experience it as a test (or trial) depends on our sincerity.

The Prisoner

In the ancient temples of Southeast Asia, nature has slowly crept in and overgrown all that man created. Originally free-standing, many of the statues have been choked by vines and tree roots. This mirrors the human condition of being trapped by something bigger than we can control, held in the grip of a relentless power that is greater than we can understand, something beyond our ability to manipulate. Even the gods, when they take human incarnation, experience the binding power of limitation in the earthly atmosphere, and they too must struggle to overcome inertia and find freedom.

When you draw The Prisoner, the way forward is not obvious, nor are the means at hand to understand any aspect of the experience. One can only surrender and fall back on faith. This is the meaning of the experience. You are being cornered, and all your human resources are being taken away so that you are naked and helpless except for faith in the divine. If this card comes up for you, the spiritual meaning it carries is : you must surrender and trust. In your mind, you must re-define your perspective and consider a new approach to life on a higher level. Emotionally, you must embrace humility and willing acceptance of what seems incomprehensible or intolerable, and you must do this with all your heart. At the physical level, you must be prepared to wait and to sacrifice. The special possibility in this situation is a delay, or a change of direction which makes you renounce your claim and give up something. You are blindfolded, suspended in time, and asked to discern from your deepest instincts what you feel is right. It is a time of transition and probing, an in-between stage which can help you re-align and awaken to something good but unsuspected. Be willing to give up what is known, to let go of your insecurity, and to step outside the mould of your social conditioning. Trust to your destiny, face your fears and accept the constraint which is at hand. An unusual turn of events will take you into something quite different from your norm, and in this there is a hidden opportunity to learn and grow.

Death

The mummified body of the great pharaoh Ramses has been preserved for thousands of years in the land where once he held supreme power. Filled with life and royal privilege in his prime, a god on earth, Ramses' physical form has become a brittle, disfigured shell of its former self. Pride has yielded to the inevitable grip of decay and mortality.

If the card Death comes up for you in divination its spiritual meaning is to signify transformation. On the intellectual level, you will have to let go of something and detach yourself. Old beliefs and views may crumble and we may feel like we are going from the known to the unknown. We may feel that we must experience something that cannot be avoided, and that it is necessary to accept the inevitable. Emotionally, release is called for. When we experience a confrontation or test that shakes us to the core, we are ready for a rebirth. We must be willing to break with the past, because a reversion to the old ways is just not possible. The loss of the old self is a necessary basis for our new awakening. So let go of outdated patterns, actions, habits and attitudes. Let the old cycle finish and be ready to move on to a new opportunity. Remember that where one door closes, another opens. At the physical level it may be necessary to reorganise your practical affairs. The special possibility that may come up for you at this time is a death. It could be a physical death of someone you know, or an inner death of sorts where something outworn and outmoded slips away from your life and lightens your burden. Embrace the experience and trust the process. This will allow you to come through in the best possible way. All students of initiation are tested, and everything hinges on the attitude and reaction we choose as we face our tests. To be forewarned is to be fully prepared.

Temperance

Poised, with hands folded and wings open for flight to heaven, the figure of Temperance is an image of balanced wholeness. Opposites are alchemically bonded into a synthesis of eternal calm. There is ancient wisdom and timeless renewal of energy in the archetype of Temperance. More than a statue from a mystery school, this figure expresses an inner, secret and sacred power of life that renews the spirit and empowers the soul.

The oldest Mesopotamian religious traditions give importance to the Simurg, a vulture-deity with great healing powers. In India, this deity became Garuda. Under various names and forms, this avian deity brings healing and higher balance to the human microcosm.

The real message of this sign, on the highest level, is that one is finding a balance of polarised energies within one's consciousness and energy-fields. Temperance reconciles opposites and achieves equilibrium, bringing balance and harmony out of disorder. It is more than moderation, composure, discipline and self-restraint, although it includes them. Temperance is really a sign of the Higher Self in action, and an indication that we are being led toward inner wholeness, or challenged to recognise our need for it. On the intellectual level, Temperance may manifest as a movement toward some kind of synthesis and blending, and this could show up in one's writing, speaking or thinking. A personal philosophy is always an amalgam of understandings that one has synthesised from various sources. Emotionally, Temperance can bring reconciliation and harmony along with a release of creative self-expression, because it is more than synthesis, it is synergy. At the physical level, balance and moderation are indicated. In other words, there arises a need to try and live the golden mean. And the special opportunity which Temperance foreshadows is an enhancement of our creativity. One may experience an inspiration for fresh artistic output in one form or another, according to one's gifts.

The Devil

Also known as The Shadow, what humanity has feared and repressed from ancient times, The Devil must be faced and resolved if we are to progress beyond our limitations. Then, his energy is released and transmuted to good. The primal reality that tests and opposes us as we seek the light, what tradition calls the Evil One, is actually a helper in disguise. Our weaknesses and self-deceptions are exposed as we face what we fear and work to change what binds us. In the end, we attain strength and purity by rising to this challenge. We grow in light, understanding and love, and in the fullness of time we outshine all that The Devil represents. *The Ancient Mysteries* card shows you that The Devil has a wry sense of humour and enjoys a good laugh.

If you pick The Devil, it suggests that temptation is facing you. Your shadow is there and you must recognise it. Shadow means those areas in your life where you still experience bondage, obsession, enslavement or addiction, where you are controlled by something that limits you, where you over-indulge or get taken in by the world's materialism. When you experience depression, doubt or negativity, when you feel mired, caught and paralysed, it is a sign that the Shadow needs to be acknowledged and dealt with. On the mental level, in addition to recognition it may help to have a sense of humour, and to be patient. Emotionally, this sign may remind you of how your desires are working against your best interests. Physically, you may have to reorganise an unhealthy or unproductive situation, or reassess something because your understanding of it is false. Are you closing your eyes to something unpleasant that is happening? The opportunity in all this is that you become more aware of your own ignorance and darkness. There is even an outside chance that negative occult forces are at work, but this too is ultimately only a test of your endurance and will, and a potential victory for the soul.

The Tower

A Tower is a construction of the human mind. When ideas are manifested on the physical level, they result in physical forms with boundaries and limits. Anything that has a fixed form traps and holds energy. Eventually, all physical forms must change, and change sometimes means an initial destruction. This ancient tower has endured for untold centuries, but one day an earthquake will topple it. The earthquake's arrival, unforeseen, is approaching. If we understand that the very nature of towers is to confine and delimit energy, we will see that all towers are like sand castles on the beaches of time. The waves of change will wash them away. The destruction of towers releases energy for new forms more appropriate to the changed conditions of the world. In this way, we outgrow the past.

When the sign of The Tower comes to you, there is a catharsis and a purification on the way. The mind will experience it as some kind of de-construction, possibly as an assault on, or challenge to the ego or its cherished beliefs. But the emotions are given the opportunity to embrace change and experience it as freedom. If we do not seize upon the opportunities of the situation, we will suffer from attachment to what is being swept away. Physically, we may have to begin some kind of reconstruction. The special opportunity in this upset is that we can make or experience a fresh beginning and a renewal.

The Star

At the physical level, our five senses tell us that a star is a point of light in the dark infinity of the night sky. But our heart, and ancient tradition, teach that stars are much more than their mere physical form. Stars transmit heavenly light. This light brings hope, peace, inspiration and guidance into our consciousness. The Ancient Mysteries card shows a heavenly star bathing an ancient stone form with light. The light imparts spiritual life and joy.

On the highest spiritual level, The Star stands for Divine Grace. On the mental plane, it brings inspiration and higher vision, while in the emotions it fosters hope and trust. On the physical level, it promotes generosity and may also attract prosperity. The special opportunity that The Star signifies is a blessing of some sort on one or several levels of one's being. It is an altogether auspicious archetype, and usually the idea of guidance is present when it comes to you. You are being helped and guided by a higher force.

The Moon

The Moon is perpetually changing her face and her light. Change relates to appearances, not to fundamental reality. The changing of appearances can be bewildering to the earthly human mind. The Moon presents us with a need to distinguish appearance from reality, to determine what is authentic, and to express authenticity in the terrestrial context of ceaseless flux.

In ancient times, The Moon was considered a divine being worthy of veneration. The role of The Moon in the cosmic scheme is to measure and mediate the effulgence of The Sun so that we can assimilate its radiance and give it expression in life on earth. Goddess Luna, known by many names in different cultures, is one of the profound primal mysteries of existence, intimately connected to our experiences of light and darkness as we struggle to grow. In ancient temples of The Moon, the cycles of waning and waxing light established the rhythms of worship and ritual. Moonlight remains the source of inspiration for bards, prophets and artists alike. They peer into the waters of consciousness and perceive the face of Reality. This they express with power and eloquence.

The Moon can be a contradictory sign. On the one hand it can bring creativity, spiritual vision and intuitive attunement, dreams which reveal divine knowledge and an awakening of our capacities for instinctual, emotional knowing. For artists, the imagination and the visionary capacity is heightened by the moon. On the other hand, the moon can trigger illusions, false pictures, distortions and unrealistic notions. It takes us into the depths of the unconscious and shows us its contents, for better or worse. In this way, it challenges our authenticity. If we have not clarified and purified ourselves from within, we may face confusion, disorientation, bewilderment and a lack of direction. But if we are using our creative energies in the right way, we may find enchantment and inspiration as well as an opening to things mystical and spiritual. At the mental level, we will have to choose how we will interpret the non-rational elements that are before us. The lunar approach would be to listen to our intuitive guidance, tune in to deep feelings and cultivate meditative insight. At the emotional level, the heightening of our creativity and imagination will create a positive flow and a harmonious expression. Physically, we may be able to tap our cellular intelligence for healing or to understand the patterns of our own self-unfoldment. The special possibility that we face is the need to deal with an illusion. This will require us to touch base with our own inner integrity and authenticity.

The Sun

Timeless symbol of the highest Truth, The Sun has been the chosen divine form of religious leaders as distant in time as Akhenaton of Egypt, and as recent as Pachakuti of the Incas. A source of light, power and inspiration for all cultures throughout history, the sun is also a divine being who illumines the minds and opens the hearts of those who seek perfection. The culmination of the spiritual path is enlightenment. Infinite light is established in the seeker's consciousness, making possible the descent of heaven upon earth, first in the human microcosm, then on a wider scale. The Ancient Mysteries card is a bas-relief from ancient Egypt where pharaoh, who incarnates Truth on earth, draws down the blessings of The Sun for the people. His earthly power comes from his inner relation to the divine. He is sometimes called 'The Son of The Sun'.

If you draw his sign, then on the spiritual level a rebirth and an inner renewal are coming your way. At the mental level, you will be touched by the light of Truth, which can bring insight, inner awakening, or some intellectual breakthrough, as well as assurance, confidence and a sense of self-worth. Emotionally, you will have an opportunity to experience fulfilment. Physically, you will sense renewed vital energy and you may feel like celebrating. Often, The Sun creates a situation where we are able to progress by collaboration with someone or something outside ourselves. It indicates that you will be successful in what you undertake and that this is a time for decisive action. Say "yes" to the opportunity before you and let your light shine. Victory and attainment are yours.

Prophecy

The Christian concept of a final judgement day derives from still older

190

prophecies of the Mystery School tradition. The sages and seers of ancient times foresaw the ultimate liberation of humanity from death and darkness. Life on earth will culminate in a triumph over ignorance and limitation, and mankind will achieve victory over death and chaos. The dance of liberation is pictured on this ancient carving found in one of the temples of Southeast Asia. The rainbow colours signify the many masteries of light which have prepared for the moment of prophecy's fulfilment, and the soul's release. The movement is upward, the feeling is one of joy and freedom. Prophecy is fulfilled when the soul's adventure of consciousness culminates in enlightenment.

The fulfilment of ancient prophecy takes place at the Hour of God. There are times when much inner work can be done for little result, and other times when little effort brings much gain. At this time, unimaginable opportunities await those who plunge into the quest for Truth, especially if they have been prepared in previous lives of seeking and dedication. There is a higher reality, a golden Truth-Light which is entering into the world for the first time in spiritual history. The ancient seers and sages foresaw that a door would be opened in the inner world to make this new chapter of spiritual history on earth possible, and their prophecy is being fulfilled even as we study these words. Vergil, in his "Fourth Eclogue" gives us one of the Sibyl's prophecies :

> Time has conceived
> And the great Sequence of the Age starts afresh.
> Justice, the Virgin, comes back to dwell with us ...
> The First-born of the New Age is already on his way
> From high heaven down to earth.
> With him, the Iron Race shall end
> And Golden Man inherit all the world...
> Enter – for the hour is close at hand –
> On your illustrious career, dear child of the gods ...
> See how the whole creation rejoices in the age that is to be!

The early Christians interpreted this as a reference to Jesus. But the Divine has incarnated a number of times in the avatars of history, and in our own lifetimes, once again, the Divine took human form on earth to accomplish this Herculean inner work. The sealed doors have been opened. A new destiny is dawning for the spiritual heroes who choose to go forward.

If you draw the archetype of Prophecy, you have been touched by a higher level of awareness. You are being given a fresh start, renewed hope; something in you is reborn and transformed. There is a call drawing you in a new direction; there is a summons that needs to be answered from within. To answer this call means to achieve reconciliation, to have the experience of being unburdened and to find atonement (at-one-ment) with Truth. On the mental level, this energy will help you achieve purification and transcend ego. On the emotional level, you will be given a chance to taste liberation and release from limitation. Physically, you will discover new goals and directions, and a special possibility of an enlightenment experience is in the air, if you take the care to recognize it. This is one of the highest energies you can access.

The World

Kouros, the heroic Greek youth set out on the journey of initiation and Gaia, the dancing figure of Mother Earth concludes his journey. She stands for wholeness, homecoming and oneness with Source. She also expresses manifestation of the light in its earthly expression. One who passes through the ancient mysteries and achieves initiation is meant for a life of service. His or her wisdom and love are not only an individual victory, they are meant to be shared with others and to be spread throughout the earth atmosphere for the benefit of all. The dancing Greek goddess pictured here celebrates The Fool's homecoming and inspires him to enter the world again in loving service. He left home as her human child and returns as her hero. The Mother's dance celebrates the attainment. She radiates joy and she dispenses blessings to all because her dream has been fulfilled.

When this sign comes up in divination, it means that spiritually one has found one's true place in the world.

The seeker has achieved a self-understanding that is equivalent to coming home. In the mind, this gives a sense of kinship with all existence, a partial or complete realization of the universal consciousness. In the heart, there is great happiness and completeness. In one's physical life, there is harmony and universality.

The special possibility which is indicated by The World is the discovery of one's soul-mission. One intuits who one is, and why one is here on earth. The sign of The World means that the best which can be is coming to you. But you have to have discerning eyes to recognise it, and the wisdom to treasure your new insights. What The World brings may be so wonderful and complete that it may just be beyond the framework of your current understanding, so be alert!

Fool: My own experiences are often brought to mind as you read from this book. The divine ones have been with me, as I see, from the time I left home and began my adventure.

Hermit: And they will continue to be present to you in the future, for you still have much to learn and many adventures lie ahead.

Fool: I want to ask you something.

Hermit: Speak.

Fool: You have been my friend and mentor. Promise that you will be with me throughout the journey, and that your help and wisdom will be there to sustain me.

Hermit: Those who go forward on the path wholeheartedly are united by bonds of unconditional love. I made this promise to you in my heart in the hour of our first meeting. I will share the fruits of my own journey with you as my inner guidance permits. But you, for your part, must always strive to let go of every limitation and to open up your full potential of receptivity. This is how you can make best use of our friendship. Will you make this effort?

Fool: It is what I wanted from the first. But I did not know how to say it.

The Sacred Numbers
A new day had dawned. The Fool was slowly catching up on lost sleep, and The Hermit was a very gracious host. The food was simple, and apart from a few words of polite concern, The Hermit was quite fond of silence.

After answering a rap at the door, The Hermit ushered The Priestess into the room, and it was clear that she and The Fool needed no introduction.

Priestess: Today, I want to take you to the temple of divination. With The Hermit's kind permission, we will use the portal that leads underground. I do not know if it has been explained to you, but this portal connects to many dimensions, controlled of course by your intention. Come, follow me.

With no further ado, she led the way through the portal and down the dim stairs to the crypt. Then, The Fool followed her up the fifteen stairs through walls of stone until they emerged in a large circular chamber, the stone walls of which were lined with niches.

Fool: We have been here before.

Priestess: I come here often. This hidden temple is very dear to me. The Hermit's portal is not the only entrance into this sacred space. As a place of divination, it helps one to see and to understand many things that lie beyond the normal awareness.

Slowly from the shadows on the opposite side of the temple, The Magician emerged into view. He walked toward the centre of the temple and stood facing The Priestess. Together, they motioned to The Fool to approach the altar, which stood at the centre of the chamber. They stood on either side of the central stone altar, gazing into a large crystal sphere which rested upon it. The Fool stood facing them.

Magician: The column of light which comes down onto the crystal from on high is a living beam of power. It brings inspiration, spiritual empowerment and creative energy into any human being who contemplates it. The crystal sphere on this stone altar stands for The World. It seems to be static, but actually it moves, because there is a transmutation happening within its surfaces. The light from above is slowly transforming the stone and releasing its power.

Priestess: On the walls, in positions that correspond to the four points of the compass, you will find the symbolism of fire, water, air and earth. Fire stands for will, vitality, energy, creativity and aspiration. In its essence, fire is the creative spiritual force that transmutes, but in humans its primary manifestation is vitality. A higher kind of vitality develops as the soul comes forward, and there we see creativity and inspiration at their maximum. In human beings, the fiery qualities include boldness, bravery, confidence, courage, daring, energy, exuberance, heroism, inspiration, inventiveness, optimism, originality, passion and wholeheartedness.

Water stands for feeling and desire, the capacity for love, harmony and relatedness, and love of beauty. Attributes of water include affection, benevolence, calm, caring, compassion, concern, empathy, gentleness, dreaminess, healing, intuition, joy, kindness, mercy, mildness, patience, peace, psychic ability, refinement, romance, sensitivity, softness, spirituality, sweetness, sympathy, tolerance and wisdom.

Air represents intellect, understanding and communication. It governs justice, truth and principles of ethics. When ego is strong, it may involve struggle or conflict. But otherwise we normally see attributes like mental clarity, analytical ability, and truthfulness. People who are well endowed with the air element are often analytical, articulate, astute, direct, discerning, forthright, honest, impartial, incisive, knowledgeable, literate, logical, lucid, objective, observant, penetrating, rational, reasonable, unbiased, and witty.

Earth, symbolised by stone, represents the physical manifestation. It includes the world of sensation, the material sphere of earthly concerns, practical affairs of business, physical attractions, security, nature, wealth and prosperity. Earthy people are characteristically trustworthy, tenacious, sturdy, steady, stable, sensible, able, careful, cautious, conscientious, constant, dependable, reliable, realistic, productive, practical, persevering, orderly, loyal, hardworking, generous, factual and efficient.

Magician: We know that matter is spirit solidified. The Mother is One, but as you have seen, Her primal powers are fourfold. Within this temple, an alcove and shrine to each of these four powers of the Mother is placed in the various compass directions, North, South, East and West. The divine light flows down the pillar into the crystal sphere, which is The World. It infuses The World, releasing its hidden perfection. Thence, the light radiates outward in time and space to the four sacred directions. Each alcove is the earthly expression of one of the Mother's four powers.

Fool: I see symbols engraved on the alcoves, symbols for fire, water, air and stone, and they are arranged by number. What does this mean?

Magician: Let us start at the centre. The pillar of light is the essence of the power of One. All numbers express forms of sacred power, but the nature of One is a potential for manifestation. The form that this manifestation takes will depend on the field of energy in which it finds itself, whether earth, water, air or fire. For example, when you place the Power of One in the energy-field of Fire, you have vital potential, capacity to achieve ideals, inspired visions, an impetus to new growth. In Fire, the Power of One can help to develop spiritual and artistic capacities. It is dynamic and energetic, promoting movement and action. But this same energy of One would promote physical expression if it were situated in Earth. It always initiates new beginnings. It is the seed or origin of something that can develop and unfold. The Power of One is always a pioneering force, independent, leading the way forward. It is active, decisive, empowering and unifying.

Priestess: Observe the placement of numbers in the four shrines. They tell the primal story of creation. When you look around at the pictures of the twenty great archetypes on the wall, you will feel their stillness. In the cards you were given, the figures of the Major Arcanum are all seated or standing, except for The World, who dances the dance of creation. She moves, but again she seems not to move. When you place number-energies in the four fields of the primal elements, earth, water, air and fire, you generate a panorama of experience.

Magician: Remember that meaning is contextual. The language of number and form has all the richness of symbolism, and little of the scientific precision which has come to be so valued these days. Symbols are first experienced intuitively and then only much later do we add the words.

At this point, The Magician and The Priestess extended their arms and they each pointed one forefinger at the crystal ball.

Priestess: Out from the power of One comes Two. This is the power of polarity, duality, the relation of opposites. It is the potential for both creation and destruction. The experience of otherness and individuality first comes into existence with the Power of Two.

When we step out of the original unity into duality, we begin a long return journey of return to our original Source. We must be divided from our original wholeness into a bi-polar existence if we are to gather experience. In order to learn, we must taste the fruit of the tree of knowledge. Darkness and light, black and white, high and low, heaven and earth, hard and soft, sun and moon, man and woman - all come into existence because of duality, the feminine principle. Duality takes unity out of the Garden of Eden. It begins the great pilgrimage. The duality of creation becomes a classroom to the embodied souls. Between the polarities of creation, a path comes into existence, a pillar of light, and a high destiny.

In the world of duality, we have choices to make. We have emotional choices in the world of water, intellectual choices in the world of air, practical choices in the world of earth or stone, and energetic choices in the domain of fire. Duality makes possible partnership and co-operation.

But it also creates the possibility of opposition and strife. Because polar opposites have come into existence from the original Power of One, we have the opportunity to learn devotion and service. We learn from the school of life how to harmonize all things so as to diminish the stress and conflict in our lives. The Power of Two is a feminine power. It is not instigating like the Power of One, but it is fruitful.

Fool: I have two eyes with which two see, two hands with which to work, two ears with which to hear and two legs with which to move forward on the path. Two is a womb of sorts, a generator of potential for action.

Magician: Now, point your finger toward the crystal sphere, the symbolic world, as we are doing. You have thereby manifested the power of three. Three is the child of Two. It is a new Sacred Power born from what preceded it.

Three is movement arising from the womb of two. It is dynamism, the dance and the play of opposites, as well as their synthesis. It is the resolution of polarity and creative tension into some form of expression. Three is progeny, new life, a material result, the fruit of partnership, the offspring of a pair. Three manifests the possibilities of two. It is the beginning of community and social life. Three moves the Power of Two beyond its static balance or its conflicting opposites into a hopeful possibility. New opportunities arise when Three is at work.

Fool: We are three. Because we come together, the temple teaching is being expressed.

Priestess: That which emerged in the Power of Three becomes stabilized in the Power of Four. Four is a securely founded sacred number, a well-rooted manifestation. Four turns the energy of Three into a solid and complete expression. The energy of Three settles down and becomes structured in Four; it ceases creative generation and becomes something secure and stable. A building, a solid construction, a foundation for future growth, an anchoring of possibilities in solid form – this is what the sacred Power of Four accomplishes. Four is at rest. It is evenly balanced and poised. Thus, it is powerful.

Four may sometimes be resistant to change, because it holds its form securely. You could say it is conservative, enduring, reliable and permanent. Where stability is important, the Power of Four comes into focus. It represents a limited success, an achievement of something solid, but not the ultimate attainment. In fact, Four may tend to stagnation, other catalysts being absent. Four suggests walls, ninety degree angles, enclosed spaces, possibly confinement.

At this point, The Priestess and The Magician each pointed two fingers into the crystal. The Fool continued to point at the crystal as well. In all, five fingers were aimed into the glowing orb.

Magician: When the Power of Five comes into being, everything changes. By now, the Power of One is receding. The equilibrium of four is de-stabilized. Turbulence, change and transformation arise. It may be resolved harmoniously, or it may be continuously disruptive, in which case conflict and wounding come about. Danger and difficulty arise with five, but also opportunity. Five hungers for freedom. Journeys and dynamic encounters come about because of this. Complacency and pretense are challenged, for Five forces us to go beyond static equilibrium and helps us achieve balanced movement. Change, uncertainty and a need for adaptation are thus the order of the day when the Power of Five is at work. This imbalance brings about fluctuations of fortune, with difficulty and even adversity at times. But in all this change one can gather experience and insight. There is variety, and a chance for progress when Five is present. There is a need for freedom of movement, a call to explore, to communicate and a need to change. Thus the challenges that lead to mastery are heralded by Five.

Fool: Now, I shall point two fingers, two streams of energy, toward the crystal sphere, just as you are both doing. This manifests the Power of Six.

Priestess: Here, we return to harmony and balance. The comfortable structure of Four has been stirred up by Five, and with Six, it has settled down into a new balance. Here we have the dynamic balance of a well developed human being. What was missing in Four and what was unstable in Five is now graciously expressed. Well balanced movement is what we find in Six. It is contentment, satisfaction, beauty and well-being.

Six is not static because it is made from a pair of threes, and threes are quite dynamic. This poised dynamism opens up a possibility for higher states of awareness. The earthbound fixity and duality of the previous even numbers are harmonised and uplifted. Marriages, relationships, and family affairs are favoured by the Power of Six.

Magician: Hold the image of six in your mind, and add to it the pillar of light. This makes seven. Seven widens the openings of Six into something higher than the earth plane. This pillar of light brings stillness into the motion and commotion of Five and mysticism into the harmony of Six. It connects earth to heaven. The energy of Sacred Seven can bring visions and dreams, spiritual knowledge and wisdom. Mystics love this number because its power favours their soul's unfoldment. Seven is the number of faith, the Higher Self and perfection. There are seven higher worlds, seven energy centres or chakras in the human microcosm and seven colours in the rainbow. There are seven notes in the musical scale before eight brings in the octave. But Seven brings to us the deeper state of calm which we need to grow into the depths of mystical experience.

Fool: Now I see that you are each pointing four fingers into the crystal sphere. This brings us to the Power of Eight.

Priestess: Eight is a number of power and weight. It is made of two Fours, and they are looped together in a powerfully balanced interaction. The momentous energy of eight can be used to achieve influence, authority and control, even victory. But it can also be channelled into regeneration and self healing. Those who have the power of eight can work magic. They can access the occult dimensions of experience and manifest prosperity. But unless great wisdom and selflessness accompany the use of the Power of Eight, these striking successes will become a limitation to further progress. So the danger of entrapment is here in Eight as well. Only if we move further are we released from this possible limitation.

Magician: And this leads us to nine. Again, picture the pillar of light, the Power of One coming to the fore. A deep unity is at work here in the sacred energy of Nine. There is a unifying force that integrates the various aspects of a human being into a harmonious expression of soul. Nine brings with it the possibility of a truly spiritual life. It is the number of teachers, because it fosters knowledge and compassion. It is a number of inner guidance, universality and true humanitarianism. It is the most mystical of the numbers, the highest synthesis of all the previous possibilities. Here, we have three Three's. Or, you can think of it as two Fours plus the power of One. Nine takes us to the frontier of our humanity and points beyond. Here, in the highlands of Nine, veils are lifted and Truth is glimpsed. Nine carries us past the limitations of mere social convention because it is full of forward momentum. Nine is expansive. It overflows with loving concern for all creation.

Priestess: With Ten, we break through the mould of everything that has gone before, and enter a new world of possibilities. But the breaking away from the past may be painful. Ten begins a new and more advanced cycle. It is a culmination and a completion of what went before. It represents mastery and wholeness. Ten means greatness and fullness. Ten opens many doors, but if we have not developed love, it can be lonely territory.

The Power of One is here again in Ten to begin a new cycle, but this new cycle will be based on experiences of many kinds gathered from all the previous numbers. Ten calls us to move on into deeper and more complex situations, with more lessons and a requirement for greater mastery. We must die to the old in order to open up what is new. Ten brings with it some hint of a need for sacrifice. But what begins as sacrifice often turns into a kind of liberation when the full possibilities of Ten are revealed.

Fool: These are all the numbers of the alcoves. These powers are expressed spiritually, intellectually, emotionally and physically in my life. I can see how they played their role. But if I had not become a seeker, I would never have learned about this pattern that underlies my experiences on the road. I think the story of my journey is summarised by the movement of One towards Ten. I have known these many energies you speak of. They brought me here to this temple.

Priestess: The powers of number will teach you the art of divination. You will see and understand the pattern of wholeness which has been brought to the fore in you by your journey. You will discover where your experiences lead and why they were necessary as building blocks to something still more wonderful in the future.

Magician: But for this, we must move to the alcoves. For here the numbers begin their work of expressing the four Mother Powers.

With this, The Magician and The Priestess lowered their arms. They reached out simultaneously and lifted up the crystal sphere. Then, they placed it in the hands of The Fool.

They led him to the Alcove of Fire and motioned him to place the sacred crystal sphere, the symbolic world, on the shrine between two fragrant beeswax candles. Suddenly, as if by magic, the candles were lit. His mentors stepped back.

The Fool stood facing the curious symbols and engravings on the wall. He pondered the mystery before him.

The Fire symbol was coloured to resemble a living flame. It contrasted with the cool darkness of the granite rock. The Fool's eyes rested on this symbol and then began to move about and take in the other symbols of the alcove. The candlelight cast faint shadows over the coloured carvings so that they seemed almost alive. Resting between the two candles was a volume bound in crimson and edged in gold. He placed his right hand on the volume and closed his eyes. He could feel warmth and energy flowing into his body, and his mind was flooded with new clarity.

The Book of Fire

The alcove of Fire was set into the curving temple wall and shaped like a stained glass window. In the uppermost portion were images of a King, a Queen, a Knight and a Page. Below this, there were groupings of fire symbols, from one to ten. The candlelight cast a soft glow onto the surface of the stone where the images were carved and painted.

Fool: Can you tell me the meaning of the court figures?

Priestess: A king is destined is to rule, which means to accomplish something for the common good. This general significance becomes coloured by the energy of the four elements. For example the king of fire will show different characteristics than the king of water.

A Queen, in general, represents the deep and inward meaning of her symbol, in contrast to the outwardly directed activity of a king. She is creative and nurturing. She brings a sense of caring, intuitive insight, inspiration and aesthetic refinement to the various concerns that come before her. Reverence, healing, and the power of love come from the Queen rather than the king. She is more intimate and spontaneous than her royal mate, because she brings the personal touch to her various relationships.

The Knight stands for action and responsibility to others. Knights are concerned with individual power, ability, attainment and they have great capacity for energetic action. But ego may be fairly prominent in a knight, and his activities are often coloured by a need to exercise personal will and individual initiative. Energy and ambition characterise the Knight, and while he is courageous, he might also be headstrong.

The Page loves to explore and study, because he still has a lot to learn and he knows it. A Page performs what is asked without question, but bringing messages is what he does much of the time (when he is not studying.) He is not yet fully informed of what transpires on higher levels such as that of the Queen, because he is still only an apprentice, a novice, a trainee. Still, the Page is eager to develop himself, he wants to search for deeper wisdom and to explore higher knowledge. Innocence and good will are his basic attitude, and oftentimes, he finds himself a herald of fresh beginnings.

Magician: Each of us has these four dispositions as part of our own nature. When a King is placed in the sign of Fire, we should understand that all his kingly capacities will be expressed in a way typical of the Fire energy. Such a King will precipitate movement, action and decisive choices. Since a King represents supreme power (and thus success) as well as social responsibility, and since fire is an energy of dynamism, the King of Fire stands for intense but well controlled energy turned to useful projects. Kings are normally strong, but a King of Fire will be very energetic indeed since the wand is a symbolic sceptre. He is very confident of his knowledge and his methods, and he expects to be obeyed. So strongly motivated is the King of Fire that he does not anticipate any resistance, and when he meets it he may seem intolerant. He acts not only on his own behalf, but more importantly for the broader, collective well being. For example, he likes to patronise the arts, music and just causes. He has strong principles and is ready to act on them.

Priestess: The Queen always represents the feminine, receptive qualities of her house. She feels and understands things intuitively, whereas the King acts. While the King of Fire is eager and even impatient, the Queen has a warm appreciation of life and its energy. She is sincere and honest like the King, but her love of life and people has no need for domination. The Queen of Fire has an artistic and creative nature that the king admires and supports. She is imaginative, nurturing and aesthetically inclined. She takes a personal interest in individuals who have some talent to develop, and she likes to have intimate relationships with those whom she admires, while remaining honest and correct in her morals. Perceptive and intuitive, she protects those for whom she cares with great loyalty.

Magician: The Knight translates the qualities of his house into action. If the King has the accomplishment of Fire, and the Queen has the awareness, the Knight is one who puts the dynamism of Fire most vigorously into action. But he is not so experienced and stable as his royal companions. He is apt to be impetuous and unpredictable. He is quite intuitive, like the queen, but he is also more impulsive. Innovation and surprise are part of his free spirit. He is passionate, curious, and adventurous. He has a strong sense of purpose, but needs to focus it so that he is not running off in all directions. His intensity comes from the heart, but his escapades may not be very well planned. He has much confidence and energy, and is an over-achiever.

Priestess: The Page is the simplest representation of the quality of his house, in its innocent, childlike form. He is playful, not calculating. New beginnings and freshness come with the Page, and often his presence indicates that a message or information is incoming. His simple eagerness is that of a faithful, uncalculating friend. Carrying the power of Fire, this Page is glowing with vitality and enthusiasm. His eagerness and adaptability make him a most helpful messenger. He studies healing, the forces of nature, artistic expression and higher visions, and he helps bring all these into expression.

Fool: I feel that I could get to know this royal family, and that if I did so, they would be very interesting friends.

The Priestess and The Magician both smiled and nodded.

Fool: The Fire symbols are arranged by number. Let me speculate now. A single flame stands for the Power of One. And because the symbol is Fire, it means that the Power of One is expressing itself in the energy of Fire.

Priestess: Remember what One means. It is a potential to manifest, capacity to achieve. It is creative and dynamic. It initiates new beginnings, pioneers fresh starts, leads the way.

Magician: Remember what the Fire stands for. It is enthusiasm, inspiration, initiative and creativity. Fire means, action, movement, optimism, and eagerness. Vitality and idealism combine in this sign.

Fool: Putting this together, a single flame could mean that there is an empowerment coming in the form of insight, artistic energy, or even mystical understanding. The situation could become quite dynamic and interesting. A single flame could indicate a new beginning of an enterprising or aesthetic or spiritual sort. The One is a powerful number, so the indication is for something important along these lines, maybe a breakthrough or a new beginning. With the fiery dynamism at work, there might be travel involved, and a lot of intense activity.

Magician: When you know what the symbols and the numbers stand for, you can put them together and they communicate a message. Tell me what you would make of Two Flames.

Fool: Two is duality. It can be a harmonious relationship which nurtures and fosters goodness, or it can be polarised, in which case there would be stress. Often there is a choice to be made when the Power of Two is at work. If we can take the path of devotion and service, we create harmony, but if we become polarised and play the role of an opponent, we nullify the potential for something fruitful to take place. Because Fire energies are involved, all of this can be unfolding in an area of spiritual or creative possibility. There is a spiritual or creative choice to make, and the result can be partnership or strife. Because the energy is fiery and dynamic, we can expect the sparks to fly sometimes, but in a good way if the person is harmonious. In any case, it would be challenging and interesting. Because the Book of Fire is the repository of high energy, the situation could challenge an individual to be true to himself, or herself. This could be the most significant result.

Priestess: You are doing well. You can see that Three Flames means the Power of Three at work. Tell me what this means now. Think how the Power of Three might express itself in the energy of Fire.

Fool: First, I will review the basics. Three means that something new is being born. It is dynamic. It synthesises polarities and tensions into some kind of creative expression. There is a result, a birth, a creation of sorts. Often, with Three, there is a social aspect to all this. Well, if this three energy is playing itself out in the field of Fire, then there is dynamic creativity and lots of energy present. We have a situation which is full of creative possibilities. There will be lots of stir, and motivation to bring about something positive and harmonious. This is even more interesting than the previous situation, because both Fire and threes represent newness. But there is a chance of being too impulsive. I would think that stability, patience and some sober reflection are called for here, to balance all the fiery creative energy.

Magician: Of course if you were trying to understand this symbol, you would consider it in context, because other symbols before or after it in a spread could modify the meaning. If air or water were present, for example, then they could colour your interpretation of Three Flames. All of that being said, you are doing quite well. Now what would you make of Four Flames?

Fool: The Power of Four is that of a solid foundation. It is a secure creation in a state of even balance. It is enduring, reliable, but perhaps too fixed and possibly confining or stagnant. If all this is expressed in the field of fiery spiritual creation, there is a very interesting contrast. Fire is dynamic, creative, and expressive, whereas squares and Fours are the opposite. Fire takes things into dynamic expression, and Fours represent an achievement that is solid, but not as rich as what might come later (for example an eight). What we can say is, something has been attained, some kind of satisfying structure, perhaps from an initial intuitive or artistic inspiration. It is now complete and it is there to be enjoyed. The creation could be something on the vital or spiritual or aesthetic level rather than the material level, but in any case it is solid. The optimistic and freedom-loving energy of Fire breaks through any feelings of confinement and keeps open the possibility of new adventures. But it also makes a solidified fixity of some kind full of creative and spiritual energy with a possibility of something magical taking place inside those same four walls. There is a stir, an excitement and a feeling of freedom here that is playing itself out against a backdrop, or inside a space, that is securely founded.

Priestess: Excellent! When you translate the language of symbols into words, remember that we are dealing with open-ended possibilities, it is not completely fixed. But your own intuition, and the overall context in which the symbols occur, will point to the likely meaning.

Magician: Now let us consider the Power of Five in the energy of Fire. What would you make of that?

Fool: First, I review the meaning of Five. This number brings in change, and the way that this change flows may be disruptive. There could be uncertainty and a need to adapt. There could also be stress and adversity. But it is a time to be alert and skilful in order to avoid mishaps. Challenges often teach us a great deal. Because this is situated in the energy of Fire, we could think of it as creative ferment, or artistic turmoil, or because Fire is a very energetic symbol, we could predict the possibility of a frenetic pace full of surprises and unexpected twists. Here, we have a testing of sorts. It may force one to choose how to react, what course to take, how to resolve imbalances or conflicts, or how to adapt to change. The fiery energy could make for hot tempers, so patience and discernment are called for. And the unexpected quality thickens the plot.

Priestess: We are doing well. We are halfway toward the turning point of ten.

Magician: How will you interpret Fire in a configuration of Six?

Fool: Six is harmony and balance. It is like a beautiful home where you find contentment, beauty and satisfaction. Fire would make this kind of setting a little more creative, interesting and inspiring. Fire would bring in some energy and some dynamism. So it is a picture of a dynamic energy in a harmonious setting. It is a perfect picture of success and a reaping of just rewards. With the energy of Six, everything is kept in healthy balance, so the rewards which one experiences at this time are less likely to make us arrogant than otherwise. It feels good to win through to a place of achievement, and possibly even some well-deserved recognition. That is what I feel about Six Flames.

Priestess: When you express what you feel and share what you see, you grow. Divination is an opportunity to hear and express your insights. When we see life intuitively, the whole world is a message about possibilities, and if we read those possibilities in the right way, we move more quickly to a place such as you described.

Magician: Seven takes us onward and upward in our journey. What do you feel about Seven Flames?

Fool: Seven is a mystical energy. It opens to higher knowledge and a sense of heavenly perfection. The seer needs inner stillness and focus to capture this vision, but Flames are a sign of movement, energy and creative ferment. The intuitive and spiritual and artistic aspect of Fire works well with the energy of seven. There is a possibility of a breakthrough in understanding and insight here. But with Fire, there is always a need for taking the initiative. If one takes the initiative and rises to the challenge then some victory is possible in the areas ruled by Fire. In this situation, I would like to be a knight or a queen because the right choices and actions could have a very beautiful result. I would use their insight and initiative to make the best of this opportunity.

Magician: You know, some artists have painted these possibilities into specific pictures, which tends to limit their meaning. The creative combining of number and symbol is a more open-ended way to handle divination than explaining the meaning of a single picture on a Tarot Card.

Priestess: All the paintings of the Minor Arcana do tend to limit the possibilities in the situation. They represent one of several possible interpretations. Knowing the grammar and vocabulary of number and the powers of the four elements helps you to see all the possibilities.

Fool: I suppose that the person to whom the symbolism applies will have a feeling for the information which he or she hears. When they hear Eight Flames being described, they will be able to feel which aspects apply to their own situation.

Priestess: We have said that the Power of Eight carries force and authority. With this power, you can control various situations and achieve a victory. But always it is the wisdom of your choices that creates the results. With great power, as they say, comes much responsibility.

Magician: If you see Eight Flames together, you would see something quite magical in its possibilities. I am a magician. I have studied the occult laws and I know how prosperity is manifested. A person who receives the energy of Eight Flames would be fortunate indeed. Eight empowers a person and indicates that some special opportunity has arrived, and that there will be much benefit. Because Fire has to do with dynamic, intuitive and creative possibilities, the benefit could be in those areas. But Eight often brings prosperity on the physical plane, and it could be that the dynamic movement of Fire has stirred up a chance for material enrichment. When an auspicious moment such as this comes, it is time to act, and Fire is ideal for situations requiring action. So the message here is auspicious. You can see a favourable culmination of some kind coming your way if you have this influence at work in your life. Fire is swift and soaring, but Eight is heavy. This can be something quite powerful.

Priestess: Nine Flames has richness and complexity about it. Nine is a mature number with much experience under its belt. Nine has travelled far and gathered much experience, growing wise in many ways. Nine has been a student of life and often becomes a teacher of others. Nine has synthesised the rich experiences of the past and has thereby developed compassion and understanding and sympathy for human suffering. When Nine is placed in the sign of Fire, its complex possibilities find themselves in a swirl of dynamic movement, creativity, and spiritual insight that demand much initiative. Some artists have painted this as a difficult or challenging situation. I see it otherwise. The maturity of Nine confers the wisdom to act decisively and wisely. It could be that the situation requires an individual to do just this. But we can see here a bringing forward of many talents and lessons and accumulated experience and a need to apply all this wisdom creatively, maturely and compassionately in order to accomplish something important. The energy of Fire always confers strength and mental alertness. Situations which involve Fire usually afford opportunities to apply such energy. This should be seen as opportunity rather than adversity, but cowards will always fear challenges. Nine has travelled far, but if the lessons of life have been well assimilated, there will now be a chance for wise choices and actions - indeed Nine Flames may call for just this.

Fool: Ten is a number of culmination and completion and a beginning of new cycles. The Fire energy sometimes acts without too much forethought. It loves to take on fresh challenges. Flames are energetic entities who use intuition over intellect in their choices. Ten completes a cycle, and should represent a victory. Everything that went before is gathered up and summarised. A new beginning is at hand. In the field of Fire, this could be a reaping of karma, good or bad, but likely there is a dynamic, inspirational or artistic overtone to it. Flames stir up excitement as they invite challenge. The Ten of Flames will not be a comfortable place of rest, but a challenge to complete an earlier phase of action, and make the best of its results, good or bad, as they accrue.

Magician: There is much more that we could see and say about the meanings recorded in this alcove. But here we are showing you a method and an approach. This approach opens all the possibilities in any situation for those who know the meaning of the symbol and the meaning of the number. It pays to learn well the four symbols and the ten numbers, for they afford you a way of contemplating the messages of creation. Contemplation brings its own rich rewards. It leads to wisdom and right action. You have done well. The numbers tell a story and the Fire energy sets the parameters of the plot. Earth, air and water tell different stories when they combine with the same numbers, as we are about to see.

The Book of Water

The Priestess carefully lifted the crystal ball and moved it to the alcove of Cups. She placed it there between two candles which burst into flame and began to cast their light over the carved and coloured surfaces of the stone tablet which was behind. At the top of the tablet could be seen the figures of a king and a queen. Below were the images of a knight and a page. Then there were a series of droplets of water carved into the granite in groupings of one through ten, and painted various shades of mottled blue. Resting in the alcove behind the crystal sphere was a large book bound in dark blue leather.

Priestess: Water is the precious liquid of spirit and life. It is holy and pure. Let your heart become a cup. Feel that it is full of the purest water. Make your heart into a sacred chalice holding the water of spirit. Then tell me what you feel.

Fool: I feel this place to be sacred ground. The images seem to come to life in the glow of the candlelight. I wish to understand the hidden teaching here. These figures before me have a story to tell which I am eager to understand.

Magician: Before the words come, the feeling must be there. Water signifies a flow of deep feeling. In the House of Water, the power of love holds sway. It brings about harmony, beauty, and a deep desire for inner fulfilment. This sign unites those who care about relationship, and they build bonds of friendship through the days of their lives. The deep water of feeling nurtures creativity and spirituality in the heart. For those who are receptive, the living waters from a deep well of spirit bring mystical vision, devotion and inner calm. But just as water flows, emotions fluctuate, and the currents of lower desire sometimes become turbid. If you seek divine wisdom, or visions of supernal beauty and if you would hear the harmonious music of the spiritual heart, this House of Water is a place where you will be at home. The pull of Eros is not to be denied. Through smiles and tears, with passion and devotion, in friendship, in marriage and in mystical union the love god calls. Open your heart to the Muse of Water and then speak what she whispers.

212

Fool: In the single droplet of Water I see and feel all that you have just expressed. The Power of One is there, a unity, in a form that expresses the depths of the primal waters and their call to the heart. Such a symbol as this single drop of Water tells me to remember my feelings and to nurture my heart's intimacy with all my love. My heart has its own way of knowing, this I have come to understand. If I pay attention to what I find loveable, and if I keep open my sympathies and my intuition, I will be able to accept some precious gift and new opportunity into my being. Love is knocking on my heart's door. Can I open my heart like the cup, and hold it open to this possibility? The Power of One in the House of Water urges me to hear the call that comes from spirit, the power of beauty and harmony to enrich my life, the joys of love that can grant me peace and sanctuary. When the energy of one is working in water, something good is approaching.

Priestess: Well done! The power of One in the house of Water expresses this profound spiritual potential for renewal and inspiration. It tells us to be alert and make the most of the coming possibility. Now let us consider Two in Water. This is a movement from the potential of One towards its actualising.

The image of Two Drops of Water describes a situation that allows heartfelt sharing and soulful communion to grow. Here we can give and receive love and affection; in fact there may be a sense of soul-connection and deep bonding with another human being. New levels of trust and intimacy can be achieved under this sign. This is a very harmonious omen that favours right relationship. If a relationship has been strained, it can now be mended; if there has been conflict, a truce can be achieved. One may experience a renewed attraction within a current relationship, or one may be drawn into a new partnership.

Magician: Three in Water gives us a very cheerful and happy message. It is a joyful celebration which is more social and possibly more dynamic than Two in Water. The love dimension may be widened into a collective expression, possibly a festive community. Dynamic interactions are all positive under this sign. With Three, the opportunity and potential of relationship is progressing.

Fool: I remember that the Power of Four stands for a certain consolidation. What has been developing in two and three now reaches a plateau.

Priestess: Yes, with Four the dynamism has settled down and there is time for reflection, evaluation, introspection. Such a lull and resting period may seem static, and we risk becoming apathetic, but the opportunity presented by Four in Water is to tap into our intuitive wisdom and finding our inner directions. This is an experience of "time out", a chance for withdrawal. There may be some dissatisfaction or uncertainty that needs to be resolved, but it is not yet the time to decide or act. Four in Water favours looking within to discover our intentions, assessing where we stand and finding guidance from our higher self.

Magician: When we place the Power of Five in the Water expression, the energy changes yet again. The situation is quite fluid, and transformative, and it brings the underlying divisions of self to the surface where they can be seen and resolved. The tendency to stagnate and to seek security in something imperfect is challenged. Five in Water motivates us to rise to some occasion of challenge and to display the required mastery. Inner turmoil will be present, but the need to deny or suppress it can be transcended. Foundations (symbolised by Four) are shaken but they should not be rebuilt in the old, limited pattern. New elements are present that do not allow the old forms to contain them. All this is necessary for growth because every construction must be outgrown if we are to progress. If we allow lesser aspects of self to fall away, we can be reborn with a more integrated wholeness.

Five demands freedom, but cups require relationship. There could be a tension for freedom within relationship, and it might take the form of a parting of ways.

Five teaches us not to defend our limitations, but to release them, not to uphold boundaries that have outlived their purpose, but to allow them to crumble. In short, we learn not to deny our full capacity. In order to overcome a boundary, you must meet a resistance and learn a new kind of mastery. Situations involving the Power of Five can be overly active, placing the onus on us to find the calm centre and look within. Five carries an empowerment within a challenge. When this comes to us in the House of Water, we may have to forego comfort and the consolations of society. There may be a lack of good communication, along with a need to find guidance from within. The ordinary social conventions can no longer slake our inner hunger, and we may have to abandon some part of our past. The sense of loss can be very strong at this time. The call is therefore to go deeper, possibly to embrace our isolation as a needed step toward the attainment of greater inner freedom. Difficulty and unfulfilled longing make us more sincere if we respond to their challenge. Sometimes they teach us how to change more swiftly and surely than our so-called successes.

Fool: The sign of Five Drops of Water speaks of difficulty and testing. You have explained it well.

Priestess: With Six we come again into the light. There are positive and creative moments of sharing, and a healing of wounds. Here, there is less struggle. Love is revitalized. Nature and beauty and harmony speak to us once more to remind us of how good life can be. The deep memories of the soul begin to rise from within us, and a feeling of oneness with others and with the world begins to shine through. We have a chance to feel our childlike nature. Its innocence and freshness are sensed within the heart. We are invited to give expression to that child of the heart in our relationships with others.

Magician: Seven in Water is a mystical sign. There is a possibility here of visionary experiences of other worlds, or dreams of a spiritual nature. The inspiration of the Muse is at work and new horizons of creative expression open up. It is important to be attuned to a higher level of consciousness when the opportunity of Seven in Water comes your way, or the energy will be expressed as mere wishful thinking or delusion. Some dreamers who lack spirituality may get lost in useless fantasy, but others get glimpses of higher truths. There may be such a wealth of imaginative imagery coming to the mind that we need to look for higher guidance from within to make the right choices. The Seven Drops of Water symbol indicates to us that the time has come to work with our soul, which means to accept any tests that come our way in the right spirit and then move forward to honour our ideals. If we can sift delusion from the true inner vision, and live what we believe, the highest possibilities of this sign can be realised.

Fool: I can see that every opportunity brings with it some test.

Priestess: And the nature of the test is a clue to the kind of blessing that lies beyond it. Eight in Water has just this blend of testing and opportunity. It tells us that we must leave the past behind and go on a journey into unexplored regions. We must let go of disappointment, give up comfort and relinquish security in order to reach a new understanding. All of this means dying to self in some way. It can help to be away from the world and to have a simplified life for a while in order to mature. Every attachment that we release makes our journey that much easier. Ask yourself : 'What is it that I need to leave behind or avoid?' 'What are my attachments to the past, and how can I be free?' 'Am I willing to make a move and a change to step beyond the past?'

Magician: Nine in Water tests us in the opposite way. Being given an abundance of all good things, are we thereby compromised? Nine is fullness, and cups exist to be filled. But when the cup is full to running over, the question arises, 'What does this mean to me?' If my happiness depends on anything outside myself, it can be lost. When we experience fulfilment, contentment, abundance of good things, we may become complacent or smug. The temptation to rest on our laurels is greatest at this point. The loving attention of others can be so rewarding that it pulls us away from our inner path to enlightenment. Emotional love can be binding, however nourishing it may seem. If the excess of our good fortune makes us passive, it will be all the harder to muster the needed willpower and choose what liberates us, in a spiritual sense. Comfort and success can be as binding as want and adversity. This is the lesson of success, the lesson of Nine in Water.

Fool: Ten is the fullness of everything that was a potential in One. Ten in Water tells me that all the good things symbolised by Water have been achieved. There is companionship, community, a collective ideal, a sharing of love and warmth and abundance. Ten in Water tells us that our desires are at the point of being realised. Here, we feel that we have lived up to our ideals, we have passed the test of Nine. Our fullness is spiritual as well as emotional. This is a time for gratitude and rejoicing.

Priestess: In this journey through the Book of Water, the story being told is your own. Every situation that can be conveyed by these symbols will be lived out, tasted and experienced by your seeking soul as you follow your spiritual quest. Tell me then, when you identify with the King of Water, who are you?

Fool: I am a mature and caring adult. A king is active, and his duties require him to be focused outwardly. He is wise and caring, he knows the world and its ways. He guides others with loving concern. He cares about all his people and he always acts compassionately. The King of Water is calm and stable. He can balance the needs of many people and help them achieve a collective goal that is in everyone's best interest. His good will is expressed by active service. His great depth and range of understanding make him tolerant and accepting of human foibles. On the spiritual level, fatherly love is what the king of water offers. Affection with a requirement for responsibility is what you get on the mental level. Emotionally, there is passion and generosity, and physically, there is balance. The King of Water always sets a good example. This is the special opportunity or significant development that may come your way when he registers his presence.

But the Queen of Water ... she is more inwardly focused. She is sweet, loving and sensitive. She is always kind and gentle. She soothes and calms those around her. She follows her inner feelings and acts with compassion. She trusts her intuition and lets her heart lead the way. Her love embraces all. She is very spiritual and helps make the world a holy place. For her, all life is sacred, and she relates to all beings as if she saw and valued the soul in them. She is very loveable, and always gracious. Nobility of spirit can be seen in the Queen of Water, and through her it expresses itself to perfection in right relations with everyone she meets. Spiritually, she brings you nurturing, either from within yourself of from someone you meet. Psychic insight can come to you at the mental level, while emotionally your feelings are touched, and there is an opening to love distinctly possible, especially motherly love. There may be sensual and seductive energies at work on the physical level. The special opportunity that may come to you from this queen is a creative or romantic experience, but if you are sincerely aspiring, it can take the form of spiritual experience.

Magician: The Knight of Water, translates the energy of Water into dynamic action. He has the good qualities of cups, but he may take them to an extreme. His love is less mature than The Queen's. He is not merely romantic, he also may be overly emotional, and lacking in self-restraint. He is imaginative, but he can be unrealistically fanciful. He is sensitive, but sometimes he may also be temperamental. He responds to life deeply, but he must be careful to avoid brooding or being petulant and sulky. Being a refined soul, The Knight must be aware not to take refinement to excess and emphasise style over substance. Being introspective, he risks introversion unless he learns the true balance. He seeks deeper understanding.   He truly does value wisdom. However, he must be able to relax and make others feel that they are valued for themselves, as The Queen does. But perhaps this is not his gift. The Knight of Water is gifted with a beautiful imagination and deep emotion. But his melodramatic moods must be controlled. He is apt to become too temperamental unless he achieves balance and self-understanding. This is the challenge that goes with his many fine qualities. On the spiritual level he will demonstrate devotion, which is love in action.   Mentally, there will be nobility and idealism. Emotionally there may be sacrifice, or dynamic change of some kind, with moodiness a distinct possibility.   Physically, there may be an experience of changeability, and the significant development that may crop up is an adventure, likely an emotional one.

Priestess: The Page, on the other hand, is less of an extremist. He is emotional, intuitive, intimate and loving, but not to an extreme. He is learning the basics of being a good servant, but he has not yet been tested. He has innate ability but has not yet developed inner power, so he cannot go to extremes. He brings the message that there is an opportunity for love. He brings you a chance to experience romance, beauty and poetry in life. The Page of Water is young at heart, and he is innately spiritual because he always approaches life through his heart. He knows he has much to learn, but because he is sincere he brings a good feeling to every situation and helps those around him to feel lighter. This Page is a person of inner purity in terms of spiritual energies. Mentally there is an explorative urge, and a tendency to be reflective. Emotionally, he is sensitive and somewhat sentimental. He is still inexperienced, and this becomes evident as events play out at the physical level. The special development that this Page may bring is an exploration or a project which is emotional in nature.

Fool: In the Book of Water, many deep realities of the heart and soul are expressed. My story, your story, the story of the queen and the knight, the numbers of my growth in relationship, they are all here. If I can master this understanding, I know that my journey can bring me fulfilment.

The Book of Air

When The Fool, The Priestess and The Magician had moved the crystal sphere into the alcove of Air, and the lit candles illumined the symbols on the wall, making them visible, a moment of silence ensued. The Priestess was first to speak.

Priestess: The Supreme Mother has assumed four aspects to release divinity from its long sleep in matter. We have seen Her in the Book of Fire as a forceful dynamism, swift and intuitive, fiery, creative and impetuous, full of spiritual power. We have seen Her in the Book of Water as the beauty and harmony of love, the blissful nectar of heartfelt accord. In the Book of Air, She is sometimes misunderstood. In essence this house expresses Her wisdom aspect. Her majesty, Her wideness, Her impartial justice open the doors of knowledge within the human mind and raise humanity's understanding to full clarity. In reality, The Mother of Air has a heart of endless and universal compassion. Her punishments are blessings in disguise, Her decrees are immutably in harmony with Truth. If mankind experiences Her presence and action most often in stress and conflict, it is because human thinking has not yet embraced wisdom. In each and every case, suffering comes to a pilgrim soul because it has departed from the path of wisdom. The difficulties experienced in the Book of Air can be attributed to this. When we cease moving toward the light, we withdraw our assent from the gentle guidance of wisdom, and suffering becomes the teacher. Who has caused this to happen? Our own choice.

Magician: In every case where adversity or suffering confront us, when limitation and conflict rear their heads, we can safely say that it is caused by a departure from the way of wisdom. The sword of intellect cuts and divides. In European Tarot traditions it is used as a symbol for Air, and for a good reason, because the human mind in its undeveloped form is a force of division and separation. Mind sees differences. In fact it usually emphasises and augments them. But the open heart feels the oneness which lies beneath the appearances of multiplicity. Mind separates the knower from the knowable and stresses the differences between things. It often entertains doubt, scepticism and cynicism. These tendencies of the immature intellect create bondage. When the power of number enters the mind of limitation, we find suffering, and in the Book of Air there are quite a few instances of this.

Fool: In divination, we always come from the essential truth of the Divine Mother into the human experience of how things work out in time and space, in our human ignorance. Air represent the mind and its works, communication, writing, logic, information, intellectual professions, philosophy, government and rational sciences. The Power of One is about beginnings, unity, solitude, origins, the primal aspect of things, and creative force. The Power of One in the Book of Air will mean, if I understand it rightly, a beginning of some mental matter. A singleness in air indicates some new concept or proposal coming into focus, some intellectual accomplishment or opportunity or achievement. In this atmosphere, there will be clarity of thought. The Book of Air resting in this alcove is coloured bright yellow, and this is the hue of the clear intellect. The power of one is analytical and rational when it is in the energy of Air, with quite a bit of self-confidence and internal power. There is good communication and excellent capacity for administration. Also, skilful teaching or adept learning can be indicated by this sign.

Priestess: The Power of Two involves duality, frequently a need to choose between alternatives. It indicates polarities, and a choice between co-operation and opposition, partnership or conflict. Two in Air takes us into something "other", something different and beyond our small selves at the mental level. It places before us alternatives, and a need for action or relationship in the face of dual possibilities. This is the beginning of creativity. We must choose or decide something. We are called upon to identify with and understand the other side of a question, or a different point of view. We are confronted with "otherness". There may be discussion, taking of positions, reviews of information, critiques of what is valid or invalid, negotiation, compromise or diplomacy. This is the mind's way to achieve understanding. In the end, we will very likely establish some agreement, truce or contract which makes us feel secure, but it may not be free of conflict.

Magician: The Power of Three is about expression. There is some new creation or synthesis or some fruition of what has been started in the position of Two. Three is the beginning of expansion. It involves production, or the creation of primary conditions that allow production. Three in Air brings us to the fruition of what was started in Two, and is an extension of some mental engagement with what is outside us. With Three in Air, we move toward a result which can later become a foundation, consolidated into Four. Under the sign of Three in Air, there is an increase of mental clarity, and a movement toward resolution of issues which have previously been raised by One and Two. Here we have a possibility to connect with wisdom, but to do this we must link mind and heart together. It is the strength of a loving heart which can alone bring our active mind to its full potential. The three elements called forth by three in air are, heart, mind and the expression of our intent by harmonious action. We can do this in different ways, which might include focusing on our ambitions, becoming more efficiently organised, articulating our needs more clearly, writing, meeting more people, garnering publicity, renewing our commitment, or acting decisively to communicate what is necessary. The action of this sign is, of course, mainly mental.

Fool: I know that The Power of Four gives rise to stability. It generates a reliable foundation. It centers things and settles them into a durable pattern. Order and solidarity are generated by Four. Four in Air would give composure to the mind and it would tend to centre and harmonise a person's thoughts.   This position would represent a plateau of mental development, a situation of stability and reliability. There is a mental foundation, possibly with more introspection than extraversion as was previously the case in Three. The busyness of the outwardly-directed mind would be moderated by the Power of Four. This refreshing break from its previous activity would help stabilise the thinking processes into some secure structure. Intellectual projects are completed and achievements are concluded when this sign is at work. Fundamental understandings are attained. The good qualities of the mind get emphasised, including a feeling of solid self-worth, well developed powers of rationality, practicality, objectivity, order, discipline, lawfulness and increased self-control. Four is a patient sign, but less dynamic than Three, and sometimes it is in danger of becoming static.

Magician: Five is always a power of uncertainty, and it places before us multiple choices. Freedom of action is required by the Power of Five. This can be a time of testing and there may be an element of inner struggle or outer conflict that requires us to make a decision. Five raises the question of whether or not we need to change directions. When we see Five in Air, the situation is indeterminate. We have freedom to choose among many alternatives, and we likely feel a need to move forward while preserving what has been achieved with Four. Five is a place of movement, but it is a limited movement that may be repetitive and circumscribed. In Five of Air, an individual may be reviewing, evaluating, prioritising and investigating his or her options. The mind has a fairly steady flow of communication and it uses new information for its detailed planning. Nothing drastically new is on the horizon under this sign but the pre-existing areas of involvement are being rounded out, with possibly some elements of worry or concern. There may be a degree of social or family connection that affects the thinking.

Priestess: The Power of Six in its own field stands for duty, service, external expression of togetherness and an involvement of the feelings in good relationships. Sixes can bring balance, co-ordination and equilibrium into our lives, being a combination of two Three's. They suggest wholeness, wholesomeness, and a degree of discipline adequate for the accomplishment of a goal. In the Book of Air, the Power of Six puts the emotions to work in the mental Plane. The individual now has an opportunity to learn to make duties and obligations more pleasant by doing them with care. There is an opening to go beyond exclusive preoccupation with one's own ego. Six in Air makes it easier for us to be concerned about the welfare of others. One includes others' needs in one's thinking, and one accepts responsibility for the collective good. The mind may be engaged in worthwhile causes which advance the well-being of those for whom we feel responsible. The heart is supporting the mind and its plans, and one feels motivated to be of service.

Fool: Seven is usually a new beginning and a new direction. It can involve an initiation, along with a test or obstacle that needs to be surmounted. Seven energises us with new ideas and insights as it stimulates us to achieve victory. It is quite a dynamic energy that promotes development, transformation and movement to higher levels of awareness. Seven in Air begins to reach out toward the mystical realities that lie beyond the five senses. It helps us to connect our work and duties and our service to a spiritual ideal of some kind. One sees, evaluates and chooses based on a growing faith in the divine. All the areas of mental activity may be present, for example education, research, calculation, measurement, comparison, moving information, publishing and writing, and the collecting and storing of information such as we find in computers and libraries. But this all takes place inside a new vision of a higher set of possibilities which are spiritual in nature. Old projects may be neglected under the influence of new ideals and there is a need to clearly define the new higher purpose. One needs to be realistic about how the new ideas can be put into action, and to avoid any temptation to be devious or deceptive.

Magician: The Power of Eight is a choice about the kind of order we wish to establish in our lives. We can choose to be compassionate and selfless. We can choose balance and harmony. Or, we can choose something less than that. In the Book of Air, the mind reaches a point of pressure where the limitations of ego are increasingly intolerable. One must become universal, or be bound and limited by the narrowness of the egocentric viewpoint. The requirements of self-giving compassion and universal love will not allow us to be self-centred any more. The mind must rationalise the process of breaking free of its self-imposed limits. It must find a way to step beyond the control of the ego. The heart challenges the mind to rise above itself, and the mind must find convincing justifications to take this step. Failing this, progress comes to an end.

Priestess: The Power of Nine brings healing, forgiveness, idealism and good will. Nine is a time to realise that true wealth is within us, within the quality of love we hold in our heart and extend in our relationships. If we have learned to love, then we pass this phase and we go forward. Nine in Air helps to pull us into the higher mind. One must become the servant of one's higher knowledge, or fall back into immaturity. Stress in this sign or any other preceding it indicates the resistance of our ego. Progress is no longer understood to be the same thing as success in the outer world. The higher mind sees that true progress must now be measured by a spiritual standard. Either we live up to our highest ideals or we can expect to encounter a disappointment.

Fool: Ten stands for completion, accomplishment, perfection. Ten in Air means that a cycle of mental learning is successfully brought to a close. The old self is outgrown, the little ego has passed away and a greater self has come to the fore. The lower levels of our mind can no longer dictate the shape of our life. Mind has now been linked to intuition, the guiding whisper of spirit. Freedom now means alignment with spiritual truth, because all lesser agendas have been seen for what they are, from the soul's perspective - incomplete and unsatisfying.

Magician: When the presence and the guidance of the soul has been felt, the leadership of the mind is experienced in just this way, as being incomplete and unsatisfying. Until the soul comes forward, the mind takes the leadership in a human being's life. But when we have begun to awaken the soul and to feel its guidance, the mind is required to listen and to follow this leadership. If the mind willingly becomes docile to this higher inspiration, it can still play a very useful role helping to organise the practical details of life. This is its true sphere of action.

Priestess: A Page is at the beginning of higher awareness. He is seeking additional experience and training, and integrating what he learns into his life. He is young at heart, open to learn new things, dedicated to service and willing to be a good messenger. In the Book of Air, The Page shows active intelligence looking to understand as much as he can. He is impressionable, investigative, curious and vigilant. He is intent to acquire knowledge, and very determined in his searching. He needs to develop his mind and to be aware that he is still rather naïve and innocent. His presence indicates that new intellectual opportunities and situations are at hand. He indicates that one can learn from mental interaction. The Page is always young in spirit, and he infuses the mind with enthusiasm and freshness.

Magician: The Knight of Air is strong and skillful. He fights for truth and cuts through obscurity. He has the courage to act on his convictions, but he often rushes into the fray before he asks all the right questions. He is impulsive, bold and clever, and he never avoids a confrontation. He has the willpower needed to create and defend good ideas. The best qualities that he brings to his intellectual chivalry are quickness of understanding and great daring. The Knight of Air honours all things righteous, but he can be domineering. He bases his intentions on reason, but he is always looking for new causes to defend, and so his changeability means that he does not focus on one theme for very long. Remember, a Knight may represent one aspect of our own being, or it may stand for an outside person who will be important to us in some way.

Priestess: The Queen of Air is clear-minded, a perfectionist who is protective, philosophical and alert. She plans and directs any given undertaking with great skill, because she is a talented leader. She does not hesitate to fight for a good cause, being dedicated to her beliefs and ideals. Her mind is active as a tool for implementing what she feels is right. She cares about justice, and her intellect concerns itself with high-minded principles and how to apply them. She keeps well informed and is a good communicator. She harnesses her mental will to achieve its maximum potential and she focuses the mind on what is needed for progress. We may meet such a person or we may see that this Queen reminds us of our own mature logical outlook, our capacity for hard work, candour and decisive but compassionate action. The Queen of Air handles emotional issues with logic and courage. She has found a good balance of mind and heart.

Magician: The King of Air defends truth with an assertive intellect. He is philosophical, alert and forthright, a good leader and tactician. He plans his projects thoroughly and keeps himself well informed. He is courageous and idealistic, much like Plato's philosopher-king. By means of disciplined mental effort, he has acquired power and authority. Naturally, he has patriarchal values, but his determination to do what is right is always principled, and based on the collective good, not his own whims or personal advantage.

Fool: A King will project his power outward in action, but the Queen plays a more discreet role, sometimes behind the scenes. The King, Queen, Knight and Page of Air are not abstract philosophical thinkers so much as rational planners who intend to put their ideas into practice.

Priestess: When mind is an instrument of wisdom, it is an effective tool. But when it wants to follow its own limited light, we find ego coming to the fore and conflict is inevitable. The European tradition is to use swords as symbols for air. Indeed, the European mind has spawned endless conflict and many wars, and conflict figures prominently in many Tarot decks in this tradition. But air does not have to be a sign of conflict. It is the presence of ego which generates strife. How quickly we can illumine the mind and link it to the guidance of the soul depends on our aspiration. In all these alcoves, we learn lessons about transcendence. This is a journey of discovery, and the discovery is a revelation of our own highest potential.

The Book of Earth

The Fool, The Priestess and The Magician stood in front of the alcove of Earth. The crystal sphere rested between a pair of lit candles, and behind it was a large volume bound in emerald green. The great slab of granite behind this volume was carved with figurative stones and court figures whose colors had faded with the passage of time. The images of stones protruded from the surface like knobs, and they were arranged by number in groups of two, three, four and so on. They were not coloured, but retained the appearance of the natural stone, with a noticeable surface texture.

Magician: If we contemplate these images in the same way that we have considered flames, water droplets and openings of air, we will complete our understanding of how the numbers work in the various fields of energy.

Priestess: But symbols always have an element of mystery and presence and power that cannot be fully explained in words.

Fool: This is what gives the temple its feeling. When I am here, I am able to connect with the symbols more strongly. I can identify better with the court figures and their powers, I can sense their characters and capacities more clearly. The stillness and the atmosphere of peace in this temples makes me more aware of just how sacred divination should be, when it is rightly practised.

Magician: The power of a symbol is more than the idea it creates in your mind. Symbols connect our earthy understanding to spiritual realities that lie beyond the mind's grasp. We can feel the beauty and the power of a symbol creatively, especially if we are poetic or musical. When a symbol speaks to you, if you listen to its whisper intuitively, then the words you choose to express your feeling will carry some of the primal energy of your inner experience. This gift is what makes a bard.

Priestess: Divination means seeing the divine.   In divination we get a glimpse of the pattern which the goddess is weaving into our lives.

Fool: I know that the four houses represent the four aspects of the goddess. But tell me now about the Book of Earth.

Magician: A stone is part of the material body of Mother Earth. A carved stone may bear the imprint and energy of some vision from a higher world. Indeed, the Egyptians used to call down spirit presences to take up residence in their stone carvings by intoning their names. The Hermit studied in this tradition, and the inner temple we have visited carries these energies.

Priestess: In the House of Earth, the Great Mother shows Her power to bring about perfection and order by means of detailed work. Here She comes closest to Nature and to physical matter, and She presides over the detailed and exacting processes by which we organise the physical world.

If Fire expresses the Mother's spiritual dynamism and her creative wisdom, if Water stand for the fullness of the heart's harmony, love and beauty, and if Air stands for the Mother's powerful impetus to move us forward by Her mental will, then Earth, symbolised by Stones, grounds the Mother's vision in the labour of giving birth.

In the Book of Earth, one becomes a worker with precise knowledge, patience, a skilful hand and a discerning judgement. In the European tradition, sometimes, the symbol of a coin is used, as if to suggest that this house governs business, investment and finance. Wealth accrues when we learn from the Earth Mother, but the true wealth is the capacity for perfect work. The worker is himself the product of the Mother's inner craftsmanship. The Mother works inwardly to perfect the worker. It is the perfecting of the soul in its capacity to work with matter that concerns the Mother of Earth. Her action is tireless, laborious and minute, persistent, gradual and flawless. In the House of Earth, the soul becomes a channel for the Mother's perfectionism in detailed labours of all kinds.

Fool: I know that a single Stone will stand for the essence of the symbol in its purest form. The Power of One initiates beginnings. A single Stone would suggest a material beginning, or some king of physical blessing, or physical accomplishment or skill. The Power of One in the physical realm could mean good health or good fortune, or it could indicate some potential for physical expression of excellence. It could mean the beginning of something which will result in material prosperity.

Priestess: Yes, One is the beginning. From One comes Two. Two Stones suggest that we have choices, questions, and interactions ahead of us. Our relationships will be either harmonious or competitive, depending on our level of consciousness. In this house of Earth-energy, experience will centre on questions of physical wellbeing, such as health and security, or on questions of finance, business and investment. There may be more than one project to take up our time, but if we link the spiritual and material aspects of our consciousness together, we will have the patience and skill to realise a complete success. By itself, material success is incomplete. But when rightly understood, working with matter is a ritual for unfolding spirit.

Magician: Three is a number of spiritual importance, and it opens a door for higher awareness as we work. Bringing together our ideals and our practical life is never easy, but the dullness of routine is redeemed when we approach work as a creative and joyful opportunity to learn. Three of Earth, symbolized by Three Stones, suggests a new level of mastery with regard to the skills we use in the marketplace. It encourages us to work with integrity and focus and to do the best we can. Through work, we can build an inner temple of the spirit, an attitude of dedication and sincerity. Spiritual growth and creative expression through work are encouraged under the sign of Three Stones.

Fool: Four Stones, for me, would mean a material foundation. It would be a kind of security derived from physical accomplishment. The security could be related to the physical body, or it could relate to business, or even law and order. Four brings with it a sense of dependability and confidence, and suggests that there is a measure of success in what has already been undertaken.

However, the successful businessman may be tempted to hang on to position, money, or friends because of an attachment to material security. Some people want to ground themselves in money and fiscal success. Then, it becomes more difficult to give, to share and to make the energy flow into creative expression. This kind of success can sometimes lead to self-limitation.

On the other hand, a good foundation of material security may be a basis for spiritual progress. It does not have to close a person off from further growth. We need to ask ourselves, 'What is wealth?' and 'What is poverty?' When Four Stones indicates covetousness, and we rely too much on material security, we will be closing doors against our further growth.

Magician: You sound like a teacher. The story of the numbers is not so strange or difficult once you learn how it goes. Tell me about Five Stones, then. As you know, the movement from four to five is often problematic. What do you make of it in this Book of Earth?

Fool: I feel that I am getting familiar with the language of numbers, and it is easier to see and speak the meanings of the elemental energies than when I first started. Of course speaking a thing is different from hearing or reading about it. In speaking, you discover what you already know, deep down. Your intuitive wisdom can be made to flow. It is a good way to learn.

Well, as I understand, Five comes in the middle of the journey from One to Ten. This makes it a transition point. If Four has been an experience of isolation caused by over-reliance on material wealth, or stagnation of energy arising from a sense of complete security, then Five Stones will have to reap the consequences. It may make us feel that the time has come to change attitudes, to discover why we feel insecure or uncertain, hesitant or restless, and choose a way forward.

Happiness is a condition of the heart. It does not depend on physical wealth. To be successful and yet not get caught up in success is never easy, but Five tests us and teaches us to do just this. If we have been ignoring our spiritual needs, we will be inwardly impoverished, and no amount of business success will make up for this emptiness of spirit. If our attention is directed outward into the world of action, and we ignore the inner soul, then we will feel dissatisfied, even if we have achieved material prosperity. Unless we turn inward, we will not discover the cause of our imbalance, we will just keep looking outside ourselves for solace. There is always a period of darkness before one turns toward the higher guidance. Five in the energy of Earth asks us whether our work in the world has been harmonized with our inner work of opening to the soul.

Priestess: Six has always communicated a sense of generosity, sincerity, sympathy and devotion. On the physical level, six could indicate physical or material favours, either giving or receiving them. It suggests nurturing, supporting oneself and others, fulfilling responsibilities and discharging obligations. In Six Stones, the soul has learned the lesson of giving, and gone beyond the need to clutch and possess. Here, a person has accumulated enough wealth to be able to share it, and six communicates or indicates the kindness we need to take care of others' needs. It is never easy to give without exacting some return, or to be in a position of power yet refrain from exerting undue control over others. Six Stones asks us to examine issues of giving and receiving, either in the material sphere, or in our relationships with other people. Do we, for example, nurture our own deeper needs? Are we grateful for our successes?

Magician: Number seven continues to be itself wherever it is placed. In the Book of Earth, Seven points to an abundance of supply, and this is a good position for harvesting what we deserve from our past investments. It is a time to take stock of our inventory, to harness our resources and choose our position with regard to the future. There is good reason to be satisfied with what has been accomplished, but the next step will be an important one. What do I need to focus on? What should I weed out? The inherently spiritual vibration of seven suggests that when we evaluate our position, we may be looking at the balance between our inner life and our outer life. Our treasure lies where our heart is, and in earth signs there is often a preoccupation with material prosperity.

Fool: Eight means mastery. A master has found what he or she loves to do and has learned to act in an inwardly fulfilling way. Every project contains possibilities for personal and spiritual growth. Work can be prayer. We begin to know this more deeply in Eight of Stone. We now have the discipline, thoroughness, skill and resources to do a good job in our chosen field. We have achieved some level of quality or expertise, and possibly some recognition of our talent. Those who have already achieved power and success face choices about where to go next. The outer concerns of a person's life are prospering in this sign, but the awareness of the spiritual dimension may not be all that it could be. Eight suggests that true mastery encompasses all levels of our being, because always in the wisdom tradition being precedes doing. First, we attain consciousness. Then, we express it.

Priestess: Nine is the apex of our previous efforts. If we have been doing good work, then we have a secure financial base, and a sense of inner satisfaction and confidence. Our success is manifested by physical abundance. It may take the form of good health, pleasant surroundings, agreeable leisure time, the harmonising influence of Nature, or possibly some enrichment by means of cultural activity. How best to enjoy all this? We need enough solitude to set our priorities, and see if any element is missing to make our happiness complete. In order to move on to the next stage, what changes need to be made? This is what we must ask ourselves. In this position, one has achieved the ability to create and maintain order on the physical plane, and one has the abundance to support others. Physical healing is one common way in which this is expressed. But abundance and happiness are not the same thing. Nine Stones asks us to notice how complete and encompassing our abundance really is.

Magician: Ten Stones brings completion, success and material prosperity. There is lasting physical security, perhaps taking the form of financial abundance, and there is a plentiful supply of good things to share with others. When you receive Ten of Earth, you will likely have physical longevity, and fulfil your projects and your objectives successfully.

There may be a stirring of interest in higher service, now that so many lessons have been assimilated. In what way can we grow further? Only the child in the heart can answer this, which brings one into the House of the Page.

Fool: Pages are good learners. In the Book of Earth, The Page is playful and active, innocent and pure, lacking experience, but eager to explore all possibilities. New opportunities, situations, events and teachers present themselves in this sign. The Page has the drive and the wish to grow and develop his potential. He has a sense of wonder, eagerness, enthusiasm and playful things that prompts him to explore and to discover. He likes to carry messages, and he is naturally affectionate.

Magician: The Knight of Earth is dependable and resourceful. He also has a drive to expand. But he combines this with a sense of duty, loyalty, service and dedication. The Knight of Earth has a mental interest in all things physical. He is interested in physical training, in craftsmanship and in projects that involve expenditure of energy. He is always eager to throw himself into such endeavours, to get the job done. He may not be as imaginative as some others but he is dependable, protective, and patient, a good agent to rely on when needed. He is respectful of authority and tradition, serviceable in whatever position he is placed, methodical and sensible. He is strong and comfortable with his earthly spheres of interest and responsibility. He helps show us how to put all our energy into the affairs of life, but he must resist becoming addicted to work.

Priestess: The Queen of Earth could help The Knight to keep his balance. She is close to nature, and she enriches the lives of those who know her by showing them how to keep a balance between inner and outer involvements. This Queen shows us that beauty and enjoyment are necessary to be complete human beings. She encourages skilful work, but she cares about the loving involvement of the worker in his craft, not just the end result. She has immense endurance, being motivated by a caring heart. As an embodiment of the Earth Mother, the Queen of Earth is interested in health, nourishment, food, healing and physical development, as well as gardening and managing household affairs. But her domestic interests express the outflow of her spirit, which is to nurture and protect and preserve.

Fool: The King of Earth is very good at managing and directing earthly energies. He is disciplined, dependable, and generous. He builds the structures we need to organise our physical lives successfully. He is a born leader with high ethical standards, and he shows excellent judgement in handling money and possessions. Always moved by high principles, the Earth King makes duty and work seem like something honourable and noble. He acts on his ideals, giving them expression in the physical world. His vast experience has made him immensely practical, a good provider with a strong sense of responsibility. His attention is mostly directed outward into discharging his duties, but being a true king, he is concerned with the wellbeing of all his subjects. He has excellent managerial skills and is a well-balanced embodiment of power in action.

Priestess: When spirit is expressed in matter, it brings mastery. A Priestess is one who listens to spirit, but she may not have the resilience to live in the turmoil of the secular world. Yet the journey can be completed only when the soul has the capacity to express spirit in the material life in all the possible circumstances which the world can bring to us. The King of Earth is a mature soul who has achieved this.

Magician: The journey of our soul through all these forms of experience leads to mastery. Magicians have focused their full attention on achieving mastery. Fire, Water, Air and Earth are four fields of mastery, but success in these fields is really the success of the soul in becoming the ruler of its own temple.

Fool: Now I understand my journey more fully and more deeply than when I began. But I am not sure that I understand divination yet. I know something about the language of numbers and the power of symbols. But how are these applied to divination?

Priestess: Divination is another topic which must be reserved for another day. It is time to complete our visit to this temple. Let us close the four sacred books, extinguish the candles, replace the crystal sphere in the central altar, and return to the outer world.

The Fool and the Magician followed The Priestess to the altar as she replaced the crystal sphere in its position at the centre of the temple.

Fool: So much we have shared and learned in this inner temple!

Magician: In dreams also, we can travel to places of learning. There are many such temples of instruction in the inner worlds

When they returned to The Hermit's cell, they could see that the sun had moved from east to west, and evening was coming on.

That night, The Fool had time to reflect on the many points which had been discussed in this inner temple of learning, and he attempted to review the details of each of the numbers in each of the alcoves. But in the end, the need for sleep overcame him and he found himself visiting far away worlds of wonder in his dreams.

The Five Tablets

When next The Fool and The Hermit had a chance to chat, the subject of dreams came up.

Fool: Normally, I do not remember dreams very clearly. But there is one dream that I vividly recall. It happened on the night after I received instruction from the Priestess and the Magician. I saw the five books all together on the central altar of the inner temple. But each of the books had turned into a stone tablet, and on the face of each tablet was a summary of all that the book contained. I walked round the altar gazing at them, and what I saw was imprinted on my mind. And the result is that I can remember what each of the seventy eight aspects signify. It was all on those tablets, five of them, summarizing the five books. But you know, it was more than a dream. I lived it so vividly.

Hermit: It may not have been a dream. It could be what we call a vision, or a revelation - a real experience in one of the inner worlds we visit while asleep. Such experiences have their own power and clarity, and this is what impresses them onto the memory with such distinctness.

Fool: Of course, during the day I had some long discussions with the Magician and the Priestess in the inner temple, and we touched on all aspects of divination.

Hermit: But your vision moves your understanding forward because now you can feel the archetypal reality of what you discussed. You now see the pattern of the whole within which each of the numbers and persons fit. You can appreciate their interconnections. This will make you much more confident of the meanings. They have their place in your personal experience now. This vision of yours has clarified your understanding. It is a very good experience.

Fool: Previously, I had my insight or opinion about one aspect or another of the seventy eight aspects of Tarot, which you call the Book of Truth, but now I have confidence, and moreover I see the overall pattern. I can hold it all in my mind's eye, like an eagle looking down on a big field, or a city. And the result is, I am much closer to being able to apply my knowledge.

Hermit: Not the least important use of your new skill will be to determine what questions you need to have answered. I am saying to you that finding your questions is every bit as important as finding answers to those questions. It may be even more important, because it opens doorways to wonder and contemplation. When you recognize what is important to you in your life, when you can formulate it in words, when you know the right questions, you have made considerable progress.

Fool: How am I closer to finding out what my questions are?

Hermit: Each of the seventy-eight positions of Tarot is a question as well as an answer. The Fire cards ask you to look at life experience in terms of vitality and creativity. The Air cards focus on questions of the intellectual realm. Water cards refer to affairs of feeling and the heart, sometimes spiritual matters, while Earth refers to the practical life and material concerns. The Major Arcanum has to do with matters of spiritual importance on the journey of your self-discovery. Where something important is coming your way, a special possibility for your growth and inner unfolding, one of the figures from the Major Arcanum will come and speak to you. And they may come to focus you on the question at hand or to indicate the nature of the answer to a question.

Fool: How then can I find my questions?

Hermit: Take out your deck of cards. That's good. Now, shuffle them, asking to find what question you should be attending to at this time. Good. Now, place the cards on the table. Good. Now divide the deck into three piles. Put them back together in the normal way. Take the top card.

Fool: It is The Moon.

Hermit: How appropriate. You have been looking to understand your dream-vision, to unravel its mystery. Well, you know all the possible meanings that The Moon has. Remember the tablet of the Major Arcanum now. Look at the five possible meanings attached to The Moon. You want to find out which of these it is. Shuffle the deck while keeping this question in mind. Good. Now divide the deck again. Now take the top card.

Fool: It is the seven of water.

Hermit: This gives you your answer. You drew a card which is fairly high on the emotional-development scale, a water card. The emotional meaning of The Moon is what you must focus on.

Fool: The emotional meaning of The Moon is creativity and imagination. It also means authenticity, finding out what is real as opposed to the surface appearances. I could think of several other things as well, but this is the main meaning it has for me.

Hermit: Something else to consider. The seven of water has its own meaning, and provides you with an angle from which to look at your question, the lens you should place over your mind's eye. Look at this question from the perspective of the seven of water.

Fool: I see the seven of water in my mind's eye. I see its spiritual, intellectual and emotional aspects and the rest as well. I think I have a feeling for how to look at this question of creativity and imagination. Yes, it is a valuable perspective on the central question.

Hermit: Can you see how some of the seven of water has been there in your life? Or why this angle may be a useful vantage on your first card, The Moon?

Fool: I do, definitely.

Hermit: Now you are ready to choose a spread to open up answers to your question.

Fool: Let me phrase the question. I know it is important to put questions into words clearly and succinctly. My question is : In what way should I approach the development and expression of my creativity and imagination? That is my question.

Hermit: What spread will you use?

Fool: What would you advise?

Hermit: It could be a spread of two, three, four or more cards.

Fool: I really need to know more about spreads.

Hermit: Ah then, let us consider this question in more depth! First, let me suggest something simple. You will be much further ahead if you can improvise your own spreads, rather than try to memorize a whole collection of different ones from other sources. Secondly, most of what you want to know can be assigned to one of three topics : The Past, The Present, and The Future. So why not begin by writing these three down at the top of a page.

Fool: That is a good idea. Alright, I am setting down these three topics as you suggest

Hermit: Now, what is it you want to know with regard to the past? Just write it down under that heading, perhaps one, two or three questions. Then, for The Present, write down what you want to know, put it into words. And the same for The Past. I'll give you a few moments to finish this.

Fool: There is much to think about in this spread-making.

Hermit: And only one person can do this thinking. Tarot can help you find your questions, and Tarot can help you answer them. Of course your cards do not actually provide answers. They suggest perspectives for you to consider. They provide hints and indications. They point to possibilities. They do not violate your free will to choose your own future and create your own destiny. Often what you will derive from a Tarot spread will be deeper insight into how your life is unfolding. You may not arrive at a fixed conclusion, or a course of action or a decision. Simply seeing more clearly and feeling your own personal truth more deeply is already a wonderful blessing.

The Hermit lit several candles and placed one on the table where the cards were spread. Others he placed on the mantle of the fire place and on the small table by the bed.

Hermit: There is something else I want to suggest, while you have pen and paper handy. This is the best time for you to write down exactly what you remember from the Five Tablets that you saw in your dream. Will you do that?

Fool: It will take a while. But yes, certainly.

In the quiet of the evening, the candles burned slowly down, and silence reigned supreme. It was very late when The Fool finally crept under the covers. The fire had burned down to a dull glow, and the candles were extinguished. On the table rested five pieces of papyrus, on which were summarizing The Fool's dream. The Moon climbed up into the sky and beamed down her silver light onto the forest clearing outside the cave. Once again, The Fool entered the land of his dreams while The Hermit, who slept very little, plunged deep into contemplation.

When The Hermit returned several hours later, he saw that The Fool had fallen asleep. A smile crossed his lips, and he began to stoke the fire in preparation for the evening meal.

The Key
One day, the Hermit awoke to find The Fool arranging his papers and putting his few possessions into his bag, as if getting ready to leave.
Hermit: Are you making a move?

Fool: Last night, I dreamed that my mother was ill, and that she needed me by her side. I fear I may be too late.

Hermit: My blessings go with you.

Fool: I have almost finished packing. But before I go, I want to ask you. Can we meditate together one last time?

Hermit: I pray it will not be the last time! But yes, of course. Come and join me by the riverside when you are finished.

In a few moments they had taken their seats on the grass beside the water, and it was not long before they had plunged into contemplative silence. Time passed. The river flowed on. Birds could be heard in the background. There was no way to measure the passing of time, but they both knew when the meditation had inwardly come to an end, and almost simultaneously they opened their eyes.

Hermit: You will arrive on time. Your mother has things to tell you. She knows you will come. All is well.

Fool: Thank you.

Hermit: Before you go, I want to explain one or two things which you can ponder as you journey. It will not take long, but it is the capstone of what I have shown you thus far.

Fool: You have been so good to me! I can never forget.

Hermit: You may not suspect how rich in meaning the cards are, the illustrations in the Tarot deck which I have placed in your keeping. The story goes back many lifetimes, to a period in the history of ancient Egypt when the mysteries were flourishing. In that lifetime, I was connected to Queen Tiy, a lady of immense spiritual depth, mother of the Divine Pharoah Akhenaton. She was like a spiritual mentor to me. I was promoted to a position of responsibility in the temple priesthood, and I mastered the arts of divination. She gave me to understand that we would be together in future lives, as spiritual seekers, teachers and devotees of Truth. I had little interest or capacity for painting, but she encouraged me to learn how pictures were made, and how to empower them with inner life. Slowly my skills developed. The style in favour in that age was very formal, but the important thing was the knowledge of symbols, the energies of colours, and the technique of empowerment which could bring images to life. This knowledge came to me then, and I have possessed it ever since.

In a later life under the Ptolemies I was privileged to have a position of some importance in the great Museion, or museum as you would call it today, of Alexandria. It was a grand temple of the Muses, a university of higher studies affiliated with the wonderful library of Alexandria where the sacred and secret texts of all the ages had been gathered together into a single collection. I had free access to this wealth of knowledge and I dived into it eagerly. Moreover, I was in charge of the museum's art collection. The curators had assembled the best of the world's paintings, sculptures and manuscripts, which were mostly papyrus, but often ornately illustrated.

Slowly, carefully and with much thought and reflection, I came to understand which of the pieces in this collection best captured and expressed the divine archetypes. As I have explained, these are the twenty one divine energies who preside over the journey of initiation and its stages of unfolding. I was an initiate myself in this life, a high priest in the temple of Serapis, and a teacher in one of the Alexandrian mystery schools. In those days we did not use Tarot cards for divination, and the word Tarot had not even come into existence. However, we understood the archetypes, and we had access to their guidance, and our knowledge of numbers and the four elements was truly profound.

I oversaw the creation of a temple of initiation dedicated to Serapis wherein the sacred presences and their images were enshrined. And in the centre of the temple was a square stone altar. And on that altar was an orb of purest crystal. And in alcoves set into the walls of stone, each member of the divine hierarchy was enshrined in a sacred image. There the sincere novices were taken for initiation. And there I passed a life of service study and quiet joy. I was doing what my soul wanted and I passed many years in satisfaction.

Later, much later, oh, hundreds of years afterwards, in a different part of the world, my beloved queen attained her full status of divinity. She incarnated as a spiritual teacher and accomplished the ancient prophecy of bringing down the highest golden light from heaven to earth. She opened a door in the inner world which had been sealed from the beginning of time, and the golden light began to enter the earthly atmosphere as it has been doing ever since. The history of the world has been radically altered because of this, but it is understood by very few.

I came to know of her attainment only after she had left the body, because we never met in person in that lifetime, only in dreams and in the depths of meditation. I continued on with my own journey of seeking and studying, service and purification. We had opened a channel of communication in the inner world, the Divine Mother and I, and Her guidance became my constant companion. Now, I rely on no other. My life is vastly simplified, and I am completely happy.

Before you came here, for reasons I did not fully understand, I was prompted to create these images on cards. They capture the spirit of the temple images in those ancient days when the glory of Alexandria was a light to the world, before the Caesars came with conquering armies, and quite some time before the birth of the Messiah in Palestine. But time's wheel is forever turning, and the teaching must be passed to new generations of seeking souls and in forms adapted to the changing cultures. And you come to me at a point in your own quest when you are ready to make use of this tradition. But you may not know its true source, its inmost power, its sacred secret.

You have made contact with the Mother's Force; you have spent time in the temple. You have the images and you understand their import.

243

What I am telling you now is the key, the capstone of all that you have built up by way of understanding.

The Mother guides her children in various and diverse ways, often beyond our capacity to comprehend. Ancient Egypt lies buried in the sand, but the life of the spirit moves forward and is ever renewed. These cards carry the power of the archetypes, the sacred numbers and the four blessed elements, and they are a book of wisdom which you can study for an entire lifetime.

The Divine Wisdom is a bottomless well of living water, it can never be drained dry. But wisdom is in essence a unity, not a duality or a multiplicity. That unity is the light of Divine Love, the smile of the Divine Mother. This love-light moves from the Power of One through all the numbers and the four elements to express and empower the story of our souls' seeking. We were lost, but slowly we have found our orientation and are making our way back home to the Source. Yes, in the end, we come home to the Divine Mother's heart of love.

May Her spirit to be with you in all your journeys, in divination, in moments of revelation, and in your service to all the seekers you will meet as you journey through the world. She was once human. She knows the trials and the difficulties of the journey. She is now divine, and her loving care is with you. Remember Her. Call on Her. She is the infinite light, the guiding love, the lasting sanctuary.

Fool: Through you, this connection with The Mother has become stronger in me. It is growing. It is a seed that must flourish and bear fruit. I will reflect on everything you have said.

Hermit: In my heart I will pray for your safety and happiness. But please pay close attention to these final points of instruction. I want to show you the way of using the cards that I myself have come to personally favour above all others. You may find also, in time, that it becomes your own preferred method.

Fool: I have my deck here. We can use it.

244

Hermit: Very well. Shuffle the deck. Move into your consciousness of divination. Find the question. Begin by asking: "I wish to understand…" – then you complete the thought. When you feel that your consciousness has connected with the inner guidance and the cards are ready, place the deck on the table and divide it as we normally do, taking the top card. Place this card face down.

Fool: I am placing this card face down.

Hermit: Good. Now we will elaborate its meaning. Consider the region of fire, which is heavenly light and vital energy, to be above the card, just as heaven is above earth, and place the second card in that quadrant. Then, place a card for earth below the first card. Then, place a card for water to the right of the first card or to its west, and a card for air to its left, or to the east. Now you have a picture of how the energies are working on these four levels of your being, your physical, emotional, and mental bodies and your vitality.   Remember that fire is vitality on its lower level and spirit on its higher planes. But the centre card can be considered the key, the spirit, the central clue to answer your query. Now, turn the cards over and read them.

Fool: There is a very solid structure to this layout.

Hermit: There is. At this point, you are ready for the complete elaboration. You have the central card indicating the primary issue. You have cards in four directions indicating how this is playing out on four levels of your being. Let us consider the card you chose for water, which is emotion. Place three cards beside it to elaborate its meaning.

Fool: What do these three cards stand for?

Hermit: You have some choices in this matter.

You might want them to mean:
a) The Inner Process b) The Outer Process and c) A Recommendation.

Or you might prefer :
a) The Worst that can be; b) The Best that can be; c) Advice on this matter.

Or again, you could use :
 a) The Challenge; b) The Opportunity; and c) Pay Attention to This.

Sometimes, I like to designate these three cards as :
a) The Origin; b) The Present Stage; and c) The Likely Outcome.

Again, I have sometimes used :
 a) The Yin Side; b) The Yang Side; and c) Consider This.

You have many choices. You determine which categories work best.

Fool: I am turning over the three cards now. They comment on the nature of the emotions involved. This spread totals seventeen cards in all.

Hermit   It can, but again, you need not elaborate on all or even any of the four cards in earth, air, fire and water positions. You might choose to look more closely into one or two of them, it is a personal choice. The spread can be elaborated in a very flexible way, according to your need.

Fool: This is a wonderful tool. Thank you for showing me this.

Hermit: One last thing. At the end of a reading, you might want to ask this question : "What energies in my life most need to be balanced?" Shuffle the cards and draw one to represent the answer.

Fool: Very well, I am doing it. I am turning the card over. There is the answer.

Hermit: Now take only the cards of the Major Arcanum, the sacred divine forces of spiritual help, and separate them from the deck.

Fool: Here, you take some of the cards and separate them out with me.

Hermit: Good, now shuffle only the Major Arcanum cards and ask this question: "Which of these forces will be most helpful to me in correcting the balance of the chosen card?"

Fool: I am dividing the deck. Here is the top card. Here is the answer.

Hermit: Not unexpected. Indeed, it makes sense. Now place them together, face to face and place them between your right and left hand. Concentrate on melding the energies of the two cards together. Visualize them combining as one. When you have finished, you may place these two cards on your meditation altar for a while, or you may keep them together and replace them into the deck. The energies involved will be working until the cards are separated and there is an intention of closure.

Fool: In this way, I can ask for help using the same tools for healing as I used for divination.

Hermit: Exactly. My master showed me this shortly before our last separation. I am giving it to you as my final teaching.

Fool: The time has come then. I am leaving a better person than when I came. My way forward is now clear. One fine day we may cross paths again.

Hermit: And perhaps in the world of dreams we will renew the encounter as well. Look to your dreams, then.

Fool: So I shall! Adieu!

APPENDIX I

What follows is a simplified overview of the meanings of the cards in the *Ancient Mysteries Tarot Deck*. The five levels of meaning for each card as laid out below are as follows: the first meaning is the Major Arcana level (spirit); the second meaning is the Fire level (will and energy); the third meaning is Air (mental); the fourth meaning is Water (emotional); and the fifth meaning is Earth (practical). These suggest what may be going on at these five levels of your being.

Major Arcana

The Fool: Purity; Adventure; Innocence; Openness; Freedom.

Magician: Opportunity to Develop; Empowerment; Mental Skill & Concentration; Confidence; Initiative, Ability to Manifest.

Priestess: Wisdom; Insight; Reliance on Inner Guidance; Intuition & Inner Feeling; Stillness.

Empress: Connection to Nature; Motherly Love; Intellectual Creativity; Abundance & Balance; Nurturing.

Emperor: Responsibility; Power; Leadership; Authority; Doing & Leading.

High Priest: Spiritual Experience; Spiritual Initiative; Tradition, Philosophy, Religion or Education; Initiation & Faith; Morality & Conformity.

Lovers: Relationship & Choice; Passion; Commitment; Devotion & Sincerity; Sexual Issues.

Chariot: Mastery; Victory; Assertion; Motivation; Perseverance.

Strength Fortitude; Brave Action; Tolerance & Endurance; Compassion & Benevolence; Patience.

Hermit Spiritual Focus; Dedicated Action; Guidance & Teaching; Spiritual Love; Solitude & Withdrawal.

Wheel: Karmic Experience; A Surprise; Karmic Insight; Turning Point; Physical Change.

Justice: Truth & Authenticity; A Reckoning; Evaluate & Discern; Re-Align & Re-Balance; Take Responsibility, Practice Integrity.

Prisoner: Re-Orientation; Surrender & Trust; Change of Perspective; Humility; Waiting & Sacrifice.

Death: Transformation; Revolution; Letting Go & Detachment; Release; Re-organization.

Temperance: Wholeness; Balanced Energy; Synthesis & Blending; Reconciliation; Moderation.

Devil: Ignorance & Darkness; Temptation; Acknowledge The Shadow; Desires & Obsessions; Sensuality, Materialism.

Tower: Catharsis & Purification; An Upset; Deconstruction (mental); Liberation (emotional); Start Again.

Star: Grace; A Blessing; Inspiration & Higher Guidance; Hope & Trust; Betterment (physical).

Moon: Authenticity; Dispel Illusion; Discern Reality; Creativity & Imagination; Cellular Intelligence.

Sun: Blessings and Upliftment; Collaboration; Light and Truth; Fulfillment; Rejoicing.

Judgement: Heightened Awareness; Release from Bondage; Transcendence of Ego; Inner Release; New Goal or Direction.

World: Fulfillment & Wholeness; Alignment with Truth; Oneness & Universality; Bliss; Ideals Manifested.

Fire

Ace: Opportunity, A New Cycle; Inspiration & Initiative; New Ideas; Optimism & Enthusiasm; Initiative.

Two: Potentials Developing; Momentum; Making Choices & Weighing Alternatives; Preparations & Alliances; Laying Foundations.

Three: A Success; An Empowerment; Investigating and Foreseeing; Conviviality & Optimism; Social Life.

Four: Foundations Secured; Solid Achievement; Harmony & Security; Contentment & Satisfaction; Consolidation.

Five: New Challenge or Opportunity; Input from the Outside; Unrest & Agitation; Struggle & Frustration; Dynamic Effort Needed.

Six: Goals Achieved; Good Fortune & Progress; Encouragement & Harmony; Satisfaction & Validation; Recognition.

Seven: Impetus for Change; Urge to Improve; New Ideas & Choices; Perseverance & Determination; Change and Competition.

Eight: Breakthrough; Energy & Speed; Complexity & Incentive; Eagerness & Zeal; Activity.

Nine: Accomplishment (proved or tested); Determination & Self Reliance; Perspective & Resourcefulness needed; Be Resolute; A Dilemma (take a stand).

Ten: Responsibility; Capacity and Opportunity; Burdens – Focus on Goals; Perseverance & Determination; Commitments.

Page: A Creative Venture; New Impetus or Directions; Intuition or

New Interests; Imagination & Artistry; Preparing to Act.
Knight: Dynamic Change; Enthusiastic Optimism; Confident Initiative; Eager, Volatile & Restless; Start a Project.
Queen: Good Fortune; Focused Competence and Self Discovery; Versatility, Creativity, Intuition; Generosity, Loyalty and Dependability; Harmonious Order.
King: A Leadership Opportunity; Decisive Implementation; Visionary Initiative; Authority, Confidence and Power; Projects Accomplished.

Air

Ace: New Beginning (Intellectual); Inspired Ideas; Mental Clarity; Intuitive New Thinking; Confidence.
Two: A Contract, or A Delay; Balance Opposites; Decision Made, or Minds Meet; Issue to be Resolved; Procrastination or Obstruction.
Three: Getting On with Life; Loss or Separation; Difficult Thoughts; Disappointment; Chagrin.
Four: Healing; Truce, Peace, Detachment; Introspection, Reflection; Quiet; A Break, Stillness.
Five: Change, Instability; Difficulty and Struggle; Strife (mental); Fear of Loss; Conflict or Opposition.
Six: An Opening to Advance; Progress (peaceful); New Perspective, Trust; Safe Passage, Calm; A Solution.
Seven: Need to Improve; Daring and Skill; Strategy or Skepticism; Stealth or Despondency; Secrecy or Subterfuge.
Eight: Opportunity; Limitation; Vacillation, Excessive Analysis; Uncertainty; Hesitation, or Confusion.
Nine: Completion; Dissolution; Mental Oppression, Regret; Sorrow or Fear or Despair; Misgiving and Hesitation.
Ten: Re-Alignment or Sacrifice; Reversal; Reconsider, Review, Look Ahead; Pain, Wounding, Fear; An Ending, A Change.
Page: An Intellectual Adventure; Quickness & Alertness; Thoughtful (but immature); Curious & Naïve; Prepared & Vigilant.
Knight: Intellectual Initiative; Crusader; New Ideologies; Loyally Defending; Vigorous.
Queen: A Solution or Realization; Perception; Clear Focus, Planning; Cool & Disciplined; Poised & Determined.
King: Wisdom, Leadership; Intellectual Initiative; Will and Authority; Steady Determination; Competence.

Water

Ace: Inner Blessing or Awakening; An Emotional Initiative; Peace and Balance (mental); Strong Feeling, Capacity for Love; Good Fortune.

Two: Love and Harmony; A Relationship Enhanced; Acceptance, Harmonious Communication; Romance and Deep Feeling; Reconciliation.

Three: Inner Fullness; An Emotional Initiative; Positive Social Experience; Joy, Expression of Positive Feeling; Community, Sharing, Celebration.

Four: Deepening, Inner Listening; Re-Focus; Introspection, Re-Evaluation; Uncertainty, Misgivings; Inertia, Time Out.

Five: A Correction; A Challenge; Regret, Endings; Emotions re: Loss or Broken Relationship; A Dislocation.

Six: Fulfillment; Satisfaction; Memories; Consolation, Pleasure, Dreams Realized; Outside Help or Gift.

Seven: Imagination, Creativity; Glamour, Indulgence; Wishful Thinking, Assessing Choices; Dreams, Inspirations, Fantasies; Need for Grounding.

Eight: Momentum; Progression and Change; Detachment, Letting Go; Poise or Stagnation; A Conclusion.

Nine: Achievement; Abundance; Appreciation, Optimism; Satisfaction; Success & Enrichment.

Ten: Blessings; Completion; Ideals Realized, Plans confirmed; Contentment (fulfilled relationship); Culmination.

Page: Purity; Emotional Adventure; Exploration and Reflection; Sentiment and Sensitivity; Immaturity.

Knight: Devotion (in action); An Exploit; Nobility & Idealism; Sacrifice & Change; Moodiness, Fickleness.

Queen: Creative Energy; Nurturing; Psychic Insight; Love and Deep Feeling (often Motherly); Sensual & Seductive Experience.

King: Fatherly Love; Dynamic Service; Affection & Responsibility; Generous Passions; Balanced Expression.

Earth

Ace: Creativity (seeking physical expression); A New Start or Opportunity; A New Idea; Stimulation or Inspiration; Energy & Initiative.

Two: Balancing Dualities; Change & Fluctuation; Alternatives, Creative Solutions; Enthusiasm while facing Dualities; Adaptation, Juggling.

Three: Initial Progress; An Achievement; Skills Unfolding, Commitment to Work; Dependability & Dedication; Business Grows.

Four: Consolidation; Conserving; Putting in Order, Protecting; Cautious, Acquisitive; Stability, Security (material).

Five: A Challenge; Crisis/Opportunity; Tension and Testing of Ideals; Need for Solace, Anxiety; Struggle.

Six: Bounty; Material Success; Fairness & Kindness; Generosity, Harmony, Satisfaction; Prosperity.

Seven: Inwardness; Time Out; Evaluation & Discernment; Satisfaction, Appreciating Various Possibilities; Pausing to Consider.

Eight: Dedication; New Initiatives; Persistence; Conscientious Work, Inspiration; Diligent Application.

Nine: Achievement; The Good Life; Relaxation, Calm, Self-Reliance; Enjoyment, Fulfilment, Leisure; Pleasure, Prosperity & Material Security.

Ten: Completion; Opportunities for Service; Looking Beyond Material Success; Giving, Providing for Others; Family, Community, Material Prosperity.

Page: Study, New Opportunities; Self-Preparation; Discovery, Communication; Wonder & Enthusiasm; New Projects and Skills.

Knight: Commitment, Material Interests; Stay The Course; Responsible, Reliable, Methodical; Dedicated & Persevering; Obligation, Overwork.

Queen: Grounding and Stabilizing; Enjoyment of Self and Nature; Practicality; Generous, Creative, Nourishing; Sensual & Pleasure-Loving.

King: Stewardship, Responsibility & Authority; Rewards for Diligence; High Standards, Care/Attention & Principled Action; Realistic & Practical; Diligence leading to Security.

Summary

When an energy or an experience is coming into your life, it is often an inner event which begins as an opportunity for growth and then ripples out into a set of blessings or challenges on the mental, emotional and physical levels. The vital level (fire) involves the central will, and the initiative to act. This is often an area of the being where Spirit connects to mind, emotion and physicality. Everything, even the most trying circumstance, provides an opportunity for us to develop our strength, capacity and talent. Blessings and positive energies lift us up while challenges and difficulties make us strong and test our determination.

We grow and benefit if we approach difficult experiences as opportunities to develop our strengths. Thus, in the tables above, the first quality listed represents the spiritual opportunity in its purest and most positive form. Then we see a reflection of this on the other levels of the being, namely Fire (vitality), Air (mind) Water (emotional life) and Earth (practical material life).

BIBLIOGRAPHY

History

Collins, A. 1996. *From the Ashes of Angels*. Penguin Books Ltd. London, England.

Baigent, M. 1998. *Ancient Traces: Mysteries in Ancient and Early History*. Penguin Books Ltd. London, England.

Baigent, M. and R. Leigh.1997. *The Elixir and the Stone: Unlocking the Ancient Mysteries of the Occult*. Penguin Books Ltd. London, England.

Bancroft, A. 1987. *Origins of the Sacred: The Spiritual Journey in Western Tradition*. Arkana Paperbacks. New York, USA.

Gooch, S. 1979. *Guardians of the Ancient Wisdom*. Fontana. Glasgow, Scotland.

Clow, B.H.2001. *Catastrophobia: The truth Behind Earth Changes in the Coming Age of Light*. Bear & Co. Vermont, USA.

Kingsley, P. 1999. *In the Dark Places of Wisdom*. The Golden Sufi Center. California, USA.

Mehler, S.S. 2001. *The Land of Osiris*. Adventures Unlimited Press. Illinois, USA.

Schoch, R.M. 1999. *Voices of the Rocks*. Harmony Books. New York, USA.

Wilson, C. 1996. *From Atlantis to the Sphinx: Recovering the Lost Wisdom of the Ancient World*. Virgin Books. London, England.

Wilson, I. 2001. *Before the Flood*. Orion Books Ltd. London, England.

Numerology

Buess, L. 1987. *Numerology for the New Age*. DeVorss and Co. California, USA.

Elinwood, E. 2003. *The Everything Numerology book*. Adams Media Corp. Massachusetts, USA.

Gruner, M. and C. Brown. 1978. *Mark Gruner's Numbers of life*. Taplinger Publishing Co. New York, USA.

King, J. 1996. *The Modern Numerology: A Practical to the Meaning and Influence of Numbers*. Blandford. London, England.

Pither, S. 2002. *The Complete Book of Numbers: The Power of Number Symbols to Shape Reality*. Llewellyn Publications. Minnesota, USA.

Roquemore, K. 1985. *It's All in Your Numbers: The Secrets of Numerology*. Harper and Row, Publishers, Inc. New York, USA.

Shine, N. 1994. *Numerology: Your Character and Future Revealed in Numbers*. Simon & Schuster, Inc. New York, USA.
Vaughan, R. 1985. *Numbers as Symbols for Self-Discovery*. CRCS Publications. USA and Canada.

Tarot
Echols, S.E., R. Mueller and S. Thomson.1996. *Spiritual Tarot: Seventy-eight Paths to Personal Development*. Avon Books. New York, USA.
Giles, C. 1996. *The Tarot: Methods, Mastery, and More*. Simon & Schuster, Inc. New York, USA.
Guiley, R.E. 1991. *The Mystical Tarot*. Signet. New York, USA.
Haich, E. 1984. *Wisdom of the Tarot*. Aurora Press, Inc. New Mexico USA.
Irwin, L. 1998. *Gnostic Tarot*. Samuel Wiser, Inc. Maine, USA.
Lammey, W.C. 2002. *Karmic Tarot*. Career Press. New Jersey, USA.
Ozaniec, N. 2002. *Initiation into the Tarot*. Watkins Publications. London, England.
Pollack, R. 1997. *Seventy-eight Degrees of Wisdom: A Book of Tarot*. Thorsons. London, England.
Thomson, S.A., R. Mueller and S. Echols. 2000. *The Heart of the Tarot*. HarperCollinsPublishers. New York, USA.
Warwick-Smith, K. 2003. *The Tarot Court Cards: Archetypal Patterns of Relationship in the Minor Arcana*. Destiny Books. Vermont, USA.

THE ANCIENT MYSTERIES TAROT DECK

Painted and designed by Roger Calverley, (author of *ANCIENT MYSTERIES TAROT)*, the *ANCIENT MYSTERIES TAROT DECK* draws it Major Arcana imagery from the mystery school traditions of pre-Christian Egypt, Greece, Mesopotamia and India. The art is primal and archetypal, suitable for Tarot practice and studies in areas such as divination and inner self development. The Minor Arcana show images of fire, stone, water and air rather than the conventional European symbols of wands, pentacles, cups and swords. This shifts the consciousness back to the primal realities which are at the basis of the ancient mystery school traditions of divination and initiation , namely 1) the primal and ancient archetypes; 2) number, especially the tradition of Pythagoras and his mentors in Egypt and Mesopotamia (such as the Magi); and 3) the four sacred elements, earth, water, air and fire. This original art, based on years of travel and meditation, opens new doorways for inner attunement and practical application.

Ask for the ANCIENT MYSTERIES TAROT DECK at your nearest bookseller or send $19.95 U.S. funds plus $2.50 for the first deck, .75 for each additional deck ordered (Wisconsin residents add 5.5% sales tax) to

Lotus Press
PO Box 325
Twin Lakes, WI
53181 USA
Telephone: 262 889-8561
Email: lotuspress@lotuspress.com
Website: www.lotuspress.com

Note: If you are interested in contacting Roger Calverley about any experiences or comments you might have with *Ancient Mysteries Tarot* or the *Ancient Mysteries Tarot Deck* you can contact Roger at

Email: calverleyr@yahoo.ca

The author will make every effort to reply to as many inquiries as possible.